Agency and the Semantic Web

Agency and the Semantic Web

Christopher D. Walton

OXFORD
UNIVERSITY PRESS

Great Clarendon Street, Oxford ox2 6DP

Oxford University Press is a department of the University of Oxford.
It furthers the University's objective of excellence in research, scholarship,
and education by publishing worldwide in

Oxford New York

Auckland Cape Town Dar es Salaam Hong Kong Karachi
Kuala Lumpur Madrid Melbourne Mexico City Nairobi
New Delhi Shanghai Taipei Toronto

With offices in

Argentina Austria Brazil Chile Czech Republic France Greece
Guatemala Hungary Italy Japan Poland Portugal Singapore
South Korea Switzerland Thailand Turkey Ukraine Vietnam

Published in the United States
by Oxford University Press Inc., New York

British Library Cataloguing in Publication Data
Data available

Library of Congress Cataloging in Publication Data
Data available

Typeset by SPI Publisher Services, Pondicherry, India
Printed in Great Britain
on acid-free paper by
Biddles Ltd., King's Lynn, Norfolk
ISBN 0-19-929248-5   978-0-19-929248-6

1 3 5 7 9 10 8 6 4 2

Dedicated to Morna

Foreword

The Web is one archetype for successful application of computing on a global scale. It works because of a simple unifying concept (linked URLs) supported by a pervasive infrastructure (the Internet) and delivered via standard communication mechanisms (Web browsers). Its unexpected effectiveness is a consequence of its scale: as more people use systems that index Web information the more sophisticated these indexing systems have become. This trick only takes us so far, however, and we already are experiencing limits to the scale of traditional Web systems. Statistics and indexing as we know them cannot cope with the volume and complexity of pages and (increasingly) programs available for us to use on the Web. The question is: where do we go from here?

This question is being answered in different ways. One reaction is to use more sophisticated links to describe information—leading database engineers to develop methods for federating information via descriptive metadata, and leading knowledge engineers to adapt their methods to ontology mediation. Another reaction is to build more scalable infrastructures and architectures for knowledge sharing—via peer to peer architectures or computational grids. Yet another reaction is to build systems that can reduce the burden on human communication by automating more of the interaction with the Web—a motivation for those interested in multiagent coordination.

Notice the breadth of topics in the paragraph above and how they cut across many of the traditional subfields of computing. It is difficult to hold in one's mind all of the concepts that could be relevant to the problem, especially since each of those concepts typically is promoted from the viewpoint of its parent subfield rather than in a broader context. We have yet to establish the gravity necessary to pull these disparate ideas together.

This is where we need texts like the book you are about to read. Its purpose is to demonstrate the range of methods that may be applied to the problem and explain how they fit together. It summarizes the most important representational languages and standards and, importantly because these languages are still evolving, explains their mathematical foundations. It charts the relevant developments in multiagent systems from localized belief systems through performative based systems to coordination based on models of interaction—perhaps the main point of contact to the Web service world. It explains how such services may be coordinated and how this has led to the development of service ontology languages and associated architectures for automating service interaction. This is done in a craftsman-like way which will appeal both to applied theoreticians and to programmers.

Perhaps the best feature of this book is that it wastes so little time in conveying these essential ideas. It is the fastest way I know to get up to speed with the key ideas that I hope will revolutionize the way we understand large-scale multiagent systems, service-based computing, and the Web.

Dr David Robertson (Director)
Centre for Intelligent Systems and their Applications (CISA)
School of Informatics
The University of Edinburgh

Acknowledgements

I would like to thank my colleagues at the 'Centre for Intelligent Systems and their Applications' in Edinburgh for their support and encouragement during the preparation of this book. Particular thanks are due to David Robertson, Jarred McGinnis, and Jessica Chen-Burger for their suggestions and comments on the content. I would also like to thank Viviana Mascardi and Giovanni Casella for proofreading this manuscript. My research was funded by the following projects while this book was prepared:

- **Advanced Knowledge Technologies (AKT)**, EPSRC Interdisciplinary Research Collaboration
- **Open Knowledge (OK)**, European Union Sixth Framework Programme, Information Society Technologies

Chris Walton

Contents

List of Figures

List of Tables

1 The Semantic Web

At the present time, the Web is primarily designed for human consumption and not for computer consumption. This may seem like an unusual state of affairs, given that the web is vast and mature computerized information resource. However, we must recognize that the computer is presently used as the carrier of this information, and not as the consumer of the information. As a result, a great deal of the potential of the Web has yet to be realized.

This book explores the challenges of *automatic* computer-based processing of information on the Web. In effect, we want to enable computers to use Web-based information in much the same way as humans presently do. Our motivation is that computers have a brute-force advantage over humans. Where we can gather and process information from a handful of Web-based sources, a computer may download and compare thousands of such sources in a matter of seconds. Nonetheless, despite the apparent simplicity of this task, there are a great many issues that must be addressed if we are to make effective use of this information. As a result, the automated processing of Web-based information is still in its infancy. In this book, we show how many different techniques can be used together to address this task.

The automated processing of information on the Web is principally an issue of *scale*. There are many existing techniques in Computer Science and Artificial Intelligence (AI) that may be appropriate to the task. However, there are significant issues that must be addressed if we are to scale up these techniques for use on the Web. Therefore, we present a detailed overview of the current state of the art, with a particular emphasis on practical solutions. The methods and technologies that we present in this book are of importance to all computer practitioners, as they will shape the future evolution of the Web.

1.1 Information and knowledge

To appreciate the challenges of computer-based consumption of Web-based information, we consider the following scenario. Suppose we are searching the Web for information on a specific ailment. In response to our query, we find a page that contains the requested keywords, but the information is beyond our comprehension, say a paper from a medical journal. We can read the paper in detail, and look up any unfamiliar words in a dictionary. We can also go further, and examine the references presented in the paper, and even contact the author. However, it is likely that we will have little more understanding of the content of the paper upon completion than we did at the start. What we are lacking is the background knowledge necessary to understand the paper, which can only be obtained through many years of study.

The scenario that we have described is very similar to the situation we face when attempting to process information on a web page automatically, by a computer program. Our program can readily count the keywords in the page, download the images, and follow the relevant hyperlinks. However, our program will have no real understanding of the content of the page, other than statistical data. We will not be able to do anything with this information beyond what can be achieved by purely statistical means. This statistical data can be used to good effect, as shown by the current generation of Web search technology. However, the limitations of this approach to Web search are often all too apparent.

We can illustrate the limitations of Web search when attempting to perform a search that goes beyond what can be accomplished by keywords alone. For example, suppose we wish to find the best recipe for making a chocolate cake. We perform a search with the keywords 'chocolate cake recipe', and are faced with over half a million matches. We can attempt to narrow the search by including additional keywords such as 'best' or 'good', but this does little to reduce the number of results. Ultimately, it will be up to us to examine the results, and decide on an appropriate recipe, though it is highly unlikely that we could examine all of the candidates. It may appear that our chocolate cake example is unrealistic, as the definition of the 'best' cake relies on personal preference. However, we have presented this exaggerated example to illustrate a problem, which results from the fact that a computer has no notion of what a 'chocolate cake' is.

A more realistic demonstration of the limitations of the Web can be obtained by considering an example that could technically be computed. For example, determining the best method for travelling to a particular destination. In this case, the relevant information can be found on the Web, and we can define 'best' mathematically, e.g. as the cheapest route. However, unless a suitable application is already available on the Web, the computer will be unable to provide us with the desired result. A regular keyword search will be of no use, other than finding a large list of candidate sites containing the relevant information. The computer cannot calculate the desired result, as it has no understanding of the information that it perceives on the Web. It is because of this lack of understanding that the computer is unable to perform any kind of automatic inference with this information. In principle, if the computer was aware of the meaning of the information, then the required calculation could be performed automatically.

The fundamental issue that we are experiencing is related to the classical problem of *information* versus *knowledge*. What exists on the Web at the present time is information, essentially a large collection of facts. To make use of this information, we need to appreciate these facts in the wider context of knowledge. By this, we mean that the information must be interpreted in light of the *concepts*, such as truths, beliefs, perspectives, judgements, methodologies, and know-how. At present, the Web relies entirely on the human user to supplement the information with knowledge to make use of the information. We later show that a computer can make many of the same kinds of inference as a human if the information on the Web is supplemented with *semantic* knowledge about this information.

The provision of semantic knowledge associated with the information on the Web will open the door to the construction of a whole new class of intelligent Web applications. A number of authors have outlined their vision of a *Semantic Web*, and the applications that this will enable. These accounts appear in the Suggested Reading section at the end of the chapter. Examples of applications include intelligent searches, automated data mining, e-science experiments, e-learning systems, personalized newspapers and journals, intelligent devices, and so on. These motivating examples provide a flavour of the power and flexibility of associating semantic knowledge with the existing information of the Web. The remainder of this book is devoted to the challenges of realizing these goals. There are essentially two main questions that we answer:

1. How do we represent the knowledge in such a way that it can be understood and processed automatically by a computer?
2. Once we have this information, how can we use it effectively in real applications?

1.1.1 Knowledge representation

In our discussion, we have identified knowledge as the key to unlocking the potential of the information held on the Web. With a suitable *representation* of this knowledge, we can perform *inference* about the information, and thereby obtain new insights. However, before we perform any kind of inference, we must consider how this knowledge can be represented, so that it can be automatically processed and shared. It is necessary to adopt appropriate conventions that can be consistently interpreted by both the producers and the consumers of the knowledge.

Before we discuss these conventions, it is important to consider the big picture of what we are trying to represent. We previously talked about knowledge in terms of concepts such as beliefs. These concepts, together with the facts on which they are defined, and the relationships between them form the basis of our representation. What we actually represent is a *conceptualization*, which is a simplified view of a part of the world.

At this point it is helpful to consider an example of a conceptualization. Figure 1.1 presents a specification that can be used to classify cameras into different categories. The boxes in the example contain the concepts, and the arrows define the relationships between them. The root of the hierarchy is a class called *Thing*, which represents the universe of discourse, i.e. everything that we could have in our conceptualization. Thing has two direct subclasses: *Tangible Thing*, which have a real physical existence, and *Intangible Thing*, which do not. This is a useful distinction as it enables us to separate real physical objects, such as the Camera itself, from properties such as Autofocus. This is a common distinction in the design of conceptual

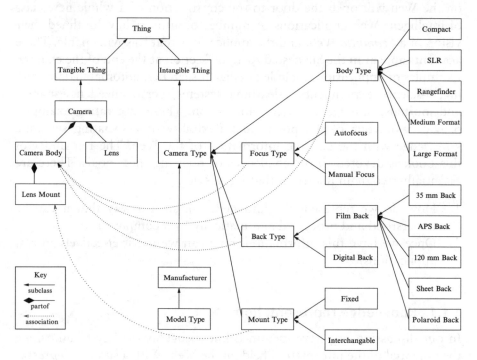

Figure 1.1 *Camera ontology.*

hierarchies. The remainder of the hierarchy identifies the key concepts that are important to photographers in categorizing different types of camera.

The style of definition that we have used should be familiar to anyone who has encountered a class hierarchy in an object-oriented programming language such as Java, though there are some important differences. The most apparent difference is that we define two kinds of relationship, in addition to the usual *subclass* relation. The *partof* relation is used in relation to Tangible things, and indicates that a thing is a physical part of another thing. The *association* relationship relates intangible things to tangible things. For example, Body Type is a property of a Camera Body. Our use of this relationship in our example indicates that we do not have a strict tree-like hierarchy, rather we have defined a graph, or network, of relationships.

To illustrate the use of our example hierarchy, we present a list of the features for a range of popular cameras in Table 1.1. This is similar to a list of cameras that may appear on the Web, for example, on a shopping website. It should be clear that we can classify all of these cameras according to the conceptualization that we have defined. By performing this classification, we are representing knowledge about each camera and constructing a *knowledge base*.

The advantage of the classification is that we can perform inference on the information. This inference can provide additional knowledge that is not readily apparent from the initial list of features. We can infer facts from our examples such as: all SLR cameras have an interchangeable lens, all compact cameras have a fixed lens, and all digital cameras are autofocus. Our confidence in these inferences would clearly be enhanced if our list of examples were larger. We can also answer questions about a specific camera, for example, what type of body does it have? Comparisons of features between the cameras can also be performed, and we can ask for all the cameras of a particular type. Further inference can be performed in relation to additional knowledge. For example, if we had a list of

Table 1.1   *Camera features.*

Camera	Features
Olympus MD3	Compact, Autofocus, APS, Fixed Lens
Canon Ixus 500	Compact, Autofocus, Digital Back, Fixed Lens
Pentax K1000	SLR, Manual Focus, 35 mm, Interchangeable Lens
Nikon D70	SLR, Autofocus, Digital Back, Interchangeable Lens
Leica M2	Rangefinder, Manual Focus, 35 mm, Interchangeable Lens
Hasselblad H1	Medium Format, Autofocus, 120 mm, Interchangeable Lens

prices available, we could infer the cheapest camera with a specific set of features.

Representing knowledge in the form of a conceptualization is central to the automatic processing of information on the Web. As we have shown, this kind of representation can be used to make inferences. In particular, we can infer facts that would be difficult or impossible to determine otherwise. Nonetheless, there are a further two important considerations that must be addressed:

1. We need a suitable conceptualization model for the information that we wish to classify.
2. We need to actually perform the classification of the information, and this is itself a difficult task.

1.1.2 Ontologies and knowledge lifecycles

We have illustrated how a body of knowledge can be represented as a conceptualization, which is an abstract view of the world. More formally, we can define an *ontology* that is a specification of a conceptualization. This term is borrowed from philosophy, where an ontology refers to the study of existence, and the fundamental categories of being. For our purposes, we define existence as that which can be represented. A formal ontology defines a set of objects, and the relationships among them. The ontology may also define axioms that constrain the interpretation and usage of the objects. More precisely, an ontology is the statement of a logical theory.

A formal ontology is usually defined as a knowledge vocabulary, rather than in a graphical notation. There are a number of different languages that can be used to define an ontology. For the Web, RDF, RDFS, and the OWL family of languages are the most relevant. These languages use XML-syntax, and have varying degrees of expressivity. The underlying semantics in these languages is provided by graph theory and description logics.

Designing a formal ontology is a difficult task. Even a simple ontology, such as our Camera example, can take a lot of effort to produce. This difficulty has long been recognized, and many kinds of methodology and tools have been produced to assist in the construction of formal ontologies. More recent thinking, principally in light of the Web, has highlighted the dynamic nature of knowledge. A formal ontology should not be considered in isolation. Instead, ontologies should be linked together, parts of ontologies should be derived from others, and ontologies should change over time in response to trends.

The dynamic view of knowledge has resulted in the concept of a knowledge *lifecycle*, as illustrated in Figure 1.2. A lifecycle expresses the craft

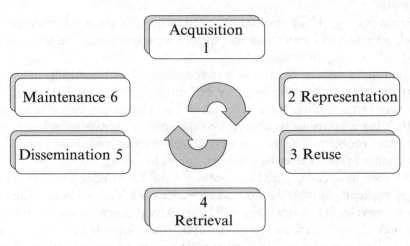

Figure 1.2 *Knowledge lifecycle.*

of knowledge management through a set of distinct tasks. The lifecycle model illustrated contains six possible tasks that express the management of Web-based knowledge. The application of these tasks can be performed in a variety of different orderings, over a range of time periods, and tasks can be omitted. The results of this application can be viewed as a flow of knowledge over time.

The first task in the lifecycle model is the acquisition of the information that we wish to represent in the ontology. This information can come from a variety of different sources such as human experts, though we are primarily interested in Web-based sources here. As we have previously stated, the Web contains a vast body of information. Therefore, this task is concerned with sifting potential sources of information to find the relevant pieces, identifying gaps in the knowledge, and integrating knowledge from different sources.

Representing the acquired information in a form suitable for problem-solving is the second task of the lifecycle. This is the point at which an ontology is constructed so that the acquired knowledge can be classified. Design decisions about the ontology must be made so that the ontology will be suitable for inference and flexible enough for future needs. In particular, the ontology must be representationally adequate for the needs of the domain in question.

Constructing an ontology and the associated knowledge base entirely from scratch is not typically a profitable exercise, particularly if existing ontologies are available in the domain. Therefore, the third task in the lifecycle is the reuse of existing knowledge sources. Typically, the representation of knowledge is designed specifically for a particular kind of problem-solving. Understanding and adapting the knowledge already at hand can result in a more general-purpose representation, and increase the utility of existing knowledge.

The fourth task in the lifecycle is the retrieval of knowledge from our representation. When the quantity of knowledge that we have available gets very large, finding the correct bit of knowledge can be a challenge in itself. It is necessary to be able to find the correct knowledge relevant to a particular problem. This task is significantly harder if we have knowledge that changes rapidly over time, such as news headlines.

Once we have constructed our ontology and knowledge base, we would like to make it available for others to use. This is addressed in the fifth task of the lifecycle. Our knowledge will be used by different users for different purposes. Some users may want to update the knowledge, while others may wish to visualize the data in ways that we did not originally envisage. Certain knowledge may be time critical, and must be made available at the right time. We may also wish to restrict the knowledge to certain kinds of users, or present only a subset of the knowledge.

The final task in the lifecycle is the maintenance of our knowledge to preserve its usefulness. This task involves the update of content to reflect changes, and the removal of obsolete content. This may involve a deep analysis of the knowledge in question. Additions or changes to the knowledge base may involve updating the underlying ontology. The verification of the accuracy of the content is also an important maintenance issue.

The lifecycle model does not prescribe a rigid methodology for the management of ontological knowledge. Instead, it provides a summary of many different kinds of operations that we would like to perform on our Web-based knowledge, from the initial acquisition to long-term maintenance. These tasks are intended to serve as a guide for the kinds of issues that we should consider in the construction of a knowledge base.

1.2 Agency and reasoning

The use of ontologies addresses the question of how to represent knowledge on the Web such that it can be understood by a computer. This is clearly a necessary requirement in automated processing of information on the Web. We now turn our attention to the second question, and consider how we can use this knowledge effectively. In answering this question, we move beyond representational issues, and consider the technologies and applications that will be used to realize the benefits of the Semantic Web.

The Semantic Web vision promotes the notion of *agents* as the primary consumers of knowledge. These agents are programs that will collect Web content from diverse sources, process the information, and exchange the results with other agents. Agents are not just arbitrary programs, rather they are programs with *autonomous* and *rational* behaviours that interact with each other. These behaviours are required for the dynamic kind of systems that we want to construct. In particular, we want to define agents that can go out onto the Web and perform tasks on our behalf, without our direct intervention. The construction of programs with this kind of behaviour continues to be an active AI research area.

There is a surprising lack of consensus over how the term *agent* should actually be defined. In surveying the literature, it quickly becomes clear that there are many different definitions. The basic principles of autonomy and rationality are present in most definitions, but there is little further agreement. This can be a considerable source of confusion in attempting to apply agent techniques to the Web. The reason for this lack of consensus is because the term is used generically to refer to a heterogeneous body of research rather than a specific notion of agency. It can be argued that a precise definition of agency for the Semantic Web is unimportant, provided that the agents can cooperate in meaningful ways. In fact, it is probably unrealistic to insist on a single definition. In this book, we adapt and apply a variety of different definitions for our purposes.

The first challenge that we address is how to construct agents that are capable of autonomous and rational behaviour. In other words, how can we design a program that can decide on its own what needs to be done, and to do it, without explicitly being told what to do. This is rather different from a typical style of programming, where the computer performs only exactly what we instruct it to do. The inspiration for this style of programming comes from the study of *human reasoning* in philosophy. In essence, this is the reasoning directed towards actions and the process of determining what to do to achieve these actions. This differs from purely *logical reasoning*, e.g. all water is wet; rain is water; therefore rain is wet.

Human reasoning can be considered to comprise two activities:

1. We decide what state of affairs we want to achieve.
2. We decide how to achieve this state of affairs.

The first of these activities is *deliberation*, and the result is a list of intentions. The second is *means–ends reasoning*, and the result is a plan of action. We can illustrate this kind of reasoning by returning to our chocolate cake example. Through some deliberation on our current state of being, we decide to make a chocolate cake, and this becomes our intention. We then undertake means–ends reasoning on how this can be achieved. In our first stage of reasoning, we decide that we need to obtain a recipe, then obtain the ingredients for the recipe, and then follow the recipe to make the cake. These decisions become our new intentions and we embark on further reasoning, for example, we decide to obtain a book of recipes, and this in turn requires money to purchase the book, and so on. Once the reasoning process is complete, we will have a plan of action that we can use to bake our chocolate cake.

Practical human reasoning can be expressed computationally by a number of different logic-based systems. The most popular of these systems is the Belief–Desire–Intention (BDI) model of Michael Bratman. The BDI model is said to take an *intentional stance* in determining the behaviour of the agent. This is a theory from philosophy, which makes predictions about the behaviour of an entity by treating it as a rational agent whose behaviour is governed by intentional states. Intentions are the driving force of the BDI model as they determine the actions of the agent. However, it is important to appreciate that intentions may have unexpected side effects. For example, I may intend to get to a meeting by the quickest route, but this does not mean that I want to swim across a river on the way.

In the BDI model, reasoning is defined by three mental states. *Beliefs* correspond to knowledge that the agent has about the domain, *desires* represent the state of affairs that the agent would (ideally) like to bring about, and *intentions* are desires that the agent has committed to achieving. In addition to these three states, we also have *goals*, which are a consistent subset of the desires as some desires may conflict, and *actions* which are derived from the intentions. Figure 1.3 illustrates the various components of the model.

The BDI model can be used to define and implement agents with rational behaviours. However, it is important to note that this is just one particular technique for defining rational agency. There are many alternative techniques that we can adopt, which may be more appropriate depending on the kinds of agents that we want to build, e.g. reactive agents, hybrid agents, planning agents, and theorem-proving agents.

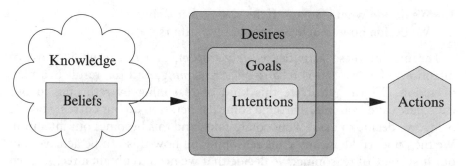

Figure 1.3 *The BDI model.*

1.2.1 Communication and societies

An individual agent is a useful entity that we can define to perform tasks on our behalf, given suitable reasoning and enactment mechanisms. For example, we can define an agent with the intention to obtain some useful piece of information, e.g. a list of banks in our area. The agent can then be let loose onto the Web and will attempt to find this information for us by utilizing a variety of knowledge sources, and performing inference on this knowledge.

The Semantic Web vision goes beyond the notion of agents acting in isolation, and views the agents acting together as a *society*. In a society, the individual agents interact closely and assume group behaviours such as cooperating, coordinating, negotiating, and so on. This is a common view of agency and is based on the idea of agents interacting in much the same way as humans interact on a daily basis. The term *Multiagent* System (MAS) is used to describe a system of agents that interact closely with a range of behaviours.

Embracing a societal view of agency introduces a range of new challenges that we must address. One of the most important is simply how to get the agents to talk together, since the agents cannot assume group behaviours if they cannot communicate. The issue goes beyond standards for communication, although such standards are a crucial first step. In addition, we need to communicate the meaning of our communication in such a way that it can be understood, e.g. to express our beliefs to another agent. The inspiration for this style of communication comes from the study of *human dialogue* in philosophy.

A popular basis for the definition of agent interaction is the theory of *speech acts* proposed by the philosopher John Austin and extended by John Searle. This theory recognizes that certain natural language utterances have the characteristics of actions. That is, they change the state of the world in a similar way to physical actions. For example, the act of moving an object changes the state of the world, as does the speech act of 'declaring war', to use a popular example. The theory identifies a class of *performative verbs*, which correspond to different types of speech acts. These verbs can be classified into five groups. *Assertives* commit the speaker to the truth of what is asserted, e.g. inform. *Commissives* commit the speaker to a course of action, e.g. promise. *Declaratives* effect some change on the state of affairs, e.g. declare war. *Directives* attempt to get the listener to do something, e.g. propose. Finally, *Expressives* express a mental state, e.g. prefer.

Speech acts are a popular basis for defining communication between agents in MASs. In this approach, the inter-agent communication is performed by exchanging messages containing performatives. Each message has an associated performative that expresses the intended meaning of the message. To ensure compatibility between different agents, a number of standard Agent Communication Languages (ACLs) have been defined. These languages define a common set of performatives, and their precise meanings. The two dominant ACLs in MASs are the Knowledge Query and Manipulation Language (KQML), and more recently the Foundation for Intelligent Physical Agents-Agent Communication Language (FIPA-ACL). KQML defines a set of forty-one performatives, and FIPA-ACL defines a set of twenty-two performatives. Figure 1.4 illustrates an example FIPA-ACL message. The example is a message from `agent1` informing `agent2` that the price of `item` is `150`. The message also specifies the content language of the message, in this case the FIPA Semantic Language (`sl`). Finally, the message specifies the ontology relevant to the communication.

In the speech acts approach, an interaction between agents will consist of the exchange of performatives over a time period. This process is akin to a *dialogue* between humans. The sequence of performatives that an agent uses will be focused on achieving a particular intention of the agent. The sequence can be quite complex and varied over time, as the agent may also cooperate with the intentions of other agents. Nonetheless, a sequence will have a definite pattern, dependent on what kind of goal the agent is attempting to satisfy. This sequence is called a *protocol*, and it is useful to consider these protocols in their own right, rather than simply a side effect of agent interaction. Treating the protocol separately is particularly useful when we consider large numbers of interacting agents.

Protocols for agents can be expressed using a finite-state representation that defines the legal sequences of performatives in a dialogue. This approach has been adopted in a number of different agent frameworks. Figure 1.5 defines an example protocol for a simple interaction between a doctor and a patient. The protocol begins with both agents in the INITIAL state. A patient agent then sends a request message to a doctor agent indicated by **request(P, D)**, where P is a patient and D is a doctor. This message is intended to represent the patient making an appointment to see a doctor. The patient then enters the WAIT state until an **accept(D, P)** message is received from the doctor. At this point the agent enters the

```
(inform
    :sender    agent1
    :receiver  agent2
    :content   (price item 150)
    :language  sl
    :ontology  english_auction)
```

Figure 1.4 *Example FIPA-ACL message.*

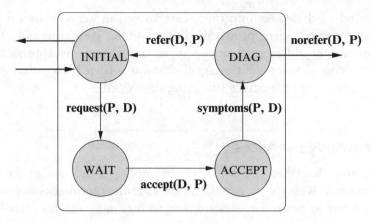

Figure 1.5 *Doctor and patient protocol.*

ACCEPT state and proceeds to send a message **symptoms(P, D)** to the doctor. The doctor then performs a diagnosis of the patient in the DIAG state and the result is that the agent is referred **refer(D, P)** for further diagnosis, or no-referral **norefer(D, P)** is made in which case the protocol terminates.

Agent protocols, or patterns of dialogue, also have a parallel in human dialogue. In any human interaction, there are always implicit rules or social norms at work. Some of these rules are more obvious than others. For example, in an auction house or in sport there are clearly defined rules. Other rules are more subtle and flexible, for example the interaction between a salesperseon and a customer. Finally, in general-purpose conversation there are different ways in which we speak to business associates and close friends.

The different kinds of human dialogue have been classified into six main categories by the philosophers Douglas Walton and Erik Krabbe. Table 1.2 summarizes the different types of dialogue that they identify. The eristic type is essentially the breakdown of rational dialogue. The

Table 1.2 *Dialogue types.*

Dialogue type	Goal	Initial situation
Persuasion	Conflict resolution	Conflicting point of view
Negotiation	Making a deal	Conflict of interest
Deliberation	Reach a decision	Need for action
Information Seeking	Spreading knowledge	Personal ignorance
Enquiry	Growth of knowledge	General ignorance
Eristic	Humiliation	Antagonism

classification of dialogues into these categories can act as a useful guide in the constructing agent protocols. For example, we can readily define templates for the different dialogue types. However, this approach is a relatively recent development in agency, and a formal theory that relates dialogue types to speech acts is still being developed.

1.3 Knowledge services

We have now described the two main technologies that are at the heart of the Semantic Web vision: *ontologies* and *agents*. Ontologies are used to represent knowledge, and agents are used to reason about this knowledge. Both of these are founded on mature AI techniques that have been under development for many years. The difference in the Semantic Web is the use of these technologies together, on the Web, with a focus on the provision of specific applications. To unite these two approaches, a third technology has been adopted, called Knowledge Services or 'Semantic Web' services.

Knowledge services are the means by which computation is performed on the Semantic Web. A *service* is a software component that can be invoked by an external entity to perform some task. There are essentially two different kinds of knowledge services: those that *provide* knowledge, and those that *transform* knowledge. The first kind of service is used to obtain knowledge, e.g. to access a resource such as a knowledge base. The second kind of service performs computation on the knowledge, e.g. to perform a particular kind of inference on a collection of knowledge. In essence, the knowledge providers are a wrapper around ontologies, and knowledge transformers a wrapper around agents.

A range of example knowledge services are shown in Figure 1.6. The most common kind of knowledge transformation is realized by an inference engine such as the BDI reasoner we outlined previously. Another kind of knowledge transformation can be achieved by combining together services into a plan according to a predefined workflow of tasks. This kind of service is appropriate where the full power of agency is not required. Finally, a knowledge transformation may be simply a predefined operation, e.g. a lexical analysis, performed by a computation engine. The most common kind of knowledge provider is a knowledge base, i.e. a database of knowledge. Alternatively, we may be interested only in obtaining the ontology, and therefore we can consult an ontology store. Thus, we may obtain our knowledge from an ordinary website containing semantically annotated information.

Knowledge services are typically implemented by encapsulating them in *web services*. Web services are a programming technique that standardizes

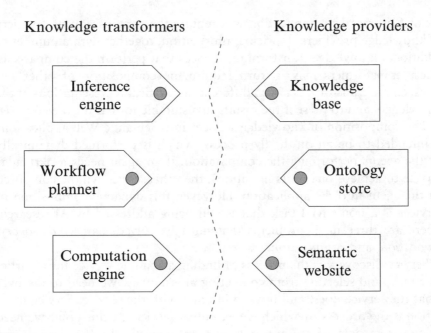

Figure 1.6   *Knowledge services.*

many aspects of distributed processing and communication on the Web. The appeal of web services over other interoperability standards, such as CORBA, is the simplicity and flexibility of the architecture. At the core of this technique there are just two XML-based standards that define the web services architecture: web services are specified in the Web Service Description Language (WSDL), and communication between web services is defined by the Simple Object Access Protocol (SOAP).

The use of a web services architecture is an important step towards the construction of a computer-processable Web. This architecture enables websites to be accessed through a standard mechanism, which is similar to procedure calls. Therefore, Web-based information can be retrieved in a suitable form for mechanized processing, rather than as an HTML-formatted document designed for human consumption. An increasingly large percentage of sites on the Web already allow their information to be accessed through a web service interface. Although this is still a long way from the full Semantic web vision, this alone is an important achievement as it provides a context for the Web-based information, and allows this information to be processed by external agents.

Semantic Web *applications* are constructed by composing together knowledge services. Consider our earlier example on the construction of a Semantic Web application to locate the cheapest camera with a specific set of features. This application will require the composition of a variety of knowledge providers of pricing information, together with a number of additional knowledge transforming services that perform the comparison. These transformers may in turn require the composition of other services, e.g. to transform between different ontological representations of the knowledge, and to present the results in a suitable format for the end user.

The composition of knowledge services into Semantic Web applications is intended to be an on-the-fly process, which is performed dynamically by the agents performing the computation. If an agent needs a particular service to achieve one of its intentions, then this service will be composed by the agent into the application. However, this dynamic composition of services is a non-trivial task that is still being addressed by AI research. There are three main problems that must be solved, namely *discovery*, *invocation*, and *composition*.

Service discovery is the process of finding a suitable service for a particular task, and selecting from competing alternatives. We need to discover what the service does, and how to interact with the service. Service invocation is the process by which we execute a service. At this point we need to construct data of the appropriate form expected by the service, and interpret the results obtained from the service. Finally, service composition is the process by which we combine together services, where the task cannot be performed by a single service.

A possible approach to addressing the three issues that we have highlighted is to equip each service itself with ontological knowledge. This knowledge classifies the service by *profile*, *process model*, and *grounding*. The profile defines what the service does in order to facilitate discovery. The process model defines how the service works so that we can determine the choreography of the service. Finally, the grounding defines how to access the service such that invocation of the service is possible. There are currently two standard ontologies for classifying services in this manner: OWL Service (OWL-S) and Web Service Modelling Ortology (WSMO).

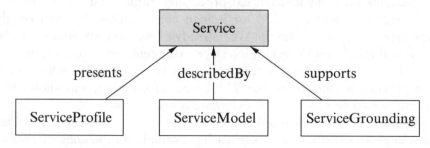

Figure 1.7 *OWL-S top-level ontology.*

Figure 1.7 illustrates graphically the top-level concepts and relationships in the OWL-S.

1.4   Book outline

This book is about the construction of the next generation of the Web, commonly called the Semantic Web. This Semantic Web will enable computers to automatically consume Web information, overcoming the human-centric focus of the Web as it stands at present. This in turn will expedite the construction of a whole new class of knowledge-based applications that will intelligently utilize Web content.

The construction of the Semantic Web will be a very difficult process. Nonetheless, there has been a decade of AI research into knowledge management and multiagent techniques that can be applied towards achieving this goal. We have presented a flavour of these techniques in this introductory chapter, and we expand on this material in the remainder of the book. Our presentation is structured naturally into four related themes, which correspond to the techniques that we have discussed:

1. Knowledge representation techniques for the Semantic Web: Chapter 2.
2. The construction of agents that can reason about knowledge: Chapters 3, 4, and 6.
3. Reasoning on the Semantic Web with agents: Chapter 5.
4. Knowledge Services for the Semantic Web: Chapter 7.

For each of these main themes, we present an overview of the state-of-the-art techniques, and the popular standards that have been defined. We are primarily interested in practical results that can be achieved using these technologies. For those who are interested in obtaining a deeper understanding, we also present the main theoretical results that underlie each of the technologies, and we summarize the main problems and research issues that remain. Our presentation is guided by the following two aims:

1. To educate the reader about the various Semantic Web techniques and technologies.
2. To give the reader a theoretical grounding in the field, so that they can perform research in the area.

We acknowledge that there will be some readers who are sceptical about the whole idea of the Semantic Web. As with many new Web technologies, there has been a lot of hype and many inflated claims on what can be achieved. It should be clear from our introduction that there are still many significant issues that must be solved before the full Semantic Web vision can be achieved. Nonetheless, we claim that it is not necessary for all of the pieces to be in place before the benefits of the Semantic Web can be realized. For example, simply implementing a web service interface to a website enables a much greater degree of computer processing of Web information, and the construction of a single agent can perform many useful tasks, without requiring the existence of a community of agents. Our opinion is that the construction of the Semantic Web will happen in a piecemeal manner, and will be driven by the applications. This is evident as the most popular uses of ontologies on the Web at present are Really Simple Syndication (RSS) feeds, and Friend-of-a-Friend (FOAF) documents.

1.5 Suggested reading

1. G. Antoniou and F. van Harmelen. *A Semantic Web Primer*. MIT Press, 2004.
2. T. Berners-Lee and M. Fischetti. *Weaving the Web*. Harper, 1999.
3. T. Berners-Lee, J. Hendler, and O. Lassila. The Semantic Web. *Scientific American*, May 2001.
4. J. Davies. *Towards the Semantic Web: Ontology-Driven Knowledge Management*. Wiley, 2003.
5. D. Fensel. *Ontologies: A Silver Bullet for Knowledge Management and Electronic Commerce*. Springer-Verlag, 2001.
6. D. Fensel, J. Hendler, H. Lieberman, and W. Wahlster. *Spinning the Semantic Web: Bringing the World Wide Web to Its Full Potential*. MIT Press, 2003.
7. A. Gómez-Pérez, M. Fernández-López, and O. Corcho. *Ontological Engineering: With Examples from the Areas of Knowledge Management, E-Commerce and the Semantic Web*. Springer-Verlag, 2004.
8. T. R. Gruber. *Towards Principles for the Design of Ontologies Used for Knowledge Sharing*. Kluwer, 1993.
9. J. Hendler. Is There an Intelligent Agent in Your Future? *Nature—Web Matters*, (3), March 1999.
10. J. Hendler. Agents on the Web. *IEEE Intelligent Systems*, 16(2): 30–7, March 2001.
11. G. Schreiber, H. Akkermans, A. Anjewierden, R. de Hoog, N. Shadbolt, W. Van de Velde, and B. Wielinga. *Knowledge Engineering and Management: The CommonKADS Methodology*. MIT Press, 1999.
12. K. Sycara and M. Paolucci. Ontologies in Agent Architectures. In *Handbook on Ontologies in Information Systems*. Springer-Verlag, 2004.
13. M. Uschold and M. Gruninger. Ontologies: Principles, Methods, and Applications. *Knowledge Engineering Review*, 11(2): 93–155, June 1996.

2   Web knowledge

In the introductory chapter of this book, we discussed the means by which knowledge can be made available on the Web. That is, the *representation* of the knowledge in a form by which it can be automatically processed by a computer. To recap, we identified two essential steps that were deemed necessary to achieve this task:

1. We discussed the need to agree on a suitable *structure* for the knowledge that we wish to represent. This is achieved through the construction of a *semantic network*, which defines the main concepts of the knowledge, and the relationships between these concepts. We presented an example network that contained the main concepts to differentiate between kinds of cameras. Our network is a conceptualization, or an abstract view of a small part of the world. A conceptualization is defined formally in an *ontology*, which is in essence a vocabulary for knowledge representation.
2. We discussed the construction of a *knowledge base*, which is a store of knowledge about a domain in machine-processable form; essentially a database of knowledge. A knowledge base is constructed through the *classification* of a body of information according to an ontology. The result will be a store of facts and rules that describe the domain. Our example described the classification of different camera features to form a knowledge base. The knowledge base is expressed formally in the language of the ontology over which it is defined.

In this chapter we elaborate on these two steps to show how we can define ontologies and knowledge bases specifically for the Web. This will enable us to construct *Semantic Web* applications that make use of this knowledge. The chapter is devoted to a detailed explanation of the syntax and pragmatics of the RDF, RDFS, and OWL Semantic Web standards.

2.1 Resource description framework

The resource description framework (RDF) is an established standard for knowledge representation on the Web. Taken together with the associated RDF Schema (RDFS) standard, we have a language for representing simple ontologies and knowledge bases on the Web. In essence, RDFS is used to define the ontology or vocabulary, and RDF is used to define the knowledge base. This separation is slightly ambiguous in that an RDFS vocabulary is defined using RDF. However, the advantage of this approach is that we need only a single representation language for both the ontology and the knowledge base.

The motivation for the RDF standard is primarily the description of metadata about Web-based *resources*, hence the name of the standard. Examples of resources are the author, title, and description of a Web page. The RDF approach is a marked improvement over the ad hoc mechanisms previously provided by HTML meta tags. The Dublin Core initiative defines a standard set of RDF metadata for describing Web pages. As we show, RDF can also represent knowledge about things that are not directly Web related, and this makes it suitable as a simple formalism for general-purpose knowledge representation.

RDF has an XML-based syntax, and we assume that the reader has a basic familiarity with XML in this book. Nonetheless, we do not use XML syntax initially in our discussion of RDF. This is because XML is overly verbose for our purposes, as it is designed primarily for automated processing. Therefore, we introduce the main concepts of RDF in a more concise manner before discussing how these concepts are represented in XML syntax.

The key to knowledge representation is expressing the structure of the information that we want to represent. For example, representing the relationships between the different components of a camera. As we have shown previously, this structure can be represented graphically as a network. To understand RDF, it is useful to view the syntax as simply a textual representation of a graph. With this in mind, we can view the basic structure of RDF as a *triple* comprising a pair of nodes and a directed edge. For example, Figure 2.1 is a triple, which states that a Nikon D70 camera has a Single Lens Reflex (SLR) body.

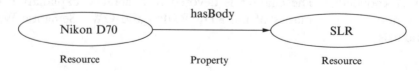

Figure 2.1 *An RDF triple.*

An RDF triple allows us to make *statements* about things. The things that we make statements about in RDF are *resources*. In our example, 'Nikon D70' and 'SLR' are the resources. A statement asserts *properties* of resources, where a property describes a relationship between resources. In our example, 'hasBody' expresses a relation between the two resources. We note that a property in RDF is considered to be a special kind of resource. Although this can cause a bit of confusion, it allows a uniform naming scheme to be used for both resources and properties, and it allows us to make statements about properties themselves. We revisit this issue later in the chapter when discussing RDFS.

RDF statements are closely related to statements in natural language. Our example statement is equivalent to the English-language statement 'A Nikon D70 has a body type SLR'. As RDF is intended for automated processing, it does not permit arbitrary statements, but instead fixes the structure of the statements so that all RDF statements have the same form. RDF takes a *logical* view of statements, where each statement has a *subject*, followed by a *predicate*, and finally an *object*. The subject is the thing that the statement is about, the predicate describes the property that the statement specifies, and the object is the value of the property. We can also think of a triple as a logical formula $p(S, O)$ where p is the predicate, S the subject, and O the object. The RDF permits only *binary* predicates comprising a single subject and a single object, although we discuss how to overcome this limitation later in the chapter.

Statements in RDF can be taken together to produce larger networks. Figure 2.2 denotes an example network that has been constructed from four individual triples. This kind of structure is often referred to as a *semantic network*. The structure of the network is a directed graph, where the edges of the graph are directed from the subject to the object, and labelled with the predicates.

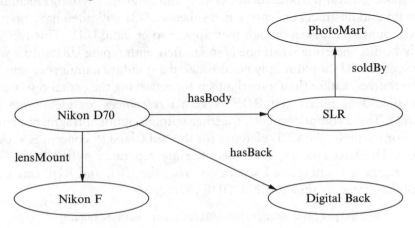

Figure 2.2 *RDF semantic network.*

The representation of knowledge as triples, and the construction of semantic networks from these triples are the principal concepts in RDF. It is important to realize that there are three equivalent views of a triple in RDF:

1. A triple relates a resource to a property.
2. A triple defines a statement with a subject, objects, and predicate.
3. A triple represents a directed edge and a pair of nodes in a graph.

Each of these views has a distinct purpose. The first view is how we represent triples within the RDF framework. The second view is how we construct triples from natural language. Finally, the third view is how an individual triple relates to other triples in a collection, and defines how these triples can be combined into networks.

2.1.1   RDF resources and representation

We have now outlined the main concepts that underlie the RDF standard for knowledge representation. Thus, it remains to illustrate how these abstract concepts are transformed into concrete definitions in XML. The use of an XML-based syntax allows us to define RDF documents that we can publish, so that others can process and share the knowledge that we represent.

An RDF statement is defined by three resources, i.e. a triple. Up to this point, we have used arbitrary names to denote these resources. However, RDF requires that we use a standard naming scheme for these resources. RDF defines a resource as anything that can be identified by a uniform resource identifier (URI) reference. This is a naming convention that is commonly used in XML documents.

The most common kind of URI is a uniform resource locator (URL), e.g. http://www.w3.org, which refers to a network accessible resource. A URI is a more general-purpose identifier that can refer to anything, including humans and abstract concepts, e.g. a subclass. URI will often have no network counterpart, even though they appear to be valid URL. This can initially be disconcerting when one is so familiar with typing URL into a web browser. A URI should simply be considered a standard naming convention for resources, rather than a mechanism for retrieving the actual resource.

It should be noted that RDF uses URI *references* for identifying resources. These comprise a URI, together with an optional fragment identifier. For example, the URI reference for the 'subClassOf' concept is shown below. The URI and fragment identifier are separated by the # symbol. The fragment is interpreted separately from the URI, and RDF fragment identifiers can contain any UNICODE characters.

```
http://www.w3.org/2000/01/rdf-schema#subClassOf
```

The subject, predicate, and object of an RDF statement are identified by URI references. However, there are some situations where it can be inconvenient to use a URI for the object of a statement. In particular, RDF statements will often be defining properties of resources. For example, if we have the statement 'Nikon D70 has price 1000' then we have a subject 'Nikon D70', a predicate 'hasPrice', and an object '1000'. The subject and predicate can readily be assigned to fixed URI. We can also assign the integer value 1000 to a URI and use this for the object. However, for efficiency, it makes more sense to simply include the value 1000 directly. Therefore, RDF permits *literal values* to be used as the object of a triple, but not as the subject or predicate. It should be noted that literal values will often be associated with a URI that defines their type.

In addition to using URI to identify resources, RDF also makes substantial use of *namespaces*. XML namespaces are a convenience that prevents us from having to repeatedly type a lengthy URI. They also serve to disambiguate elements that are imported from different locations, but have the same name. For example, the elements that we use to define an RDF document all begin with:

```
http://www.w3.org/1999/02/22-rdf-syntax-ns#.
```

We can avoid the need to retype this URI in every element by making a namespace definition at the top of the document that has the form:

```
xmlns:rdf = "http://www.w3.org/1999/02/22-rdf-syntax-ns#"
```

The `rdf` string that appears after `xmlns:` refers to the entire URI. Therefore, we can now type `rdf:Description` in our document instead of using the full URI each time, as shown in Figure 2.3.

In XML, namespaces are only used as a shorthand notation to avoid ambiguity. However, in RDF, the external namespace definitions are assumed to refer to real RDF documents, which define resources that we can use. When we define an RDF document that uses an external namespace, we are essentially constructing a knowledge base that reuses and extends this external knowledge with our own definitions. In this way, RDF constructs a 'web of knowledge', linking together external knowledge into larger knowledge bases.

A final consideration, before we present the XML syntax of RDF, is the representation of predicates with more than two arguments, e.g. tertiary predicates. As we have stated earlier, RDF is restricted to binary predicates, i.e. predicates with two arguments. This appears to be a serious restriction as we often want to make statements with more than two arguments, e.g. a camera is constructed from a body and a lens. The intuitive way to represent this statement in the tertiary predicate *construct*(*Camera*, *Body*, *Lens*). To represent this in RDF we must decompose into the binary predicates: *construct*(*X*, *Camera*), *compose*(*X*, *Body*), and *compose*(*X*, *Lens*). In general, such a decomposition will always be possible, thus a little tedious. As we see in the following section, RDF contains some additional syntactic sugar that simplifies the representation of *n*-ary predicates.

2.1.2 An XML syntax for RDF

An RDF document consists of a list of *descriptions*. Each of these descriptions is in essence the definition of an RDF triple. The following fragment shows the basic representation of an RDF triple in XML syntax:

```
<rdf:Description rdf:about="NikonD70">
   <camera:hasBody>SLR</camera:hasBody>
</rdf:Description>
```

The above representation is equivalent to the triple previously depicted in Figure 2.1. The triple is defined by a single `rdf:Description` element. The subject of the triple is defined by the `rdf:about` attribute. The element that appears inside is a property–value pair, which corresponds to the predicate and object of the triple. The predicate is identified by the name of the element `camera:hasBody`, and the object `SLR` appears inside the element.

We now consider a complete example, shown in Figure 2.3, which illustrates all of the necessary parts that make up a basic RDF document. The line numbers in this example are purely for reference and would not appear in the document. The example encodes the network previously illustrated in Figure 2.2. To define a complete RDF document, we encompass a list of `rdf:Description` elements by an enclosing `rdf:RDF` element.

```
1   <?xml version="1.1"?>
2   <rdf:RDF xmlns:rdf="http://www.w3.org/1999/02/22-rdf-syntax-ns#"
3            xmlns:camera="http://www.mycamera.org/photo#">

4      <rdf:Description rdf:about="NikonD70">
5        <camera:hasBody rdf:resource="SLR"/>
6        <camera:hasBack rdf:resource="DigitalBack"/>
7        <camera:lensMount>Nikon F</camera:lensMount>
8      </rdf:Description>

9      <rdf:Description rdf:about="SLR">
10       <camera:soldBy>PhotoMart</camera:soldBy>
11     </rdf:Description>

12  </rdf:RDF>
```

Figure 2.3 *An RDF document.*

We also define two namespaces: `xmlns:rdf` (line 2), which is the main RDF namespace, and `xmlns:camera` (line 3), which references an external RDF document that defines the key concepts relating to cameras. The `rdf:Description` elements are as described. However, we define three triples together in the first description rather than a single triple as before. We use an `rdf:resource` attribute (line 5) to state that the type of the camera is an SLR. This creates a link between the two descriptions. If we were simply to give the label, then it would be ambiguous as to whether we meant the description that we have defined or simply the string.

There are a number of additional RDF features that we now consider. These features are largely for syntactic convenience over the basic definitions that we have already described. Figure 2.4 presents a more complex network that we use as the basis for our discussion.

The encoding of our network in RDF is presented in Figure 2.5. The first thing to note is that we use `rdf:ID` in line 6 to identify the tuple. This has the same meaning as the `rdf:about` definition used previously, but it allows the description to be referenced externally. For example, we can write the URI: `http://www.mycamera.org/nikon#NikonD70`, where the base URI (`http://www.mycamera.org/nikon`) is our RDF document, and the fragment identifier `NikonD70` is the definition inside the document. In this way we can choose to make definitions visible externally or internally. It is important to note that when we use the ID attribute, we must add a # symbol when we refer to the attribute within the defining document, i.e. `rdf:resource="#NikonD70"`.

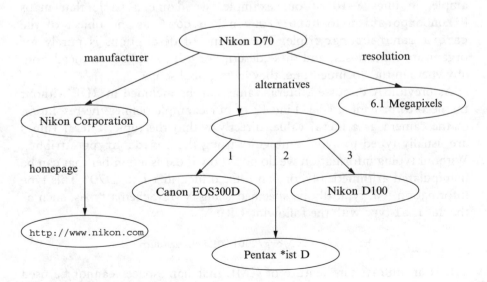

Figure 2.4 *RDF features.*

```
1   <?xml version="1.1"?>
2   <!DOCTYPE rdf:RDF [
3      <!ENTITY xsd "http://www.w3.org/2001/XMLSchema#">]>

4   <rdf:RDF xmlns:rdf="http://www.w3.org/1999/02/22-rdf-syntax-ns#"
5           xmlns:camera="http://www.mycamera.org/photo#">

6      <rdf:Description rdf:ID="NikonD70">
7        <camera:manufacturer>
8          <rdf:Description rdf:about="NikonCorporation">
9            <camera:homepage rdf:resource="http://www.nikon.com/"/>
10         </rdf:Description>
11       </camera:manufacturer>
12       <camera:resolution rdf:datatype="&xsd;decimal">
13          6.1</camera:resolution>
14       <camera:alternatives rdf:nodeID="alt"/>
15     </rdf:Description>

16     <rdf:Description rdf:nodeID="alt">
17       <camera:1>Canon EOS300D</camera:1>
18       <camera:2>Pentax *ist D</camera:2>
19       <camera:3>Nikon D100</camera:3>
20     </rdf:Description>

21  </rdf:RDF>
```

Figure 2.5 *RDF syntax example.*

Nested definitions can be made within an RDF document. For example, in lines 8–10 of our example, we define a triple that maps NikonCorporation to http://www.nikon.com/, as the object of the camera:manufacturer triple. The nesting of descriptions is purely for organization purposes, and these descriptions can still be referenced from anywhere in the document, i.e. they have global scope.

As previously discussed, literal values can be included in RDF without the need to provide a URI. Line 12 of our example defines the resolution of the camera as a literal value, directly within the tuple. Literal values are usually typed to avoid ambiguity using the rdf:datatype attribute. Without typing information we do not know if 6.1 is a number that can be manipulated arithmetically, or is it a fixed identifier like 'D70'. This type information will typically be specified using XML Schema types, such as the decimal type with the following URI:

http://www.w3.org/2001/XMLSchema#decimal

It is an unfortunate feature of XML that namespaces cannot be used within strings, and therefore we are forced to write the complete URI every time or use an alternative mechanism. The alternative is to use an XML *entity* declaration, as shown in line 3 of the example. An entity associates a name with a string, and substitutes this name for the string when used within the document. In this case, we associate the name xsd with the string http://www.w3.org/2001/XMLSchema#. The name is substituted for the string in line 12 when we write &xsd; and in this way obtain the correct type in our example.

RDF permits the definition of network nodes that do not contain resources, by using *blank node* identifiers. In line 16, we define a blank node using the rdf:nodeID attribute, and in line 14 we refer to this node using the alt ID that we assigned to the node. Unlike the rdf:ID attribute, the blank node is invisible outside the document in which it is defined. Blank nodes have a variety of uses, e.g. a placeholder for unknowns, or for grouping resources together. In our example, we use the blank node to structure the alternative camera models into a separate group.

We can avoid the need for a blank node in our example by making use of RDF *containers*. A container is a resource that contains members, which are either resources or literals. Containers are used to group together a collection of things that we want to talk about as a whole. Three types of containers are available in RDF. A *bag* is an unordered container of members, which may contain duplicates. A *sequence* is an ordered container, which may also contain duplicates. An *alternative* is a container where the members are alternatives for each other. The first element of the alternative is considered to be the default, and the order of the remaining members is not significant. We note that containers simplify the representation of predicates with more than two arguments in RDF.

The following RDF fragment illustrates the encoding of the alternative cameras from Figure 2.4 as an alternative container. We could equally use a bag or a sequence container by replacing rdf:Alt with rdf:Bag or rdf:Seq respectively. We can write rdf:li instead of explicitly numbering the members as rdf:_1. This is convenient when the members may need to be reordered. A container is itself a resource, and can be used directly as the object of a triple, in which case the rdf:about attribute would be omitted.

```
<rdf:Alt rdf:about="alt">
  <rdf:_1>Canon EOS300D</rdf:_1>
  <rdf:_2>Pentax *ist D</rdf:_2>
  <rdf:_3>Nikon D100"</rdf:_3>
</rdf:Alt>
```

There is no way to state that an RDF container is closed, i.e. it contains all possible members. Therefore, RDF provides an alternative *collection* construct for describing a closed list of things. In the following example, we use `rdf:parseType="Collection"` to indicate that the list which follows is closed. This has the effect of saying that a camera can have either a film back or a digital back, and no other.

```
<rdf:Description rdf:about="camera">
  <camera:hasBack rdf:parseType="Collection">
    <rdf:Description rdf:about="FilmBack">
    <rdf:Description rdf:about="DigitalBack">
  </camera:hasType>
</rdf:Description>
```

The final feature of RDF that we consider is the ability to make statements about other statements, which is called *reification*. For example, we can currently define a statement such as 'D70 is manufactured by Nikon'. However, we may want to state that 'Photomart says that the D70 is manufactured by Nikon'. The meaning of this is not the same as the original statement and one does not imply the other. In other words, the statement 'Photomart says that the D70 is manufactured by Nikon' does not mean that the D70 *is* actually manufactured by Nikon, only that Photomart has stated that it is so.

To perform reification, we need to be able to treat a whole statement as a resource with an identifier, without actually defining the statement. To accomplish this, RDF provides a reification mechanism that expresses a statement as a resource. The following example expresses the statement 'Photomart says that the D70 is manufactured by Nikon'. Note that we define an `rdf:Statement` rather than a description. We explicitly define the subject, predicate, and object that we are talking about. This statement is equivalent to the network illustrated in Figure 2.6.

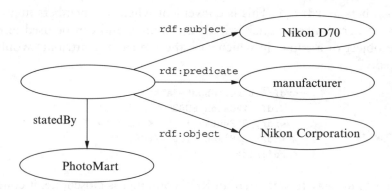

Figure 2.6 *RDF reification.*

```
<rdf:Statement rdf:about="StatementAboutD70">
  <rdf:subject rdf:resource="NikonD70">
  <rdf:predicate rdf:resource="&camera;manufacturer">
  <rdf:object rdf:resource="NikonCorporation">
  <camera:statedBy rdf:resource="PhotoMart">
</rdf:Statement>
```

2.2 RDF schema vocabularies

At the beginning of the chapter, we discussed two tasks that are key to the representation of knowledge on the Semantic Web. To recap, we define ontologies that provide structure to the knowledge, and we construct knowledge bases according to these ontologies that hold the knowledge. The RDF language, which we have now described in detail is appropriate for the second of these tasks. We now turn our attention to the RDFS language, which addresses the first task. Our reason for approaching these tasks in reverse order is that RDFS is defined using RDF, and so it is necessary to first obtain an understanding of RDF.

An RDF *knowledge base* comprises a collection of RDF documents that are linked together by their namespaces. These RDF documents will typically be made publicly available using standard web server technology, e.g. Apache. Therefore, an RDF knowledge base is constructed in essentially the same way as a collection of interlinked web pages. RDF documents can also be directly placed in an RDF store, such as 3Store or Jena, which facilitates the ordered retrieval of the knowledge through queries, similar to a database system. We discuss RDF queries in more detail in Chapter 5.

It should be apparent that we can build large collections of data from RDF documents. However, up to now we have been deliberately loose in discussing how this knowledge should be structured. For example, the RDF triples that we presented used predicates such as camera:hasType and camera:subTypeOf without any discussion of their definition. The reason for this omission is that these concepts are defined externally to the knowledge base, i.e. in an ontology.

The RDFS is a very simple ontology description language for defining the structure of RDF knowledge. It is principally a language for defining a *vocabulary* of terms that can be used in constructing RDF statements. It is important to realize that RDFS does not itself define the vocabulary, as this will be specific to the kind of knowledge that we define. Instead, RDFS provides us with the means to define our own vocabulary. By restricting ourselves to a particular vocabulary, rather than arbitrary terms, we impose structure on the RDF knowledge base. RDFS can be considered a *type system* for RDF documents.

As we have stated previously, RDFS is itself defined using RDF. The RDFS facilities are presented as a special set of predefined RDF resources that have specific meanings. An RDFS vocabulary is defined as an RDF document using these resources. This can be a little confusing as it blurs the distinction between the knowledge base and the ontology, but there are many advantages in using a common syntax. We discuss the main features of RDFS at an abstract level before we describe the RDF-based syntax of RDFS.

2.2.1 RDF schema concepts

The RDFS allows us to construct a vocabulary for a particular domain of knowledge. The modelling of knowledge in RDFS is similar to object-oriented design. This makes the language easy to understand for anyone familiar with this style of definition, though there are some important differences that we highlight. However, RDFS is missing many features that would be desirable for a complete ontology description language. As a result, these deficiencies have subsequently been addressed in the Web Ontology Language (OWL) described later in the chapter, which is (loosely) defined as an extension of RDFS. Nonetheless, RDFS is still useful for performing certain kinds of inference.

The main purpose of RDFS is to identify the various kinds of things that we want to represent in our knowledge base, and subclass relationships between them. In keeping with the object-oriented model, RDFS is structured around the notion of a *class hierarchy*. A *class* is a type of thing that we want to represent, and the hierarchy defines the relationships between the different classes. Figure 2.7 is an example hierarchy taken from the camera ontology that we defined in Chapter 1.

An *object* in RDFS is considered to be an RDF resource. An object that belongs to a particular class is referred to as an *instance* of the class. We define an object as an instance by assigning the *type* of a class to the object. For example, if we have an RDF resource 'Nikon D70' and we want to say that this is a type of Camera according to our class hierarchy, then we assign the 'Camera Type' to this resource. This is achieved in RDF simply by stating that the resource has a particular type, i.e. $type(NikonD70, CameraType)$ in logical notation.

The class hierarchy establishes a relationship between the different classes. There is principally just one kind of relationship between classes which is permitted in RDFS: the *subclass* relation. When we connect two classes by an arrow in Figure 2.7 we are stating that one class is a subclass of another, e.g. 'Digital Back' is a subclass of 'Back Type'. The *superclass* relation is the inverse of subclass, e.g. we can also say that 'Back Type' is a superclass of 'Digital Back'. We note that unlike many

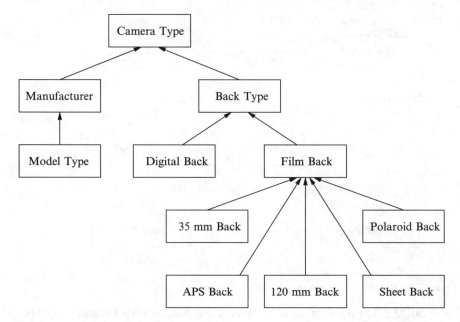

Figure 2.7   *Example class hierarchy.*

object-oriented languages, the classes together do not need to form a strict tree-like hierarchy, and a class can have multiple superclasses.

The subclass relation implies that one class is more specialized than another. For example, '35 mm Back' is a more specialized kind of 'Film Back'. This specialization is captured by the subclass relation in RDF through *inheritance*. When we define an object to be an instance of a class, we are also stating that the object is an instance of any superclass of this class. In effect, a subclass inherits all of the classes defined above it in the hierarchy, i.e. the subclass relation is *transitive*. For example, according to Figure 2.7, if we state that a resource has the type '35 mm Back', then we are also saying that it has the type 'Film Back', 'Back Type', and 'Camera Type'. However, it is important to note that we do not inherit down the hierarchy. For example, if we state that a resource has the type 'Film Back', then it is not the case that it has the type '35 mm Back'.

The RDFS class hierarchy is primarily useful for providing structure to a knowledge base. In general, when we define an RDF document we associate each resource with a class defined in a separate RDFS document. By making this association, we impose a standardized structure on the knowledge base. This is particularly useful when we have many RDF documents that conform to a standard schema.

An additional use of classes is to impose restrictions on what can be stated in an RDF document. In particular, we want to disallow invalid statements, e.g. 'Nikon D70 is manufactured by 35 mm Back'. It is helpful

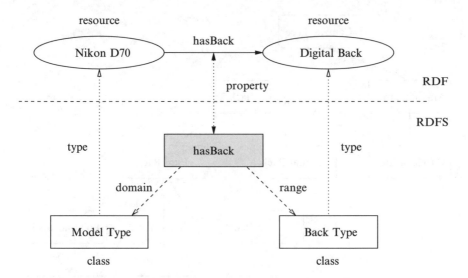

Figure 2.8 *RDFS property restriction.*

to recall that an RDF statement asserts the *properties* of resources, where a property describes a relationship between resources. RDFS allows us to place restrictions on the properties that we define. We can restrict a property to certain classes of resources. In mathematical terms, we restrict the *domain* and *range* of the property. Figure 2.8 illustrates the connection between RDF and RDFS, and the restrictions on the domain and range of an RDF statement.

An interesting feature of RDFS is that we can define a hierarchy of properties in addition to the hierarchy of classes. That is, we can specialize a property using the `subPropertyOf` relation. For example, we may define 'hasFilmBack' to be a subproperty of 'hasBack'. In the subproperty hierarchy, the domain and range restrictions are inherited from the superproperty, or they must be subclasses of the classes in the superproperty.

It is worth noting that there is a significant difference between the object-oriented paradigm and the RDFS treatment of properties. In object-oriented design, the properties of a class are generally defined directly in the definition of the class. In RDFS, properties are defined globally and are not related directly to specific classes. The advantage is that we can define new properties that apply to a class, without changing the definition of the class. However, the disadvantage of this global approach is that it is not possible to specify properties with different ranges depending on the class they are applied to. This restriction is relaxed in OWL, which allows properties to be defined for specific classes.

The most important difference between RDFS and object-oriented programming is that schema definitions are not *prescriptive*. In a typical object-oriented programming language, when we define a property for a class, this property must be satisfied, or the program will be invalid. However, in RDFS the interpretation of the schema is decided by an external application, which may or may not insist on full compliance with the schema. The RDFS schema is treated merely as a description of the structure of the knowledge. It will often be perfectly acceptable to define a knowledge base that contains additional properties or classes outwith the schema, or that violates certain constraints. This is due to the flexible nature of Semantic Web knowledge, which will often undergo rapid change.

2.2.2   An RDF syntax for RDF schema

RDFS gives us the ability to define a vocabulary for RDF documents. This vocabulary is a simple kind of ontology, which provides structure to the knowledge defined in RDF. As we have shown, there are two main kinds of definitions that are found in the vocabulary. The first of these is the definition of classes and the class hierarchy. Classes give us the ability to structure the knowledge according to a predefined set of types, and the class hierarchy enables us to connect together the classes by defining subclass relations. The second is the ability to define properties and typing restrictions. Properties are used to ensure that the statements that we make in our knowledge base are well-formed and valid. This is achieved by defining a specification of the property where the domain and range are restricted to a specific class.

As we have stated previously, RDFS is defined using the same syntax as RDF. This is not altogether surprising, as it should be evident from our discussion that RDFS is simply describing a network (of classes and properties), and RDF is a language for specifying networks. All of the definitions in an RDFS vocabulary can be readily represented in RDF, using a set of predefined resources with specific meanings. We now describe the XML-specific features of the representation of RDFS in RDF.

The basic representation of the class hierarchy uses the RDFS resources `rdfs:Class` and `rdfs:Resource`, and the `rdf:type` and `rdfs:subClassOf` properties. We can represent a simple class hierarchy using standard RDF as illustrated in the following XML fragments:

```
<rdf:Description rdf:ID="CameraType">
  <rdf:type
    rdf:resource="http://www.w3.org/2000/01/rdf-schema#Class"/>
</rdf:Description>

<rdf:Description rdf:ID="Manufacturer">
  <rdf:type
    rdf:resource="http://www.w3.org/2000/01/rdf-schema#Class"/>
  <rdfs:subClassOf rdf:resource="#CameraType"/>
</rdf:Description>
```

```
1    <?xml version="1.1"?>
2    <rdf:RDF xmlns:rdf="http://www.w3.org/1999/02/22-rdf-syntax-ns#"
3             xmlns:rdfs="http://www.w3.org/2000/01/rdf-schema#"
4             xml:base="http://www.mycamera.org/photo#">

5    <rdfs:Class rdf:ID="CameraType"/>

6    <rdfs:Class rdf:ID="Manufacturer">
7      <rdfs:subClassOf rdf:resource="#CameraType"/>
8    </rdfs:Class>

9    <rdfs:Class rdf:ID="ModelType">
10     <rdfs:subClassOf rdf:resource="#Manufacturer"/>
11   </rdfs:Class>

12   <rdfs:Class rdf:ID="BackType">
13     <rdfs:subClassOf rdf:resource="#CameraType"/>
14   </rdfs:Class>

15   <rdfs:Class rdf:ID="DigitalBack">
16     <rdfs:subClassOf rdf:resource="#BackType"/>
17   </rdfs:Class>

18   <rdfs:Class rdf:ID="FilmBack">
19     <rdfs:subClassOf rdf:resource="#BackType"/>
20   </rdfs:Class>

21   </rdf:RDF>
```

Figure 2.9 *RDFS class hierarchy.*

It is possible to abbreviate the syntax of RDF to make the representation cleaner. For description elements with an `rdf:type` element, we can use the type name in place of `rdf:Description`. This leads us to the typical representation of an RDFS class hierarchy, shown in Figure 2.9. A clear advantage of this syntax is that we can use the `rdfs` namespace directly, e.g. `rdfs:Class`.

To create an instance of a class in RDF, we define a statement with the class name as the type of an RDF resource. Once again we can use the abbreviated syntax to make things clearer. For example, in the following RDF fragment we state that `NikonCorporation` is an instance of the `Manufacturer` class. This definition would typically appear in a separate document from the schema.

```
<Manufacturer rdf:ID="NikonCorporation"/>
```

In our discussion of RDFS, we stated that the properties are defined separately from the class hierarchy. Part of the reason for this separation is that properties are already present in RDF, while the class hierarchy

```
1   <?xml version="1.1"?>
2   <!DOCTYPE rdf:RDF [
3     <!ENTITY xsd "http://www.w3.org/2001/XMLSchema#">
4     <!ENTITY rdf "http://www.w3.org/1999/02/22-rdf-syntax-ns">]>

5   <rdf:RDF xmlns:rdf="http://www.w3.org/1999/02/22-rdf-syntax-ns#"
6            xmlns:rdfs="http://www.w3.org/2000/01/rdf-schema#"
7            xml:base="http://www.mycamera.org/photo#">

8     <rdfs:Datatype rdf:about="&xsd;decimal"/>

9     <rdf:Property rdf:ID="manufacturer">
10      <rdfs:domain rdf:resource="#CameraType"/>
11      <rdfs:range rdf:resource="#Manufacturer"/>
12    </rdf:Property>

13    <rdf:Property rdf:ID="model">
14      <rdfs:range rdf:resource="#ModelType"/>
15      <rdfs:subPropertyOf rdf:resource="#manufacturer"/>
16    </rdf:Property>

17    <rdf:Property rdf:ID="resolution">
18      <rdfs:domain rdf:resource="#CameraType"/>
19      <rdfs:range rdf:resource="&xsd;decimal"/>
20    </rdf:Property>

21    <rdf:Property rdf:ID="alternatives">
22      <rdfs:domain rdf:resource="#CameraType"/>
23      <rdfs:range rdf:resource="&rdf;Alt"/>
24    </rdf:Property>

25  </rdf:RDF>
```

Figure 2.10 *RDFS property restrictions.*

is purely a feature of RDFS. The properties are defined in RDF as a special kind of resource, identified by rdf:Property. RDFS provides the additional properties rdfs:domain and rdfs:range for expressing restrictions, and rdfs:subPropertyOf for defining a property hierarchy. Figure 2.10 illustrates the syntax that is used to express these features.

The first definition that we make is applied to the manufacturer property (lines 9 to 12). This property associates a Camera Type with a Manufacturer. We make the restriction that the camera, which appears as the domain of the property, must have the type CameraType. This type was previously defined in Figure 2.9. The range is similarly restricted to the Manufacturer type from the class hierarchy. The model property (line 13–16) is defined as a subproperty of manufacturer (line 15). The domain restriction is inherited, while the range is further restricted to ModelType.

```
1    <?xml version="1.1"?>
2    <!DOCTYPE rdf:RDF [
3      <!ENTITY xsd "http://www.w3.org/2001/XMLSchema#">]>

4    <rdf:RDF xmlns:rdf="http://www.w3.org/1999/02/22-rdf-syntax-ns#"
5             xmlns:rdfs="http://www.w3.org/2000/01/rdf-schema#"
6             xmlns:camera="http://www.mycamera.org/photo#"
7             xml:base="http://www.mycamera.org/canon#">

8      <camera:Manufacturer rdf:ID="CanonInc"/>
9      <camera:ModelType rdf:ID="EOS300D"/>

10     <camera:CameraType rdf:ID="CanonEOS300D">
11       <camera:manufacturer rdf:resource="#CanonInc"/>
12       <camera:model rdf:resource="#EOS300D"/>
13       <camera:resolution rdf:datatype="&xsd;decimal">
14         6.3</camera:resolution>
15       <camera:alternatives>
16         <rdf:alt>
17           <rdf:li rdf:resource="#NikonD70"/>
18           <rdf:li rdf:resource="#Pentax*istD"/>
19           <rdf:li rdf:resource="#CanonEOS20D"/>
20         </rdf:alt>
21       </camera:alternatives>
22     </camera:CameraType>

23   </rdf:RDF>
```

Figure 2.11   *RDF instance declaration.*

The range of a restriction can be given by a literal *type*, as in the third
definition (line 17–20). The meaning of this definition is that the range of
the `resolution` property must be a literal value with the XML Schema
type `decimal`. We specify that `xsd:decimal` is a literal type, as opposed
to a literal value, in line 8. This is not a definition of the datatype, only
a statement that the datatype exists. Datatypes must be defined externally to the RDF and RDFS specification, typically in the XML Schema
language.

In our final definition, we show that a restriction can be defined using
an arbitrary RDF resource. For example, we would like the range of
our `alternatives` property (lines 21–24) to be more than one resource.
Therefore, we specify the RDF alternative container `rdf:Alt` as the range
of the property. We use an XML entity for the `rdf` namespace (line 4), as
the definition appears inside a string literal.

We present an example in Figure 2.11 that illustrates how to create an RDF document matching a schema. Our schema is taken from

the definitions in Figures 2.9 and 2.10, and assigned to the `camera` namespace. The RDF document is primarily an instance of the `CameraType` class, called `CanonEOS300D` (lines 10–22). We also define instances of the `Manufacturer` class (line 8) and the `ModelType` class (line 9) in order to satisfy the properties. Lines 11–21 define instances of all the properties shown in Figure 2.10.

We have now described all of the main features of the RDFS language. At this point, it is a useful exercise to examine the RDF and RDFS definitions that we have been including in our documents. The RDF and RDF namespaces shown below refer to real RDFS documents that can be downloaded from the given web addresses:

```
http://www.w3.org/1999/02/22-rdf-syntax-ns
http://www.w3.org/2000/01/rdf-schema
```

These documents provide a good exemplar of the use of the RDFS language. It may be somewhat surprising to see that RDF itself is defined by a set of RDFS classes and properties. The RDF class hierarchy and properties are illustrated graphically in Figure 2.12. We indicate the domain and range of the properties with D and R respectively. Note that the RDF and RDFS definitions are interdependent, e.g. the root of the RDF class hierarchy is the `rdfs:Resource` class.

A number of additional RDFS properties are used in these definition documents, primarily to make them more human-readable. The `rdfs:comment` property provides a description of a resource, and the `rdfs:label` property provides an alternative (informal) labelling scheme. The `rdfs:seeAlso` property is used to indicate that another resource may provide related information, and the `rdfs:isDefinedBy` subproperty indicates that the definition of the resource is given elsewhere, e.g. in a text document.

2.3   The web ontology language

The RDFS approach to defining RDF vocabularies is limited in expressibility. This was a deliberate choice in the design of RDFS, as it is intended to be a simple language that is easily understood. Nonetheless, in many cases it would be desirable to have a more expressive ontology language for the Semantic Web. To this end, a number of researchers proposed richer ontology languages that extend the facilities of RDF and RDFS. This work culminated in the definition of the Web Ontology Language (OWL) standard that we now describe. To give a better picture of OWL compared

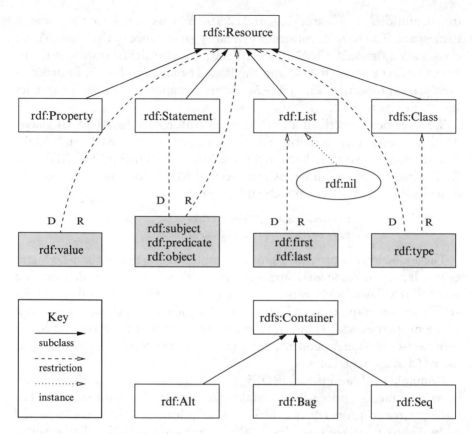

Figure 2.12 *RDF definition in RDFS.*

to RDFS, we list below a few of the additional features that can be defined in OWL:

1. We can define classes as Boolean combinations of other classes using the set operators *union, intersection*, and *complement*. For example, we may wish to define a camera class as a union of a body and lens class.
2. We can state that classes are *disjoint*, for example, a camera is either a film or a digital camera and never both.
3. We can state that two classes (with different URI) are the same class, and that two different instances actually represent the same individual.
4. We can specify *cardinality* restrictions on properties, for example, a camera uses only one film size, or a camera requires at least one lens.
5. We can specify that a property is *transitive*, e.g. if A has B and B has C, then A has C. We can also state that a property is *unique* and can be used as a key, e.g. a serial number.

In defining an ontology language for the Semantic Web, there is a trade-off between expressibility and efficient reasoning. In general, the more features that we have in the language, the more difficult it is to reason with the language. In other words, although we can represent more knowledge, the computation becomes more inefficient and eventually becomes undecidable. Depending on the kind of application that we are constructing, we may prefer to have more expressibility, or more efficient reasoning. For example, we may be only interested in representing a body of knowledge, in which case we would prefer a more expressive language. Alternatively, we may be interested in building a tool that can rapidly use our knowledge, in which case we would favour efficient reasoning.

To address the needs of the Semantic Web, OWL is not a single language but rather a family of three languages: OWL-Lite, OWL-DL, and OWL-Full. These languages form a sequence of increasing expressibility, where OWL-Full is more expressive than OWL-DL, which is more expressive than OWL-Lite. Expressibility is directly related to the number and kind of OWL language primitives that are permitted in each. The languages are also compatible, in that a legal OWL-Lite ontology is also a legal OWL-DL ontology, and a legal OWL-DL ontology is a legal OWL-Full ontology. OWL-Lite is intended to be easy to support in applications. OWL-DL is equivalent to a well-defined Description Logic (DL) with efficient reasoning. OWL-Full uses all of the OWL language primitives, though the reasoning is undecidable. We simply write OWL in our discussion to refer to the superset of all three sublanguages.

OWL is closely related to RDFS, and is similarly defined using the RDF XML-based syntax. When we use OWL, our knowledge base is defined in RDF as before. Similarly, an OWL ontology is associated with the instances in RDF by providing typing information in the RDF document, just as we did for RDFS. In effect, OWL can be considered a direct substitute for RDFS. Ideally, OWL would be defined as a pure extension of RDFS with extra language primitives to add expressiveness. However, despite the limitations of RDFS, the language has some very powerful primitives that would lead to undecidable reasoning if combined with OWL. For example, the RDFS primitive `rdfs:Class` is very expressive as it defines the class of all classes. Only OWL-Full is completely downward compatible with RDFS, with the result that the language is undecidable.

To avoid the problem of undecidability, OWL defines `owl:Class` that is a specialization of `rdfs:Class` and has a more restricted meaning. Figure 2.13 illustrates the relationship between the RDFS and the OWL primitives. Every individual defined in OWL has the special class `owl:Thing` as a superclass, which is an alternative to the 'class of all classes' in RDFS. OWL also defines the empty class `owl:Nothing`. In OWL, properties

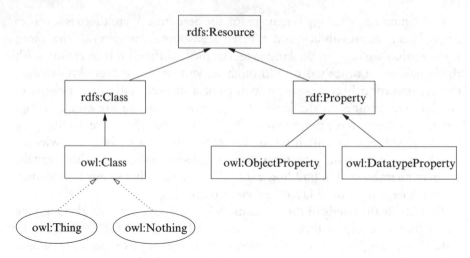

Figure 2.13 *Relationship between OWL and RDFS.*

are specialized into `owl:ObjectProperty` and `owl:DatatypeProperty`, which partition the vocabulary into properties that apply to objects, and properties that apply to values.

It should be noted that OWL makes an *open-world assumption* that resources are not confined to a single document in either definition or scope. For example, classes may be extended by other ontologies. Consequently, any extensions to a class are monotonic; they cannot retract previous information. This has important consequences for the design of ontologies in the global environment of the Web.

2.3.1 An RDF syntax for OWL-Lite

OWL is structured around the notion of a class hierarchy, and a separate hierarchy of properties just as in RDFS. There are many shared concepts between the two languages, and it is relatively straightforward to adapt to the OWL notation from RDFS. The key difference between the two is in the kinds of properties that we can express. For this reason, we use the XML-based syntax of OWL from the beginning, rather than presenting a separate discussion of the concepts. We begin by discussing the OWL-Lite language, and briefly discuss the OWL-DL and OWL-Full extensions in Section 2.3.2.

A class hierarchy can be defined in OWL using `owl:Class` together with the `rdfs:subClassOf` property. To create a member of an OWL class, we define an RDF triple with the property `rdf:type`, and a class name as the object of the property. The usage of these classes is illustrated in the code fragment below. We can also create an individual member using the abbreviated RDF syntax, e.g. `<Manufacturer rdf:ID="CanonInc"/>`.

```
<owl:Class rdf:ID="CameraType"/>

<owl:Class rdf:ID="Manufacturer">
  <rdfs:subClassOf rdf:resource="#CameraType"/>
</owl:Class>

<rdf:Description rdf:ID="CanonInc">
  <rdf:type rdf:resource="#Manufacturer"/>
</rdf:Description>
```

Ontologies in OWL will often be constructed as extensions of existing OWL ontologies. To assist in this process, OWL enables us to define *equality* and *inequality* between resources. This is useful when we combine two ontologies that define the same concept under a different name, or two knowledge bases that classify the same knowledge in different ways. We can use the `owl:equivalentClass` property to indicate that two classes have precisely the same instances. For example, the following definition declares the class `SingleLensReflex` to be equivalent to the class `SLR`:

```
<owl:Class rdf:ID="SingleLensReflex">
  <owl:equivalentClass rdf:resource="#SLR"/>
</owl:Class>
```

OWL does not have a *unique name* assumption for individuals. A single individual may be referenced using different names. We can assert that two distinct names refer to the same individual using `owl:sameAs`, or that two names refer to different individuals using `owl:differentFrom`. These properties are illustrated in the following code fragment, which states that a Pentax MZ50 is the same as a Pentax ZX50, and different from a Pentax MZ5N.

```
<ModelType rdf:ID="PentaxMZ50">
  <owl:sameAs rdf:resource="#PentaxZX50"/>
  <owl:differentFrom rdf:resource="#Pentax MZ5N"/>
</ModelType>
```

It is often necessary to ensure that the individuals belonging to a group are all distinct. For example, we may want to categorize a camera as either 'Digital', '35 mm', or 'Polaroid'. It can be cumbersome to define all of these differences, and so we can use the `owl:AllDifferent` property to assert that a group of resources are pairwis distinct, e.g:

```
<owl:AllDifferent
  <owl:distinctMembers rdf:parseType="Collection">
    <BackType rdf:about="#Digital"/>
    <BackType rdf:about="#35mm"/>
    <BackType rdf:about="#Polaroid"/>
  </owl:distinctMembers>
</owl:AllDifferent>
```

The majority of additional features in the OWL-Lite language concern the property hierarchy. The key difference between properties in RDFS and OWL is the grouping of properties into different categories. OWL defines two main kinds of properties:

1. An *object property* relates an object to another in some way, e.g. hasLens and hasFilmType.
2. A *datatype property* relates an object to a datatype value, e.g. price and resolution. As in RDFS, OWL relies on an external datatype language such as XML Schema. OWL does not directly define any datatypes, or provide any datatype definition facilities.

The basic declarations of properties and restrictions in OWL are very similar to RDFS. However, OWL permits multiple domain and range restrictions for a property, and takes the intersection of the identified classes. For example, if we restrict the manufacturer property to a range of lens manufacturers combined with a range of camera manufacturers, then the property would only permit manufacturers of both lenses and cameras. The following fragment illustrates the definition of an object property hierarchy, and a datatype property in OWL:

```
<owl:ObjectProperty rdf:ID="manufacturer">
  <rdfs:domain rdf:resource="#CameraType"/>
  <rdfs:range rdf:resource="#Manufacturer"/>
</owl:ObjectProperty>

<owl:ObjectProperty rdf:ID="model">
  <rdfs:range rdf:resource="#ModelType"/>
  <rdfs:subPropertyOf rdf:resource="#manufacturer"/>
</owl:ObjectProperty>

<owl:DatatypeProperty rdf:ID="resolution">
  <rdfs:range rdf:resource="&xsd;decimal"/>
</owl:DatatypeProperty>
```

OWL allows us to assert that properties as *equivalent* and *inverse*. An equivalent property will typically have been imported from an external source under a different name. We can define two properties to be equivalent using the owl:equivalentProperty. We can also relate a property to its inverse. For example, in the following fragment we define a manufactures property that is the inverse of the manufacturer property defined above. We also define this property to be equivalent to a producer property.

```
<owl:ObjectProperty rdf:ID="manufactures">
  <rdfs:domain rdf:resource="#Manufacturer"/>
  <rdfs:range rdf:resource="#CameraType"/>
  <owl:inverseOf rdf:resource="#manufacturer">
  <owl:equivalentProperty rdf:resource="#producer"
</owl:ObjectProperty>
```

We can state a number of property features directly in OWL. In particular, a property may be identified as *symmetric* or *transitive*. For example, if camera model A is an alternative to camera model B, then it will usually follow that camera B is also an alternative to camera A. We can assert this by defining the property to be symmetric using the type owl:SymmetricProperty. Similarly, we can assert that a property is transitive using the type owl:TransitiveProperty. For example, if camera A is an alternative for camera B, and camera B is an alternative for camera C, then it follows that camera A is also an alternative for camera C. The example below illustrates how we define a property that is both symmetric and transitive. To make the definition we require an XML entity declaration that associates owl with the URI: http://www.w3.org/2002/07/owl#.

```
<owl:ObjectProperty rdf:ID="alternative">
  <rdf:type rdf:resource="&owl;SymmetricProperty"/>
  <rdf:type rdf:resource="&owl;TransitiveProperty"/>
  <rdfs:range rdf:resource="#CameraType"/>
</owl:ObjectProperty>
```

It is often useful to assert the uniqueness of a property. This is achieved in OWL by declaring *functional* and *inverse-functional* properties. A functional property has at most one value, e.g. a film size. An inverse-functional property asserts that different objects cannot share the same value, e.g. a serial number. The range of an inverse-functional property can be considered as a unique *key* for the domain.

Functional and inverse-functional properties are defined using OWL types owl:FunctionalProperty and owl:InverseFunctional Property. We note that in OWL-Lite (and OWL-DL), we can only specify inverse, symmetric, and uniqueness of object properties, and not of datatype properties. This is because we are not permitted to define properties that have both class and datatype values, as this would make it both an object property and a datatype property.

The kinds of restrictions that we have encountered so far are all global in the sense that they apply to all instances of the property. In OWL, we can also define properties that are *local* to a particular class. For example, we may wish to define a property that states: 'if we have a Pentax camera then we must use a Pentax lens'. We can accomplish this with the following definition:

```
<owl:Class rdf:about="PentaxCamera">
  <rdfs:subClassOf>
    <owl:Restriction>
      <owl:onProperty rdf:resource="#usesLens"/>
      <owl:allValuesFrom rdf:resource="#PentaxLens"/>
    </owl:Restriction>
  </rdfs:subClass>
</owl:Class>
```

This example requires careful consideration as it introduces a number of new OWL features that we have not encountered before. To define a restriction that is local to a particular class, we make the restriction on the class itself, rather than on the property as we might have expected. The restriction is defined as an `owl:Restriction` class. The property on which the restriction is applicable is defined by the `owl:onProperty` element. The restriction states that all values (i.e. the range) of the property must come from the class `PentaxLens`. This is achieved by the use of the `owl:allValuesFrom` restriction.

The means by which we achieve the restriction are somewhat unusual. Rather than placing the restriction directly in the `PentaxCamera` class, we define the class to be a subclass of a new class containing the restriction, using `rdfs:subClassOf`. This is necessary as we may have multiple restrictions, and these would all be defined in separate classes. By stating that the `PentaxCamera` class is a subclass of the new class, all instances of `PentaxCamera` are also instances of the new class, and therefore they inherit the restriction. The new class that we define is an *anonymous* class in that it has no separate identity, and the definition of this anonymous class appears directly inside the `PentaxCamera` class.

An `owl:allValuesFrom` property restriction requires that all values of the property come from the given class. This is called a *universal quantification* in logic. We can also state that at least one of the values of the property is from a specific class by using the `owl:someValuesFrom` restriction, called an *existential quantification*. The following example defines a class of individuals where at least one uses a Pentax camera:

```
<owl:Restriction>
  <owl:onProperty rdf:resource="#usesCamera"/>
  <owl:someValuesFrom rdf:resource="#PentaxCamera"/>
</owl:Restriction>
```

A cardinality constraint allows us to give an allowed range for the number of elements in a relation. We can specify that a relation must always have a value, or a given number of values, or that the value is optional. We use `owl:minCardinality` and `owl:maxCardinality` to specify the range of cardinality values. The OWL-Lite language permits a cardinality of only 0 or 1, where 0 means that the value is optional, and 1 means that it is required. A cardinality of 1 is a stronger assertion than a functional property as the former states that we must supply a value, while the latter states that only one value is permitted. OWL-DL and OWL-Full permit any positive integer values to be used. In the following example we specify the restriction that an individual (e.g. a camera) takes exactly one film size. The `owl:cardinality` element is a convenience that defines the minimum and maximum cardinality to be the same value.

```
<owl:Restriction>
  <owl:onProperty rdf:resource="#filmSize"/>
  <owl:cardinality rdf:datatype="&xsd;nonNegativeInteger">
    1</owl:cardinality>
</owl:Restriction>
```

We have now presented all of the features of the OWL-Lite language. This language clearly allows us to express many more features of an ontology than were possible in RDFS. In particular, we can specify many different kinds of properties such as inverse, symmetric, and transitive properties. OWL-Lite also enriches the class hierarchy with the ability to specify equivalent classes, and restrictions that apply only to specific instances. In essence, OWL-Lite provides us with a straightforward ontology language for defining classification and restrictions. As previously stated, the OWL-Lite sublanguage is intended to be easy to implement. The restrictions in the language that we have noted are designed to make the language easy to reason about.

2.3.2   OWL-DL and OWL-Full

We now discuss the OWL-DL and OWL-Full languages, which directly extend OWL-Lite. These languages relax the restrictions of OWL-Lite, such as the cardinality limitations, and enrich the language with a number of additional features. Both of these languages have the same basic vocabulary, though OWL-DL imposes a number of restrictions that OWL-Full does not. The restrictions in OWL-DL are designed to permit maximum expressiveness while retaining completeness and decidability of reasoning. OWL-Full relaxes all restrictions on the language, and permits any combination of language features that result in a valid RDF document.

The additional features that are present in OWL-DL and OWL-Full primarily enhance the expressiveness of the class hierarchy. The first of these is the ability to specify a class by a direct *enumeration* of the members of the class. The enumeration completely specifies the class, i.e. any individual that does not appear in the list cannot belong to the class. An enumeration is defined using the `owl:oneOf` element as illustrated below. We use an RDF collection `rdf:parseType="Collection"` to specify that the list of members is closed.

```
<owl:Class rdf:ID="BodyType">
  <owl:oneOf rdf:parseType="Collection">
    <owl:Thing rdf:about="#Compact"/>
    <owl:Thing rdf:about="#SLR"/>
    <owl:Thing rdf:about="#Rangefinder"/>
    <owl:Thing rdf:about="#MediumFormat"/>
    <owl:Thing rdf:about="#LargeFormat"/>
  </owl:oneOf>
</owl:Class>
```

We can specify that two classes are *disjoint* so that a member of one class cannot be simultaneously considered a member of another specified class. This is more general than the `owl:AllDifferent` property that we described earlier, as it applies to whole classes rather than individuals. The following example defines the class 35mmBack as disjoint from the other subclasses of FilmBack. It is important to note that this definition does not assert that the classes APSBack and 120mmBack are disjoint from one another, only that they are disjoint from 35mmBack. To assert that the classes are mutually disjoint there must be a separate definition for each pair.

```
<owl:Class rdf:ID="35mmBack">
  <rdfs:subClassOf rdf:resource="#FilmBack"/>
  <owl:disjointWith rdf:resource="#APSBack"/>
  <owl:disjointWith rdf:resource="#120mmBack"/>
  <owl:disjointWith rdf:resource="#SheetBack"/>
  <owl:disjointWith rdf:resource="#PolaroidBack"/>
</owl:Class>
```

In defining a class by enumeration, and specifying two classes to have disjoint members, we are treating a class as a *set* of individuals. OWL permits us to define classes as Boolean combinations of other classes, using the set operators—*union, intersection*, and *complement*. With this style of definition, the members of the set are completely specified by the set operation. In the following example, we define a Camera class as the union of the CameraBody and Lens classes using the `owl:unionOf` operator.

```
<owl:Class rdf:ID="Camera">
  <owl:unionOf rdf:parseType="Collection">
    <owl:Class rdf:about="#CameraBody"/>
    <owl:Class rdf:about="#Lens"/>
  </owl:unionOf>
</owl:Class>
```

In our earlier discussion on property restrictions, we showed how a local restriction can be made on a particular class by defining an `owl:Restriction`. The restriction was treated as an anonymous class in the definition. We can also treat such a restriction as a class when using the Boolean set operators. For example, in the following fragment we use the `owl:intersectionOf` operator to define a class of `CanonCameras`. The class is constructed from the intersection of the `Camera` class with a restriction to cameras manufactured by Canon. This example also introduces the `owl:hasValue` property restriction, which requires that a property has a particular value.

```
<owl:Class rdf:ID="CanonCameras">
  <owl:intersectionOf rdf:parseType="Collection">
    <owl:Class rdf:about="#Camera"/>
    <owl:Restriction>
      <owl:onProperty rdf:resource="#manufacturer"/>
      <owl:hasValue rdf:resource="#Canon"/>
    </owl:Restriction>
  </owl:intersectionOf>
<owl:Class>
```

A complement of a class is the set of all individuals who do not belong to the class. It is defined as the set difference between `owl:Thing` and the class. The resulting set of individuals may be very large, since all of the individuals in the domain of discourse will be considered. Therefore, the complement is typically only used in conjunction with the other set operators. In Figure 2.14 we define a class of 'Point and Shoot' cameras using the `owl:complementOf` operator.

The `PointAndShoot` camera class is defined as a camera type with a fixed lens mount, an autofocus facility, and a camera body that is neither medium format nor large format. We use all three set operators in our definition. In lines 23–28 we construct a class that is the union of the `MediumFormat` and `LargeFormat` classes. In lines 20–30 we construct a new subclass of `BodyType` (line 21), which is the complement of our previous class, i.e. all body types that are neither medium format, nor large format. Finally, in lines 15–32 we construct a new `CameraType` subclass (line 16), which is the intersection of the individuals of the complement class, the `FixedMount` class, and the `AutoFocus` class.

```
1   <?xml version="1.1"?>
2   <!DOCTYPE rdf:RDF [
3     <!ENTITY rdf "http://www.w3.org/1999/02/22-rdf-syntax-ns">
4     <!ENTITY rdfs "http://www.w3.org/2000/01/rdf-schema#">
5     <!ENTITY owl "http://www.w3.org/2002/07/owl#">
6     <!ENTITY camera "http://www.mycamera.org/photo#">
7     <!ENTITY base "http://www.mycamera.org/photo/abbrev#">]>

8   <rdf:RDF xmlns:rdf="&rdf;" xmlns:rdfs="&rdfs;" xmlns:owl="&owl;"
9            xmlns:camera="&camera;" xml:base="&base;">

10  <owl:Ontology rdf:about="">
11    <rdfs:label>Point and Shoot Ontology</rdfs:label>
12    <owl:versionInfo>0.1</owl:versionInfo>
13    <owl:imports rdf:resource="http://www.mycamera.org/photo"/>
14  </owl:Ontology>

15  <owl:Class rdf:ID="PointAndShoot">
16    <rdfs:subClassOf rdf:resource="&camera;CameraType"/>
17    <owl:intersectionOf rdf:parseType="Collection">
18      <owl:Class rdf:about="&camera;FixedMount"/>
19      <owl:Class rdf:about="&camera;AutoFocus"/>
20      <owl:Class>
21        <rdfs:subClassOf rdf:resource="&camera;BodyType"/>
22        <owl:complementOf>
23          <owl:Class>
24            <owl:unionOf rdf:parseType="Collection">
25              <owl:Class rdf:about="&camera;MediumFormat"/>
26              <owl:Class rdf:about="&camera;LargeFormat"/>
27            </owl:unionOf>
28          </owl:Class>
29        </owl:complementOf>
30      </owl:Class>
31    </owl:intersectionOf>
32  </owl:Class>

33  </rdf:RDF>
```

Figure 2.14 *Complex class construction.*

Figure 2.14 illustrates a complete OWL ontology as an RDF document. The document construction and layout is clearly very similar to RDFS. Lines 3–7 contain the XML entity declarations used in the document. In particular, line 5 defines an entity for the classes used in OWL. The XML namespaces are declared in lines 8 and 9. We declare a namespace that corresponds to each entity. Thus, we can use the entities and namespaces interchangeably as required. We use the entities in our namespace declarations. This is standard practice as it avoids duplication of the URI.

An OWL *ontology header* is defined in lines 10–14 of Figure 2.14. The header is an `owl:Ontology` element that contains a list of assertions. The purpose of these assertions is to support housekeeping tasks, such as comments, and version control. Typically, Dublin Core metadata elements are used for these assertions. Only the `owl:imports` assertion has any actual effect on the ontology. This assertion lists other ontologies whose content is imported and becomes part of the current ontology. A namespace declaration allows us to reference resources in other ontologies, while an import declaration includes the external resources in the current ontology. In our example, the camera ontology that we import will become part of the ontology that we define. The `owl` namespace is not imported as we only wish to use the OWL vocabulary, not extend the OWL language. We note that importing an ontology O will also cause the import of all the ontologies that O imports, i.e. importing is transitive.

In line 12 of Figure 2.14, we define a version identifier for the ontology. This can be an arbitrary string that relates the ontology to some version information. OWL defines several additional elements that are useful in managing different ontology versions. These elements are useful for tracking revisions, which will typically occur in any knowledge lifecycle. It is possible to link an ontology to a previous version using an `owl:priorVersion` element. We can strengthen this with an indication of compatibility using `owl:backwardCompatibleWith`, which indicates that all the definitions in the previous version have the same meaning, and `owl:incompatibleWith` to indicate that an upgrade is not possible without making changes to the knowledge base. Finally, OWL defines two classes that may be used to indicate that a class or property will likely be changing in an incompatible manner: `owl:DeprecatedClass` and `owl:DeprecatedProperty`. It should be noted that none of these compatibility elements carry a formal meaning in OWL, and their interpretation is left to the user of the ontology. The following fragment illustrates the use of the version fields in the OWL header, and the deprecation of a class.

```
<owl:Ontology rdf:about="">
  <owl:versionInfo>0.2</owl:versionInfo>
  <owl:priorVersion
    rdf:resource="http://www.mycamera.org/photo/abbrev"/>
  <owl:backwardCompatibleWith
    rdf:resource="http://www.mycamera.org/photo/abbrev"/>
</owl:Ontology>
<owl:DeprecatedClass rdf:ID="&camera;SingleLensReflex"/>
```

We have now described all of the main features of the OWL language. At this point, it is necessary to examine the difference between OWL-Full and

OWL-DL in detail. As previously stated, OWL-Full and OWL-DL have the same vocabulary. In OWL-Full we are permitted to mix OWL with RDFS, and no restrictions are placed on the language, beyond the requirement that we have a valid RDF document. By contrast, OWL-DL places a number of restrictions on the language that are necessary for decidable reasoning. These restrictions are summarized below.

1. The key restriction in OWL-DL is that a resource is only permitted to assume a single type. This restriction is called *vocabulary partitioning*. In particular, a resource cannot be treated as both a datatype value and an individual at the same time.
2. The type of a resource must be declared explicitly. We are not permitted to infer the type from the usage of the resource. For example, if we use a property as an object property, then we must have a declaration in our ontology of the form:

    `<owl:ObjectProperty rdf:ID="manufacturer"/>`

3. The type restriction means that the following cannot be defined for datatype properties: `owl:inverseOf`, `owl:SymmetricProperty`, `owl:FunctionalProperty`, and `owl:InverseFunctionalProperty`.
4. A cardinality restriction may not be placed on a transitive property, defined with `owl:TransitiveProperty`.
5. Anonymous classes may only appear as the range, and not the domain, of an `rdfs:subClassOf` relation.

At this point it is a useful exercise to examine some real OWL ontologies in order to obtain a better understanding of the principles. A good place to begin is the OWL vocabulary definition that we import as the `owl` namespace in Figure 2.14. The OWL vocabulary is specified as an OWL-Full ontology. The top-level structure of this document was previously illustrated in Figure 2.13. The AKT Reference Ontology in the Suggested Reading section is a good example of a real-world OWL ontology.

We note that the manual construction of complete ontologies in XML is a difficult and error-prone task. This task can be made significantly easier by the use of graphical ontology editing tools. These tools permit the ontologies to be readily constructed and validated for consistency. Examples of such tools include the popular Protégé and Swoop ontology editors.

2.4 Summary

In this chapter we have presented a detailed summary of the syntax of the RDF, RDFS, and OWL Semantic Web languages. These languages are designed to address the representation of knowledge on the Web. A summary of the main features of these languages is given below:

- The RDF is a formalism for knowledge representation based around the notion of a knowledge triple. There are three equivalent views of a triple in RDF:

  1. A relation between a resource, a property, and a value.
  2. A statement with a subject, a predicate, and an object.
  3. A pair of nodes and a directed edge in a semantic network.

- The RDFS language is a simple ontology description language for defining the structure of RDF knowledge. RDFS gives us the ability to define a vocabulary for RDF. There are two key structures that this vocabulary defines:

  1. The class hierarchy defines the relationships between classes, which represent concepts in the knowledge base. Classes are related to RDF by assigning types to the resources. A class hierarchy is structured as a directed graph of subclass relations. The subclass relation defines one class to be more specialized than another through inheritance.
  2. The property hierarchy defines the relationships between RDF properties. However, the main purpose of the property hierarchy is to place restrictions in the form of the RDF triples, and thereby impose structure on the knowledge base. Specifically, we can restrict the domain and range of a property to specific classes or literal values.

- The OWL is an ontology description language that is more expressive than RDFS. OWL is defined in conjunction with an RDF knowledge base, as in RDFS. OWL is a non-strict extension of RDFS with many more features for defining the class hierarchy and property restrictions. There are three sublanguages in the OWL definition, which trade between expressibility and efficient reasoning. These three languages have the following features:

  1. OWL-Lite is a restricted form of OWL that is intended to be easy to understand, and easier to implement in applications. In particular, OWL-Lite excludes enumerated classes and disjoint statements, and allows only restricted cardinality. This simplicity comes at the expense of expressibility.
  2. OWL-DL is equivalent to a well-defined DL. OW-DL contains all of the OWL language primitives, but imposes restrictions on their use.

OWL-DL is designed to maximize expressiveness while retaining decidability and completeness of reasoning.

3. OWL-Full uses all of the OWL language primitives, and allows arbitrary combination of these primitives with RDF and RDFS. This flexibility comes at the expense of decidable reasoning.

The classes and properties of the RDF, RDFS, and OWL languages are summarized in Tables 2.1 and 2.2 respectively. This information is taken directly from the definition documents that we include as XML namespaces. We note that the definition documents do not provide the full formal definition of these languages. In particular, they define only the syntax

Table 2.1 *RDF, RDFS, and OWL classes.*

Class	Superclass
rdf:Property	rdfs:Resource
rdf:Statement	rdfs:Resource
rdf:Bag	rdfs:Container
rdf:Seq	rdfs:Container
rdf:Alt	rdfs:Container
rdf:List	rdfs:Resource
rdfs:Resource	
rdfs:Class	rdfs:Resource
rdfs:Literal	rdfs:Resource
rdfs:Container	rdfs:Resource
rdfs:ContainerMembershipProperty	rdf:Property
rdfs:Datatype	rdfs:Class
owl:Class	rdfs:Class
owl:Thing	
owl:Nothing	
owl:AllDifferent	
owl:Restriction	owl:Class
owl:ObjectProperty	rdf:Property
owl:DatatypeProperty	rdf:Property
owl:TransitiveProperty[†]	owl:ObjectProperty
owl:SymmetricProperty[†]	owl:ObjectProperty
owl:FunctionalProperty[†]	rdf:Property
owl:InverseFunctionalProperty[†]	owl:ObjectProperty
owl:AnnotationProperty	rdf:Property
owl:Ontology	
owl:OntologyProperty	rdf:Property
owl:DeprecatedClass	owl:Class
owl:DeprecatedProperty	rdf:Property
owl:DataRange	

[†] Restricted in OWL-Lite and OWL-DL.

Table 2.2 *RDF, RDFS, and OWL properties.*

Property	Domain	Range
rdf:type	rdfs:Resource	rdfs:Class
rdf:subject	rdf:Statement	rdfs:Resource
rdf:predicate	rdf:Statement	rdfs:Resource
rdf:object	rdf:Statement	rdfs:Resource
rdf:value	rdfs:Resource	rdfs:Resource
rdf:first	rdf:List	rdfs:Resource
rdf:rest	rdf:List	rdf:List
rdfs:subClassOf	rdfs:Class	rdfs:Class
rdfs:subPropertyOf	rdf:Property	rdf:Property
rdfs:comment	rdfs:Resource	rdfs:Literal
rdfs:label	rdfs:Resource	rdfs:Literal
rdfs:domain	rdf:Property	rdfs:Class
rdfs:range	rdf:Property	rdfs:Class
rdfs:seeAlso	rdfs:Resource	rdfs:Resource
rdfs:isDefinedBy	rdfs:Resource	rdfs:Resource
rdfs:member	rdfs:Resource	rdfs:Resource
owl:equivalentClass	owl:Class	owl:Class
owl:disjointWith‡	owl:Class	owl:Class
owl:equivalentProperty	rdf:Property	rdf:Property
owl:sameAs	owl:Thing	owl:Thing
owl:differentFrom	owl:Thing	owl:Thing
owl:distinctMembers	owl:AllDifferent	rdf:List
owl:unionOf‡	owl:Class	rdf:List
owl:intersectionOf†	owl:Class	rdf:List
owl:complementOf‡	owl:Class	owl:Class
owl:oneOf‡	owl:Class	rdf:List
owl:onProperty	owl:Restriction	rdf:Property
owl:allValuesFrom	owl:Restriction	rdfs:Class
owl:hasValue‡	owl:Restriction	
owl:someValuesFrom	owl:Restriction	rdfs:Class
owl:minCardinality†	owl:Restriction	xsd:nonNegativeInteger
owl:maxCardinality†	owl:Restriction	xsd:nonNegativeInteger
owl:cardinality†	owl:Restriction	xsd:nonNegativeInteger
owl:inverseOf	owl:ObjectProperty	owl:ObjectProperty
owl:imports	owl:Ontology	owl:Ontology
owl:versionInfo		
owl:priorVersion	owl:Ontology	owl:Ontology
owl:backwardCompatibleWith	owl:Ontology	owl:Ontology
owl:incompatibleWith	owl:Ontology	owl:Ontology

† Restricted in OWL-Lite.   ‡ OWL-DL and OWL-Full only.

and not the *semantics* of the languages. For example, the definition of `rdfs:subTypeOf` states only that the domain and range must be classes. It does not capture the underlying meanings of specialization and inheritance. These semantics are provided by the reasoning systems that operate over our ontologies. We discuss reasoning with ontologies and knowledge in Chapter 5.

Finally, it is important to note that the ontology description languages discussed in this chapter do not represent the final word on knowledge representation for the Semantic Web. Although OWL is currently the proposed standard for Web ontologies, there are many suggestions for extensions, improvements, and alternatives to OWL in the Semantic Web community. In particular, we discuss the Semantic Web Rule Language (SWRL), and F-Logic—based ontologies in Chapter 5.

2.5 Exercises

1. Design a semantic network for a topic that interests you. For example, cooking, gardening, DIY, automobiles, artists, pets, or films.
2. Convert your semantic network into an XML-based RDFS vocabulary.
3. Extend your semantic network with some interesting properties or classes that cannot be represented in RDFS.
4. Construct an OWL-DL ontology for your extended semantic network using the Protégé ontology editing tool, available on:

$$\texttt{http://protege.stanford.edu/}$$

5. Construct a small RDF knowledge base that matches your OWL-DL ontology.
6. Create an FOAF description for yourself. Details about FOAF can be found at:

$$\texttt{http://www.foaf-project.org/}$$

2.6 Suggested reading

1. H. Alani, S. Harris, and B. O'Neill. Ontology Winnowing: A Case Study on the AKT Reference Ontology. In *Proceedings of International Conference on Intelligent Agents, Web Technology and Internet Commerce (IAWTIC'05)*, Vienna, Austria, November 2005.
2. S. Bechhofer, R. Volz, and P. Lord. Cooking the Semantic Web with the OWL API. In *Proceedings of the Second International Semantic Web Conference (ISWC'03)*,

volume 2870 of *Lecture Notes in Computer Science*, pp. 659–75. Springer-Verlag, 2003.

3. T. Bray, D. Hollander, and A. Layman. Namespaces in XML. Available at: http://www.w3.org/TR/REC-xml-names/, 1999.

4. T. Bray, J. Paoli, C. Sperberg-McQueen, E. Maler, and F. Yergeau. Extensible Markup Language (XML) 1.0 (3rd edn.). Available at http://www.w3.org/TR/REC-xml/, 2004.

5. D. Brickley and R. Guha. RDF Vocabulary Description Language 1.0: RDF Schema. Available at: http://www.w3.org/TR/rdf-schema/, 2004.

6. M. Dean and G. Schreiber. OWL Web Ontology Language Reference. Available at: http://www.w3.org/TR/owl-ref/, 2004.

7. E. R. Harold and W. S. Means. *XML in a Nutshell*. O'Reilly, September 2004.

8. S. Harris and N. Gibbins. 3store: Efficient Bulk RDF Storage. In *Proceedings of 1st International Workshop on Practical and Scalable Semantic Systems (PSSS'03)*, pp. 1–15, Florida, USA, October 2003.

9. M. Horridge, H. Knublauch, A. Rector, R. Stevens, and C. Wroe. A Practical Guide To Building OWL Ontologies Using The Protégé-OWL Plugin and CO-ODE Tools. Available at: http://protege.stanford.edu/doc/users.html, August 2004.

10. A. Kalyanpur, B. Parsia, E. Sirin, B. Cuenca-Grau, and J. Hendler. Swoop—A Web Ontology Editing Browser. *Journal of Web Semantics*, 4(1), 2005.

11. L. W. Lacy. *OWL: Representing Information Using the Web Ontology Language*. Trafford Publishing, 2005.

12. F. Manola and E. Miller. RDF Primer. Available at: http://www.w3.org/TR/rdf-primer/, 2004.

13. D. McGuinness and F. van Harmelen. OWL Web Ontology Language Overview. Available at: http://www.w3.org/TR/owl-features/, February 2004.

14. S. Powers. *Practical RDF*. O'Reilly Inc., 2003.

15. M. Smith, C. Welty, and D. McGuinness. OWL Web Ontology Language Guide. Available at: http://www.w3.org/TR/owl-guide/, 2004.

3 **Reactive agents**

In the previous chapter we described three languages for representing knowledge on the Semantic Web: RDF, RDFS, and OWL. These languages enable us to create Web-based knowledge in a standard manner with a common semantics. We now turn our attention to the techniques that can utilize this knowledge in an automated manner. These techniques are fundamental to the construction of the Semantic Web, as without automation we do not gain any real benefit over the current Web. There are currently two views of the Semantic Web that have implications for the kind of automation that we can hope to achieve:

1. An expert system with a distributed knowledge base.
2. A society of agents that solve complex knowledge-based tasks.

In the first view, the Semantic Web is essentially treated a single-user application that reasons about some Web-based knowledge. For example, a service that queries the knowledge to answer specific questions. This is a perfectly acceptable view, and its realization is significantly challenging. However, in this book we primarily subscribe to the second view. In this more-generalized view, the knowledge is not treated as a single body, and it is not necessary to obtain a global view of the knowledge. Instead, the knowledge is exchanged and manipulated in a peer-to-peer (P2P) manner between different entities. These entities act on behalf of human users, and require only enough knowledge to perform the task to which they are assigned.

The use of entities to solve complex problems on the Web is captured by the notion of an *agent*. In human terms, an agent is an intermediary who makes a complex organization externally accessible. For example, a travel agent simplifies the problem of booking a holiday. This concept of simplifying the interface to a complex framework is a key goal of the Semantic Web. We would like to make it straightforward for a human to interact with a wide variety of disparate sources of knowledge without becoming mired in the details. To accomplish this, we want to define *software* agents that act with similar characteristics to human agents. In doing so, we must adopt an alternative programming paradigm, that is not limited to the definition of monolithic applications on a single machine.

The programming model envisioned for the Semantic Web is based on the notion of software agents as the key consumers of knowledge. These agents act collectively as a community, rather than as a single entity. The agents are responsible for the collection, processing, and dissemination of knowledge in order to achieve specific goals. Agents exhibit a form of intelligent behaviour, in that they rationalize and can act autonomously. A community of agents that act together is termed as MAS. In Chapter 1 we outlined the main concepts in the construction of MASs. We identified two key considerations that must be addressed in any such system, which we summarize below:

1. The first consideration is the design of the internal *reasoning processes* of an agent. In essence, how we construct programs that can reason about the world in similar ways to humans.
2. The second consideration is the design of the *communicative processes* of the agent, as we want to define agents that can interact. To construct agents that can interact, we typically take our inspiration from the study of human dialogue.

Our presentation in this chapter and the next is based around a definition of the first of the two processes described above. We show how to define agents that can make decisions and reason about their environment. We present a variety of different techniques by which agents can assume rational behaviours. However, our presentation is independent of the tasks to which the agent will be applied. We discuss the use of these techniques for solving problems specific to the Semantic Web in Chapter 5. The communicative processes, by which agents interact and form societies are addressed in Chapter 6.

A key consideration in the definition of any agent system is the *environment* in which the agents will operate. Multiagent have been designed for a wide variety of different environments, e.g. robots, sensor networks, embedded systems. In this book, the environment of the agent system is the Semantic Web. For this reason, we restrict our attention to the definition of agent systems that can operate in this domain. In particular, the assumptions that we make in the design of our agents are directly related to the capabilities of the Web and the Internet.

3.1 Rational agency

A *rational* agent is one that acts to further its own interests in light of its beliefs about the world. For example, if an agent has the goal to purchase a camera at the lowest price, and it believes that the lowest price is available at PhotoMart, then it would be rational for the agent to obtain the camera from PhotoMart. The agent would be *irrational* if it decided to purchase the camera elsewhere in light of the stated goal, and its beliefs. An agent can still be considered rational if it acts in accordance with erroneous beliefs. This raises the important issue of how to design computational agents that can act rationally.

In acting rationally, an agent exhibits a form of *intelligence*. Consequently, the design of rational agents has been an active area of AI research for many years. As a first step, it is necessary to define what we actually mean by a rational agent. We do this by defining characteristics that such an agent should possess. The following four properties have been suggested as key for rational behaviour: *autonomy*, *reactivity*, *pro-activeness*, and *social ability*. These properties have significant implications in the design of our agents, and we now examine each in turn.

1. Autonomy is the freedom that an agent has to make decisions. There are varying degrees of freedom of choice that we can permit an agent to have. We can allow an agent to make only a few choices, or to make many different decisions. Full autonomy is not necessarily a desirable goal for an agent system. In general, the more freedom an agent has, the more difficult it is to implement and to ensure that it performs correctly. If we think of an agent as an abstraction for a human being, then we can argue that full autonomy is not necessarily a human trait. In any situation, a human is constrained by social conventions, and their own limitations. For example, if I go into a shop to purchase an item, then there are a whole set of conventions that I must follow, such as paying for the item before I leave. Therefore, to construct a useful agent system it is desirable to give the agents a degree of autonomy, but constrain this autonomy according to the situation the agent is in.

2. A reactive agent is one that responds to changes in the environment. As stated earlier, we assume that the environment of our agent systems is the Semantic Web. An agent can have varying degrees of reactivity. A purely reactive agent responds continually to the changes, while a hybrid agent may deliberate on the nature of the changes, and decide on an appropriate response. For example, if we consider a hypothetical agent that is designed to monitor the stock price for a particular company. In a purely reactive design, the agent would be

programmed to buy and sell the stock directly in relation to the price, while a hybrid agent may make these decisions based on a long-term strategy or in response to additional analysis of trends. Purely reactive systems are relatively straightforward to implement, as we can map environment states directly to actions. However, systems that balance between deliberative and reactive processes are more difficult to design. We present a number of techniques for designing reactive agents in this chapter, and discuss hybrid agents at the end of Chapter 4.

3. Proactiveness means that an agent will exhibit *goal-directed* behaviour. A passive agent that never tries to achieve anything is not proactive. We define goal-directed behaviour as a sequence of actions that the agent performs towards a goal. Each action involves preconditions, which are assumptions that must hold to perform the action, and post-conditions, which are the effects of performing the action. For example, if we imagine an agent that has a goal to convert a sum of money from dollars into euros. The preconditions on the conversion may be that the agent knows the current exchange rate, and has the necessary sum of money in dollars, with the post-condition that the money is now in euros. Goal-directed behaviour may be accomplished by AI planning techniques, which we describe in Chapter 4.

4. Social ability means that an agent can successfully interact and co-operate with other agents, i.e. in a society. Given that the agents are autonomous entities, they must often perform tasks on behalf of other agents that they would not necessarily choose to perform otherwise. In such situations, the agents will be required to coordinate and negotiate for mutual benefit. In doing so, an individual agent may be required to understand and reason about the goals and beliefs of other agents. For example, in order to obtain a document from another agent it may be necessary to pay for the document, and also understand that the document should not be shared with others. Social ability is one of the most complex tasks in the design of agent systems. In this book, we embrace an approach based on agent protocols, which define patterns of social interaction. An agent can examine this template in advance to determine whether or not to proceed. We return to this issue during our discussion of agent communication in Chapter 6.

We have identified four properties that are important considerations in the design of individual agents and MASs. However, these properties should not be considered as definitive, and their definitions are subject to different interpretations. For example, there are many different definitions of what it means for an agent to be truly autonomous. In addition, there are many other properties that can be argued as important in certain classes

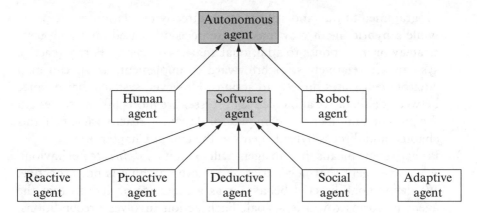

Figure 3.1 *An ontology of agent properties.*

of agent systems. For example, an *adaptive* agent is one with actions that are flexible and may be learnt through interaction, and an *emotional* agent is one that has a personality or character, with properties such as reliability and truthfulness. A basic ontology for describing the properties of an autonomous agent is presented in Figure 3.1. Our interest here is restricted to software agents, and therefore we have only expanded this part of the ontology. An agent instance would typically be ascribed more than one property, e.g. a reactive and proactive agent.

The properties that we have discussed give us a flavour of the sort of programs that we are seeking to construct. As we have previously stated, there is no single definition of the term *agent*. The actual definition and implementation of the agent is specific to the kind of task that we are seeking to perform. All that we require is that our agent can interact with other agents, and do useful work for us. We cannot hope to describe all of the possible approaches to implementing agent systems in this book. Therefore, in this book, we consider four distinct styles of agent implementation: *reactive* agents, *practical reasoning* agents, *deductive reasoning* agents, and *hybrid* agents. These styles can be considered as representing the most popular proposals for rational agency.

3.1.1 Distributed agent systems

On a casual reading of this chapter it may appear that MASs are little more than conventional distributed systems, and the reader would be forgiven for thinking that there is nothing new here. There is undoubtedly some overlap, as agent systems are necessarily distributed and concurrent in nature. However, there are essentially two subtle differences that will become more apparent in Chapter 4:

1. We have highlighted autonomy as a key property of an agent. Therefore, it is assumed that the agent makes decisions about synchronization and coordination at run-time. However, in a distributed system, these mechanisms are typically hardwired by design.
2. Rational agents are primarily self-interested entities. Therefore, it is assumed that an agent is primarily interested in furthering its own goals on behalf of a particular user. In a distributed system, the entities are generally assumed to share a common goal.

In considering these differences, we acknowledge that an agent has many characteristics in common with conventional distributed systems. However, where a distributed system prescribes a static pattern of behaviour towards a common goal, an agent system is more dynamic with individual agents acting autonomously towards their own goals. There are important meta-issues that we must address in an agent system, such how we gather together a group of agents to perform a task, how the agents actually come to specific decisions, and how agents can reach agreement with others whose motivations are unknown.

3.2 Reactive agent systems

The most straightforward way to construct an agent with a specific pattern of behaviour is simply to engineer all of the required behaviour directly into the agent. This is the approach taken in the construction of a *reactive agent*. A purely reactive agent does not perform any kind of deduction, and so its behaviour is easier to test and to predict, i.e. it should always act the same way in response to a given sequence of events. However, despite this apparent lack of reasoning power, the reactive approach to agent design can capture a wide range of useful agent behaviours.

Figure 3.2 illustrates the principles that govern the behaviour of a reactive agent. The agent is engineered to respond to changes in the environment, which we represent as input events. An input event causes the agent to perform some predefined behaviour that may result in an output action on the environment, e.g. a message is sent. An output action will cause a change in the environment, which may result in further input events for the agent. In effect, the agent is acting as a *sensor* on the environment. We can readily construct an MAS from reactive agents, where a single trigger event causes a cascade of events and actions between the agents.

More formally, we can define a reactive agent A as a function from an environment state e to an action a: $A(e) \rightarrow a$. The effect of enacting an action in one environment state is a new environment state: $e(a) \rightsquigarrow e'$.

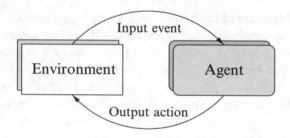

Figure 3.2 *A reactive agent.*

The following example illustrates the definition of the agent function for a trivial stock brokering agent. The agent buys stock when the price is less that 10 units, and sells the stock when the price is greater than 100 units.

$$A(e) = \begin{cases} e(stock) < 10 & \to a = \text{buy} \\ e(stock) > 100 & \to a = \text{sell} \\ otherwise & \to a = \text{do nothing} \end{cases}$$

We can define a run for a reactive agent as a sequence of environment states and actions. When we have more than one agent acting on the environment, then the actions of the different agents will be interleaved. The following definition illustrates a run r for a reactive agent system with initial environment e_i and final environment state e_n.

$$r = e_i \overset{a_0}{\rightsquigarrow} e_0 \overset{a_1}{\rightsquigarrow} e_1 \overset{a_2}{\rightsquigarrow} \cdots \overset{a_n}{\rightsquigarrow} e_n$$

Our definition illustrates the processes that occur in a reactive agent. However, there are many pragmatic issues that must also be considered if we are to construct an actual system according to this model. For example, we imply that the agent will execute continuously. However, we do not define how long the execution will last, or how quickly the agent will respond. These issues merit a closer examination of how we design our reactive agents.

The reactive agent system that we have described is driven by *events* that occur in the environment. An input event to a reactive agent can be internally or externally triggered. An *internal* event is one which the agent makes by observing the environment, e.g. checking the time, while an *external* event is made by external intervention, e.g. sending a message to the agent. An event is by definition a discrete entity, though it may be a one-time occurrence, or it may occur many times in succession. The kind of events that we want to handle have a direct effect on the kind of implementation that we choose. In general, if we are handling an event that will occur many times, such as a price fluctuation, then an *equation-based* approach is best. However, if the events are largely one-time, such as messages, then a *state-based* approach is most suited. Both the equation-based and state-based models are purely reactive formalisms. These models are driven by a domino-like behaviour; an initial event causes a cascade of agent actions and reactions in the environment.

3.2.1 Equation-based reactive systems

The equation-based style of design for reactive agents is inspired by system-dynamics modelling. This is a methodology used for studying and managing complex feedback systems, such as those found in business and social systems. This style of design is useful for understanding complex systems with multiple parts, and is therefore readily applicable to MASs. In adopting this approach we can first construct a model of the agent system to understand its dynamics, and then encode the equations from the model into our agents. The advantage of this approach is that the techniques for constructing system-dynamics models are well understood, and tool support is available. For brevity, we only provide a flavour of this system-dynamics modelling here. More information on this style of modelling can be found in the Suggested Reading section at the end of the chapter.

A complete system-dynamics specification consists of a *conceptual* model and a corresponding *quantitative* model. The conceptual model is specified as a graph-structured diagram, called a *flow diagram*. This structure is complemented by a quantitative model of linear and/or non-linear differential equations. The equations model change in the system, with the rates of change defined as functions in terms of the current state of the system. Typically, these equations are defined with respect to a time parameter, which is global to the entire system.

Figure 3.3 denotes a flow diagram for a simple *supply chain* scenario. This is a commonly occurring structure in agent systems, particularly those concerned with business processes. The supply chain begins with an initial

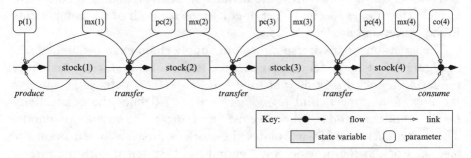

Figure 3.3 *Supply chain flow diagram.*

production of stock, which proceeds through a number of stages where it is either stored or modified, before final consumption. There are four different kinds of elements that appear in our flow diagram:

1. *State variables* in the model represent entities that will change over time. In our model, we use state variables to represent the level of stock at a particular point in the chain.
2. *Parameters* are fixed values (i.e. constants) that determine the behaviour of the model. We define two parameters associated with each state variable: the *mx* parameter defines the maximum stock for a particular stage, and the *pc* parameter defines the purchase coefficient for a stage, i.e. the rate at which stock is accumulated at a stage. The p parameter defines the rate of production in the initial node, and the co parameter defines the rate of consumption in the final node.
3. *Flows* represent the transfer of entities between the state variables. A flow may be incoming or outgoing with respect to a state variable. The ends of a flow can be unconnected, such as the production and consumption flows in our example. A flow represents a continuous transfer between state variables, where the rate of flow can be changed. It is helpful to think of a flow as analogous to a water tap.
4. *Links* are used to represent a transfer of information, as opposed to the transfer of entities in the flows. A link can be viewed as an *influence* between different parts of the model. For example, the three links into the production flow show that this flow is influenced by the production parameter, the maximum stock parameter, and the level of stock at the first node in the chain.

A flow diagram defines the structure of a system at a conceptual level. The emphasis of this definition is on the connections between the various components, rather than the behaviour of the components themselves. This is a useful distinction as it allows us to construct an abstract description of a system, before considering the details of its implementation. The behaviours of the components are defined in a corresponding quantitative model. This model specifies a set of equations for each of the components in the conceptual model.

The equations that correspond to our supply chain example are defined in Figure 3.4. The model comprises three functions: (a) $state(n, t)$ defines the level of stock for node n at time t, (b) $rate(F, t)$ defines the rate for the flow F at time t, and (c) $flow(F, n_1, n_2)$ defines the connectivity between nodes n_1 and n_2 where we use _ to indicate the absence of a node. The $state(n, t)$ function calculates the stock recursively based upon the level of stock at the previous time period $t - 1$, summed with the rate of transfer for all incoming flows F_i, and less the rate of transfer of stock

$$state(n, \ 0) = initial\_value(n)$$
$$state(n, \ t) = state(X, \ t-1) +$$
$$(\Sigma\{rate(F_i(n_i, \ n), \ t-1) \ | \ \exists n_i . \ flow(F_i, \ n_i, \ n)\}) -$$
$$(\Sigma\{rate(F_o(n, \ n_o), \ t-1) \ | \ \exists n_o . \ flow(F_o, \ n, \ n_o)\})$$

$$rate(transfer(n_1, \ n_2), \ t) = pc(n_2) * state(stock(n_2), \ t) *$$
$$(1 - \tfrac{mx(n_1) - state(stock(n_1), \ t)}{mx(n_1)}) *$$
$$(1 - \tfrac{state(stock(n_2), \ t)}{mx(n_2)})$$

$$rate(produce(\_, \ n), \ t) = p(n) * state(stock(n), \ t) *$$
$$(1 - \tfrac{state(stock(n), \ t)}{mx(n)})$$

$$rate(consume(n, \ \_), \ t) = co(n) * state(stock(n), \ t) *$$
$$(1 - \tfrac{mx(n) - state(stock(n), \ t)}{mx(n)})$$

$$flow(F, \ n_1, \ n_2) = \text{true if } n_1 \text{ and } n_2 \text{ are connected.}$$
$$flow(F, \ \_, \ n) = \text{true if } n \text{ is the initial node.}$$
$$flow(F, \ n, \ \_) = \text{true if } n \text{ is the final node.}$$

Figure 3.4 *Supply chain equations.*

for all outgoing flows F_o. The $rate(transfer(n_1, \ n_2))$ function defines the rate of flow from n_1 into n_2. The transfer is determined by the stock level of n_2 at the current time period scaled by the purchase coefficient. The transfer rate is also dependent on the level of stock in n_1 and n_2: the rate will be throttled as the level of stock in n_1 diminishes, and also as the rate of stock in n_2 approaches the maximum. The *produce* and *consume* functions are similarly defined: production is throttled as the producer reaches the maximum stock level, and consumption is throttled as the consumer reaches the minimum stock level.

The flow diagram and the equations completely specify the behaviour of a system-dynamics model. Thus, we can perform a *simulation* by evaluating the model over a specified number of time steps. For each time step, we re-calculate the values of the equations, and update the corresponding variables in the flow diagram. Typically, the values of one or more variables will be plotted against the time step to produce a graphical representation of the model behaviour. There are a number of tools available to assist with the construction and simulation of models such as Simile.

Figure 3.5 illustrates a simulation of the model with the following parameters: $p(1) = 1$, $mx(1) = 20$, $mx(2) = 50$, $mx(3) = 100$, $mx(4) = 50$, $pc(n) = 0.5$, $co(4) = 0.5$, $initial\_value(n) = 1$. Each graph exhibits an oscillation as the supply from the producer and the demand from the

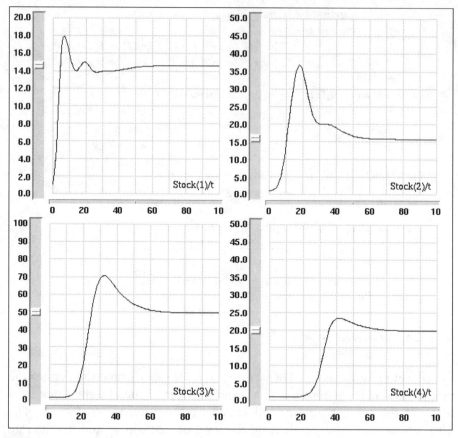

Figure 3.5 *Stock level oscillation.*

consumer balance out. This effect is most visible at the beginning of the supply chain. After approximately eighty time steps, the system reaches a stable state, and the level of stock at each node remains constant.

The system-dynamics approach is very useful in the design of reactive agent systems as we can study the behaviour of a model as a whole before we commit to a specific agent implementation. The implementation in an agent system requires us to define a *mapping* between the model and the agents, i.e. we need to decide which parts of the model correspond to our agents. The natural candidate is to map each state variable in the flow diagram, together with the corresponding equations and parameters, to a distinct agent. For example, each state variable in our supply chain would typically be defined by a separate reactive agent. However, many other mappings are possible, and the decision is ultimately dependent on the purpose of the system.

3.2.2   State-based reactive systems

The equation-based approach to reactive agent design is appropriate when the system has a regular cyclic behaviour. However, for systems that have a more dynamic behaviour, a state-based approach is often more readily applicable. In particular, if our agent system is designed around the exchange of messages, and the pattern of these messages varies over time, then this is more naturally represented in a state-based model, often called a transition-system. The state-based approach to reactive agent design is derived from automata theory, and is commonly used in specifying reactive hardware systems, such as embedded controllers. As with the system-dynamics approach, the techniques for constructing and simulating state-based models are well understood. State-based models can be efficiently implemented using tableau methods.

A state-based agent system is defined as a graph of states: the edges in the graph are directed transitions between states, and the annotations on the edges are the events in the environment that trigger the change of state. An example of a state-based model is given in Figure 3.6. This example defines the well-known *two-phase commitment* (2PC) protocol, used to ensure agreement between a group of participants. For example, to ensure that all participants agree to a transfer of money. The protocol is implemented by a collection of agents, one of which acts as the coordinator for the other participants. These two roles are defined by separate state-graphs in our example. In the first phase of the protocol, the coordinator asks all the participants to vote on the course of action. The participants then decide if they wish to proceed (commit), or to abort, and subsequently return their vote to the coordinator. In the second phase of the protocol, the coordinator tallies the votes and informs the participants of the outcome. If any of the participants voted to abort, then they must all abort. The protocol can only proceed if all of the participants commit to the action. We note that a participant will abort immediately after voting without waiting for the final result from the coordinator. This is acceptable as their abort vote will cause all the other participants to abort.

A state in the graph that has more than one exiting transition is a *choice point* in the system. When an agent is in such a state, it must make a choice as to which transition to follow. Often, this choice is entirely determined by the state of the environment, e.g. the CAN COMMIT state in the participant. However, in other cases, the agent must make a choice between states. This choice is generally determined by a *decision procedure* within the agent. For example, in the WAITING state of the coordinator we require a decision procedure that tallies the votes of the participants and makes the final decision to commit or abort. This procedure is entirely deterministic,

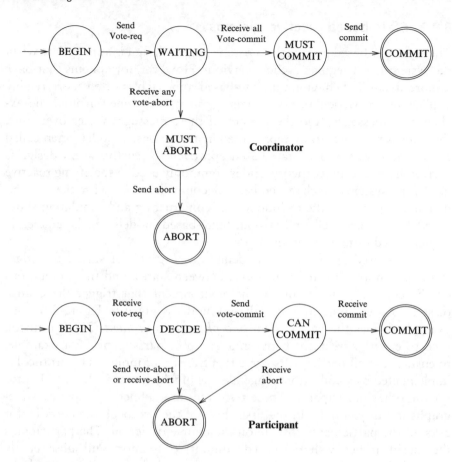

Figure 3.6 *State-based commitment.*

i.e. the same sequence of messages will always produce the same outcome. By contrast, each participant makes an internal decision to commit or abort in the DECIDE state. This procedure is non-deterministic as it relies on factors internal to the agent, and the scenario in which the protocol is applied. For example, in a transfer of money, the decision may be dependent on the agent having the necessary funds.

Our example is entirely driven by *message passing* between the agents. All of the events that occur in the environment are messages sent between the participants and the coordinator. Similarly, all of the actions that the agents perform result in the transmission of further messages in the environment. Furthermore, the agents are synchronized by these messages: an agent cannot proceed to a new state until an appropriate message has been received. This approach is in contrast to the equation-based approach, where the agents were explicitly synchronized by global time steps. Consequently, the equation-based approach is termed *synchronous*, while the state-based model is termed *asynchronous*.

The method of synchronization that we choose has fundamental implications in the way that we design and implement reactive agent systems. It can be argued that the synchronous approach is more difficult to implement as it relies on a global clock to synchronize the agents. If the agents are widely dispersed, e.g. across the Internet, then there will typically be a significant overhead in maintaining this level of synchronization. By contrast, the asynchronous approach is dependent only on the receipt of messages, and the agents can all perform at their own speed without the need to compute in lockstep. Thus, an asynchronous model is more straightforward to implement in a distributed setting, because it is difficult to impose real-time constraints on the system. For example, to state how long an agent should wait for a message, or to indicate that a message is urgent and the reply must be received in a certain time period. Thus, the approach that we follow is dependent on the kind of reactive system that we wish to construct, and whether we require tightly or loosely synchronized agents.

The asynchronous nature of the state-based approach has further implications on the *simulation* and *verification* of such systems. In the equation-based approach, we can readily simulate the behaviour of the system by evaluation of the equations, as shown previously. We can also verify properties of the system by observing the simulation, or by algebraic manipulation of the equations. For example, we can prove that the stock level of a node in our example never exceeds the maximum level specified. However, for the state-based models, we require a different approach. The asynchrony and non-determinism present in a state-based model imply that each time we simulate the system, it will behave in a different way. For example, the ordering of the messages may differ, or different choices may be made. Therefore, we cannot be certain that the system will behave as we would like. Similarly, we cannot verify properties of the system simply by observing the simulation, or by direct examination of the definition. A solution to these problems can be found in the use of a formal verification technique called *model checking*.

3.2.3   Verification of state-based reactive systems

Model checking is a technique for automatically verifying properties of finite-state concurrent systems, such as state-based agent systems. A model checker normally performs an exhaustive search of the state space of the system to determine if a particular property holds. Given sufficient resources, the procedure will always terminate with a yes or no answer. This makes the model-checking technique of significant practical value as a verification tool. We now describe the model-checking process formally, and then show how model-checking can be used to verify the 2PC protocol.

A model checker operates on an abstract model of a system, typically specified by a state-transition graph called a *Kripke structure*. This graph is defined as a four-tuple $M = (S, S_0, R, L)$, where:

1. S is a finite set of states, and $S_0 \subseteq S$ is the set of initial states.
2. $R \subseteq S \times S$ is a reachability relation. We note that R must be *total*, i.e. for every state $s \in S$, there is a state $s' \in S$ such that $R(s, s')$ is defined.
3. $L : S \rightarrow 2^{\mathcal{P}}$ is a function that labels each state with the set of atomic propositions $\mathcal{P}$ that are true in the state.

Given a system defined as a Kripke structure, we want to specify properties of the system for the model checker to verify. For example, we may wish to check that the system always terminates. These properties are typically defined using temporal-logic formulae. Conceptually, these formulae define properties of *computation trees*. The tree is formed by designating a state in the Kripke structure as the initial state, which will form the root, and then unrolling the remaining structure into an infinite tree. Figure 3.7 defines an example Kripke structure for a simple system with three states. Figure 3.8 shows a graphical representation of this Kripke structure, and its corresponding computation tree. In this representation, the nodes represent the states in S, the edges define the transition relation R, and the labels associated with each node describe the function L.

We can think of each branch of a computation tree as a *path*, where each path corresponds to a different simulation of the system. Formally, a path is defined as an infinite sequence of states $\sigma = s_0\ s_1\ s_2\ \cdots$, such that for every $i \geq 0$, $(s_i, s_{i+1}) \in R$. The view of a Kripke structure as a computation tree leads to the definition of two different kinds of temporal-logic formulae over these trees: *linear-time* and *branching-time*. In a linear-time temporal logic we express properties over all possible paths of the tree, and in a branching-time temporal logic we express properties over a single path of the tree.

Model-checking systems typically use the Linear Temporal Logic (LTL) and Computation Tree Logic (CTL). Both of these logics share the same basic syntactic operators (in addition to the standard first-order operators): always $\square$, eventually $\diamond$, and until $\mathcal{U}$. However, the semantics of these temporal operators differs depending on the logic in question. Figure 3.9

1. $S = \{s_0, s_1, s_2\}$ $S_0 = \{s_0\}$
2. $R = \{(s_0, s_1), (s_0, s_2), (s_1, s_0), (s_1, s_2), (s_2, s_2)\}$
3. $L = (s_0 \mapsto \{a, b\}, s_1 \mapsto \{b, c\}, s_2 \mapsto \{c\})$

Figure 3.7 *Example Kripke structure.*

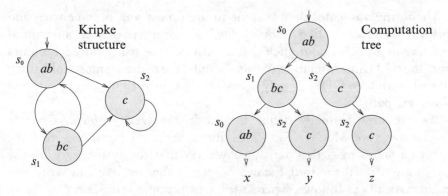

Figure 3.8 *Unrolling to a computation tree.*

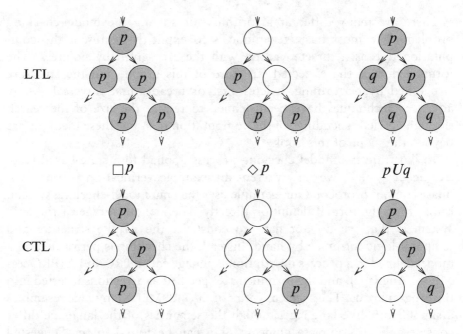

Figure 3.9 *Linear and branching temporal logics.*

illustrates the difference between LTL and CTL with reference to a computation tree. The operators $\Box$ and $\Diamond$ can be thought of as temporal variants of the first-order quantifiers: $\forall$ and $\exists$ respectively. The (strong) until property $p \, \mathcal{U} \, q$ states that p remains true until at least q becomes true. In LTL we must satisfy the property along every path in the tree, while in CTL it is sufficient that the property is satisfied along one particular path. As an example, consider the following temporal-logic formula:

$$\psi = \Diamond a \, \wedge \, \Diamond b \, \wedge \, (a \, \mathcal{U} \, b)$$

The formula ψ states that at some future time a will become true, and this will be the case until b becomes true. This formula expresses a temporal *ordering* between a and b, such that a must become true before b becomes true. In an LTL interpretation of this formula, the ordering must hold along all paths, while in CTL it is only necessary that the formula can be satisfied along one path.

We can now formally define the *model-checking problem*. Given a Kripke structure $M = (\mathcal{S},\ \mathcal{S}_0,\ R,\ L)$ and a temporal formula ψ, find the set of all states in $\mathcal{S}$ that satisfy ψ. We say that the system satisfies the specification if all the initial states $\mathcal{S}_0$ are in this set. We can write this mathematically as follows, where a $\models$ b means that a satisfies b.

$$\mathcal{S}_0 \subseteq \{s \in \mathcal{S} \mid M,\ s \models \psi\}$$

There are many different algorithms for solving the model-checking problem. The most basic technique is to explicitly represent the computation tree as a directed graph with the arcs given by pointers. The formula defines the expected structure of this graph, and the structure is checked by performing a depth-first or breadth-first traversal. Many advanced techniques have been defined to reduce the size of the search through efficient encodings of the computation tree, but these methods are beyond the scope of this book.

To illustrate the model checking process applied to a state-based reactive agent system, we now present an example verification of our two-phase commit protocol. Our example uses the Spin model-checking system, rather than the formal definition directly. The key advantage of the Spin system is that we do not have to construct the Kripke structure and temporal-logic formulae by hand. Instead, the checking is performed on a model defined in a process description language called PROMELA (PROcess MEta-LAnguage), and the formulae are specified as assertions inserted into the program code. The surface syntax of the PROMELA language resembles a simplified C-like language, though the semantics of the language differ considerably. A complete guide to Spin can be found in the Suggested Reading section at the end of the chapter. However, we now provide a brief overview of the language for the purpose of explaining the verification of our example.

The PROMELA language defines a system of concurrently executing sequential *processes*. Processes are the only unit of execution in PROMELA and are defined in a similar way to functions in a typical programming language. A process is declared using proctype declaration and executed using a run statement. Processes can take argument values when they are created, analogous to call-by-value parameter passing of arguments to functions. All of the processes run concurrently and independently with respect to one another. The processes can only interact by the exchange of messages, and by the use of shared global variables.

A process is defined as a sequence of guarded commands. In this approach, there is no difference between conditionals and statements. Statements are either *executable* or *blocked*. For example, the statement (a == b) can only be executed when it holds. If it does not, then the process containing the statement is blocked until a later time when the condition does hold. Statements are sequenced by a semicolon, or an arrow -> that indicates a causal relation between two statements. Guarded commands give us a means to express non-determinism. This is best illustrated by the iterative do statement in the language, which has the following form:

```
do
   :: sequence_1
   :: sequence_2
   :: ...
   :: sequence_k
od
```

The body of a do loop contains a sequence of statements, each preceded by a double colon. The first statement in the sequence is called a *guard*, as the remainder of the sequence can only be executed if the guard is executable. Only one of the sequences may be executed on each iteration of the loop. In the case where more than one guard is executable, a non-deterministic choice is made between the executable sequences. If none of the guards are executable, then the process containing the loop is blocked until at least one of the guards becomes executable. An else guard is selected if all of the other guards are blocked. A loop can only be exited by a break statement. An if statement has the same non-deterministic behaviour as the do loop, but performs only a single iteration.

The basic types permitted in PROMELA are all integer datatypes of various lengths, e.g. bool (1-bit), byte (8-bit), and int (32-bit). Arrays of a single dimension can be declared, e.g. int x[10]. User-defined record types can be constructed as combinations of the basic types, e.g. typedef Msg {byte id, int content}. There is also special message type mtype, which defines an enumeration of symbolic constants, e.g. mtype = {TRUE, FALSE}. Finally, there is a type of channels that are used to pass messages between processes, e.g. chan Pipe = [2] of {mtype}. Each channel has an associated length that is the size of the buffer in which messages can be stored, and a type that can be a message type or any record type. A buffer size of zero means that the channel is synchronous, i.e. the sender and receiver will be unable to proceed until the message is passed.

```
1    #define PART 4
2    mtype = {VOTEREQ, COMMIT, ABORT, NODECISION}
3    chan pchannel[PART] = [0] of {mtype}
4    chan cchannel = [0] of {mtype}
5    int final = NODECISION;
6    proctype coordinator() {
7      int count1 = 0, count2 = 0, count3 = 0;
8      mtype vote;
9      do
10       :: (count1 < PART) -> pchannel[count1] ! VOTEREQ ; count1 ++
11       :: else -> break
12     od;
13     do
14       :: (count2 < PART) ->
15         cchannel ? vote ; count2 ++ ;
16           if
17             :: (vote == ABORT) -> final = ABORT
18             :: (vote == COMMIT) -> skip
19           fi
20       :: else -> break
21     od;
22     if
23       :: (final == NODECISION) -> final = COMMIT
24       :: (final == ABORT) -> skip
25     fi;
26     do
27       :: (count3 < PART) -> pchannel[count3] ! final ; count3 ++
28       :: else -> break
29     od
30   }
```

Figure 3.10 *Coordinator specification.*

The basic operations on a channel are a send, e.g. Pipe ! TRUE, and a receive, e.g. Pipe ? value.

We can now define the 2PC example using the PROMELA syntax that we have described. Figure 3.10 specifies a PROMELA process for the co-ordinator of the system. Our specification allows for a varying number of participants, and we fix the number of participants with a PART macro in line 1. In line 2, we define the basic message types that we use in the protocol. A VOTEREQ message type is a request from the coordinator to the participant for a vote. The COMMIT and ABORT message types are used by the participants to indicate their vote, and by the coordinator to inform the participants of the final vote. The NODECISION message type is used as a convenience to indicate that no final decision has yet been made. In line 3, we define an array of channels pchannel[PART], one for each participant, that are used to communicate with the participant. In line 4, we define a single channel cchannel that is used to communicate with the coordinator. Our channels are unbuffered (length 0), and so all the message exchanges in our system are synchronous. In line 5, we declare a global variable final that is used to store the final commit/abort decision. This variable is globally defined, as it will be subsequently used to verify that all the participants arrive at the same decision.

The coordinator process is defined as a sequence of four stages. In the first stage (lines 9–12), a VOTEREQ message is sent to all the participants to inform them that a vote is required. There is no for loop in PROMELA, and so we must maintain a count of the messages that have been sent. In the second stage (line 13–21) we receive a vote from each of the participants. The communication is synchronous, and so the coordinator will be blocked until the receive operation cchannel ? vote can execute (line 15). If any of the votes in an ABORT, then the final decision is updated (line 17). Otherwise the coordinator remains undecided (line 18), i.e. final == NODECISION. In the third stage (line 22–5), a COMMIT decision is taken (line 23) if none of the participants voted to abort. In the final stage (lines 26–9), the participants are informed of the final decision.

The coordinator process that we have defined is deterministic, in that the final outcome is entirely dependent on the votes that it receives from the participants. Therefore, the same sequence of votes will always result in the same final decision. The non-determinism in the system comes from the participants, which make the actual decision to vote or abort. Figure 3.11 contains the PROMELA specification for a participant process of the system. We also specify the initialization of the system by means of an init process (lines 11–18), which is automatically evaluated at the start. The initial process creates a separate process instance for each participant, and a single coordinator process.

The participant process is specified in the same way for each participant (lines 1–10). Therefore an integer id that uniquely identifies the participant is passed as an argument to the process (line 1). This identifier determines the relevant communication channel for the participant. We declare a local variable decision (line 2), which will hold the final decision of the participant. In line 3, the participant is blocked until a VOTEREQ message is received from the coordinator. Subsequently, a decision to commit or abort is made in lines 4 to 8. As both of the guards cchannel ! COMMIT and cchannel ! ABORT are executable, a non-deterministic choice is made between these two options. If we make a decision to commit (line 5), then our final decision is determined by the coordinator. However, if we decide to abort (line 6), then we can immediately determine that our decision will be to abort. It should be noted that we cannot simply ignore the

```
1  proctype participant(int id) {
2    mtype abort, decision = NODECISION;
3    pchannel[id] ? VOTEREQ ->
4      if
5        :: cchannel ! COMMIT; pchannel[id] ? decision
6        :: cchannel ! ABORT ; decision = ABORT;
7              pchannel[id] ? abort
8      fi;
9    assert(final != NODECISION && decision == final)
10 }
11 init {
12   int count = 0;
13   do
14     :: (count < PART) -> run participant(count); count ++
15     :: else -> break
16   od;
17   run coordinator();
18 }
```

Figure 3.11 *Participant specification and initialization.*

final decision from the coordinator if we vote to abort (line 7), as the communication is synchronous, and the coordinator will be unable to terminate if we do not receive the final reply.

In any system verification task, it is necessary to decide what properties to check. Most model-checking systems are capable of verifying a range of generic properties automatically. For example, the Spin model checker can verify that all of the processes reach a valid end state, i.e. terminate correctly. This property is equivalent to the following LTL formula, where end1 is the end state for the first process, and end2 is the end state for the second process, etc.:

$$\Box(\, \Diamond(\text{end1} \,\wedge\, \text{end2} \,\wedge\, \text{end3} \,\wedge\, \cdots))$$

In addition to these generic properties, there are usually properties that we wish to check, which are specific to the definition of the system in question. While these properties can be defined as explicit LTL (or CTL) formulae, it is considerably more convenient to state properties using PROMELA *assertions* and *never-claims* internal to our specification. Assertions are statements that a property is always true at a particular point. Never-claims state that a property will never be true at a particular point, for example:

```
assert(even % 2 == 0)
never(odd % 2 == 0)
```

An assertion of the form `assert(cond)` is equivalent to an LTL formula of the form $\Box(s \wedge \text{cond})$, where s is the state in which the condition `cond` should hold. A never-claim is equivalent to the negation: $\Box(s \wedge \neg \text{cond})$. The advantage of placing these statements directly inside the PROMELA program, instead of defining separate formulae, is that we do not have to explicitly define the state s, and we can embed assertions inside loops and other constructs. In our 2PC example, we wish to check that all the participants reach the same final decision, which is the decision of the coordinator. To accomplish this, we include an assertion in the definition of our participant process (line 9). This assertion states that the coordinator reaches a decision, and that our local decision `decision` is the same as the decision of the coordinator `final`.

The PROMELA specification that we have presented gives us an abstract model of the 2PC algorithm. We can use this model for both simulation and verification in Spin. A simulation of the model corresponds to the execution of a single path through the system. Figure 3.12 describes a single simulation of our example as a message sequence chart. This figure illustrates the sequence of exchanges between the coordinator and the four participants. Although a single simulation does not provide a complete picture of the execution, it is useful to be able to view the message sequence in order to confirm that the system behaves broadly as expected. In addition, Spin allows us to replay a simulation of the system along a path that generated an error during verification, providing us with a useful debugging aid.

The verification process is performed by exhaustively searching the state space of the model. In our example, the state space corresponds to the combination of votes that the participants can make, and the different orders in which they reply, e.g. in Figure 3.12 the third participant voted to abort, and was first to reply to the coordinator. The remainder of the algorithm is deterministic, and therefore does not cause an expansion of the state space. The verification process does not give any visual feedback during operation. For our specification, the Spin model checker simply reports that no errors are found, i.e. our assertion was not violated in any state, and every process terminated. Thus, we obtain the desired confidence in the correctness of our agent system. In general, it should be noted that this confidence is entirely dependent on the quality of our specification, and on the kinds of properties that we check.

3.3 Summary

In this chapter, we have described the reactive approach to agent construction. Reactive agents do not perform any complex kind of reasoning,

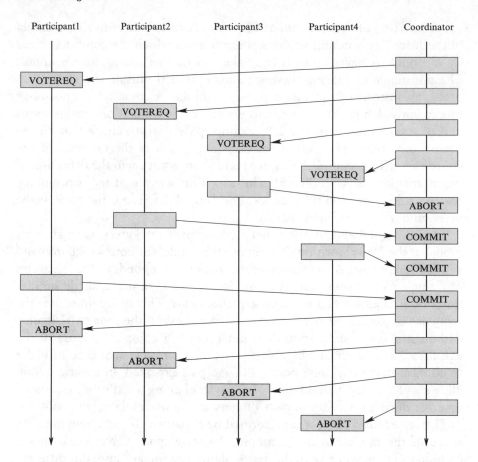

Figure 3.12 *2PC message sequence chart.*

instead they act as a sensor on the environment and are triggered by specific events. In effect, they simulate intelligent behaviour by reacting to changes in the environment, but their behaviours are largely deterministic. Nonetheless, the reactive approach can be useful in many situations, for example, in highly dynamic environments where rapid decisions are required. We detailed two different approaches to reactive agent construction, which are summarized below:

- An *equation-based* reactive agent is defined entirely by a series of mathematical equations. Its responses are predictable, and determined by external events in the environment. This approach is inspired by *system-dynamics* modelling techniques, commonly used in the study of business and social systems. In this approach, we specify the behaviour of the entire agent system. This specification comprises a conceptual model, which defines the parts of the system and the flows between these parts, and a corresponding quantitative model that defines the behaviours of the parts by differential equations. The entire system is synchronized by a global clock, which is represented by a time parameter within the equations. The resulting mathematical specification can be used directly as a basis for an implementation of the agent system.

- A *state-based* reactive agent is defined by a finite-state model, which expresses the internal states of the agent, and the transitions between these states. This approach is inspired by the design of concurrent processes and protocols in distributed systems. In contrast with the equation-based approach, the model is asynchronous as there is no global notion of time. Instead, the model is synchronized entirely by the exchange of messages between agents, which trigger changes in state. The resulting models are straightforward to implement, though their behaviours can be complex and difficult to understand intuitively.

A key feature of the reactive approach is that we can verify properties of our agents before we implement them in a real agent system. This can give us a measure of confidence in the behaviours of our agents that is not possible with more advanced reasoning techniques. In the equation-based approach, this verification is performed by *simulation* and mathematical analysis of the equations that comprise the system. In the state-based approach, we cannot usefully construct a simulation as the system behaviours are non-deterministic. Consequently, to ensure the

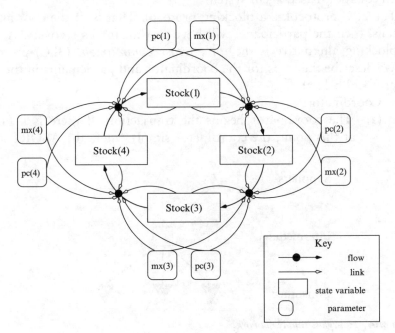

Figure 3.13 *Supply Ring.*

correctness of these systems, we define properties that we would like to preserve in a temporal logic, and then verify our model against these properties. The key technique that we use is *model checking*, which performs an exhaustive search of the state space of the model.

3.4 Exercises

1. A variant of the supply chain is a *supply ring*, as shown in Figure 3.13. In this model, the resources are continually transferred around the ring, rather than travelling from one end to the other. Modify the equations shown in Figure 3.4 to define this ring.
2. Use the Simile tool to explore the properties of your supply ring. An evaluation version of Simile is available at:

   http://simulistics.com/

3. An alternative to a supply chain (or ring) is an *hourglass* supply network, as illustrated in Figure 3.14. This network represents exchanges between groups of suppliers and groups of consumers, through a common intermediary. For example, a travel agent that organizes bookings for clients to a number of different hotels. Construct a system-dynamics model for this supply network, suitable for use in an equation-based agent system.
4. The 2PC protocol is a blocking protocol. That is, if the coordinator fails, then the participants will have to wait for its recovery. A non-blocking alternative is the *three-phase commitment* (3PC) protocol. We describe the steps for the coordinator and participants in the 3PC protocol below:
   - Coordinator:
     (a) The coordinator begins the transaction. If there is a failure at this point, the coordinator simply enters the ABORT state.

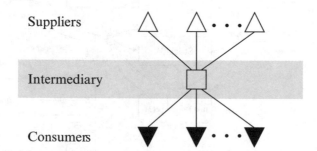

Figure 3.14 *Hourglass supply network.*

Otherwise, the coordinator sends a 'vote request' message to all of the participants and moves to the WAITING state.

(b) If there is a failure, a timeout, or if the coordinator receives a 'vote abort' message in the WAITING state, the coordinator sends an 'abort' message to all of the participants and enters the ABORT state. If the coordinator receives a 'vote commit' message from all participants within the time window, it sends a 'commit' message to all of the participants and moves to the PREPARED state.

(c) If the coordinator fails in the PREPARED state, it will move to the COMMIT state. However, if the coordinator timesout while waiting for an 'acknowledged' message from a participant, it will abort the transaction. In the case where all of the 'acknowledged' messages are received, the coordinator moves to the COMMIT state.

- Participant:

(a) The participant receives a 'vote request' message from the coordinator. If the participant decides to commit, it sends a 'vote commit' message to the coordinator and moves to the PREPARED state. Otherwise it returns a 'vote abort' message and moves to the ABORT state. If there is a failure, it moves to the ABORT state.

(b) If the participant fails, or receives an 'abort' message from the coordinator, or timesout waiting for a 'commit' message in the PREPARED state, it enters the ABORT state. If the participant receives a 'commit' message, it sends an 'acknowledged' message back to the coordinator and enters the COMMIT state.

Produce a model of the 3PC protocol suitable for use in a state-based agent system.

5. Construct a PROMELA specification of your 3PC protocol.

6. Use the Spin model checker to validate the 3PC protocol. Under what circumstances can the protocol fail? The Spin model checker and documentation are available on:

http://www.spinroot.com/

3.5 Suggested reading

1. E. M. Clarke, O. Grumberg, and D. A. Peled. *Model Checking*. MIT Press, 1999.
2. J. Ferber. *Multi-agent Systems: Introduction to Distributed Artificial Intelligence*. Addison-Wesley, 1999.

3. S. Franklin and A. Graesser. Is it an Agent, or Just a Program?: A Taxonomy for Autonomous Agents. In *Proceedings of the Third International Workshop on Agent Theories*, volume 1193 of *Lecture Notes on Artificial Intelligence*, pp. 21–36. Springer-Verlag, Budapest, Hungary, 1997.

4. N. Gilbert and S. Bankes. Platforms and Methods for Agent-Based Modelling. *Proceedings of the National Academy of Sciences of the United States of America*, 99(3), May 2002.

5. G. J. Holzmann. *The SPIN Model Checker: Primer and Reference Manual*. Addison-Wesley, September 2003.

6. N. R. Jennings. On Agent-Based Software Engineering. *Artificial Intelligence*, 117(2): 277–96, 2000.

7. C. W. Kirkwood. System Dynamics Methods: A Quick Introduction. Available at: `http://www.public.asu.edu/~kirkwood/sysdyn/SDRes.htm`, 2001.

8. Z. Manna and A. Pnueli. *The Temporal Logic of Reactive and Concurrent Systems: Specification*. Springer-Verlag, 1992.

9. R. Muetzelfeldt and J. Massheder. The Simile Visual Modelling Environment. *European Journal of Agronomy*, 18: 345–58, 2003.

10. H. S. Nwana. Software Agents: An Overview. In *Knowledge Engineering Review*, volume 11, Chapter 3, pp. 1–40. Cambridge University Press, September 1996.

11. Y. Shoham. Agent-Oriented Programming. *Artificial Intelligence*, 60(1): 51–92, 1993.

12. C. Walton. Model Checking for Multi-Agent Systems. *Journal of Applied Logic (Special Issue on Logic-Based Agent Verification)*, 2006.

13. G. Weiss. *Multiagent Systems: A Modern Approach to Distributed Artificial Intelligence*. MIT Press, 2000.

14. M. Wooldridge. *Reasoning About Rational Agents*. MIT Press, 2000.

15. M. Wooldridge. Semantic Issues in the Verification of Agent Communication Languages. *Autonomous Agents and Multi-Agent Systems*, 3(1): 9–31, 2000.

16. M. Wooldridge. *An Introduction to MultiAgent Systems*. John Wiley & Sons, 2002.

4 Practical reasoning and deductive agents

In constructing a reactive agent system, we explicitly define the behaviour of each agent. This behaviour is predefined, and dependent on events in the environment. We now consider a more powerful kind of agent that can make decisions on its own, i.e. an agent with proactive behaviour. Our motivation is the construction of agents with capabilities that are closer to the way that we reason as human beings. Our starting point in this approach is to base the internal processes of the agent directly on current understanding of how human reasoning is performed. This is the principle behind the design of a *practical reasoning agent*.

Practical human reasoning is directed towards actions, that is, figuring out what to do. This is different from purely logical reasoning, which is directed towards beliefs. Human reasoning is believed to consist of two distinct phases:

1. The first phase is *deliberation*, in which we decide what state of affairs to achieve.
2. The second phase is *means–ends reasoning*, in which we decide how to achieve the desired state of affairs.

To better illustrate human reasoning, it is helpful to consider a small example. Suppose that I wish to find a method of transportation in order to get to work each day. I would typically proceed by considering the various available options and weighing up the pros and cons. For example, I may consider travelling by car, but the available parking may be insufficient. This process of decision-making is deliberation. Once I have fixed upon an appropriate method of transport, e.g. by bicycle, then I must decide how to bring about a situation where this method of transport is possible. This process is means–ends reasoning, and the result is a plan of action. For example, my plan may involve: obtaining the money for the bicycle, finding a shop that sells an appropriate bicycle, and then purchasing the bicycle. If I am able to successfully follow the plan, then I will have reached the intended state of affairs, i.e. I will be able to travel to work by bicycle.

A practical reasoning agent attempts to replicate the process of human practical reasoning by performing deliberation and means–ends reasoning as computational processes. These processes can be defined using AI planning technology. However, the end result is only a poor approximation to real human reasoning as there are inherent limitations that arise when we move from our description of human reasoning to a computational model. We now discuss four key restrictions that we must address when designing a computational model of human reasoning.

1. Any computational model of a real world system is subject to inherent *resource bounds*. In particular, an agent will have only a finite amount of memory and a limited amount of computational power available. As a result of these restrictions, the agent is limited in the power and scope of the deliberation that can be performed. The agent will often be forced to stop deliberation prematurely and commit to a state of affairs. This may lead to a non-optimal course of action, which may have been alleviated if further deliberation were performed.

2. A Web-based agent exists in a highly *dynamic environment* that may be subject to rapid change. When the agent begins deliberation, it will typically operate on a snapshot of the world state at that particular point in time. However, as deliberation itself can take a significant length of time to complete, it may often be that the outcome will already be invalid due to changes in the environment. This requires us to make trade-offs in the design of our agents between the speed of response, and the optimality of the decision-making.

3. The reasoning process will often result in the possibility of *alternative actions*, all of which may appear equally compelling. At this point the agent is forced to make a selection based on appropriate heuristics. For example, the shortest plan, or the one that has the least associated cost. This may again result in non-optimal decision-making.

4. The final restriction that we consider is based on the need for an *abstract view* of the world. Thus, the decisions of the agent are necessarily restricted by the quality of the representation. For example, if our agent is reasoning with ontological knowledge about the world, then the deliberation is limited to the facts that can be deduced from the knowledge base. If the knowledge base contains invalid information, then the decisions that the agent makes may be incorrect.

4.1 The BDI model

The practical reasoning agents that we discuss in this section are based on the BDI model. This is currently the dominant model for defining agent-based practical reasoning. In this model, agent behaviour is determined by three distinct mental states. The *beliefs* of the agent define the knowledge that the agent has about the current state of the environment. The *desires* represent the state of affairs that the agent would (ideally) like to bring about. The *intentions* are the desires that the agent has committed to achieving. In general, an agent will not be able to achieve all of its desires, and some of the desires may be inconsistent. Therefore, the intentions are a subset of the desires that the agent has actually committed to achieving. Intentions can be viewed as characterizing the agents' state of mind. In other words, once an agent has committed to a particular intention, then the focus of attention of the agent is on achieving this intention.

There is a close correspondence between the BDI model and practical reasoning. The state of affairs that an agent commits to during deliberation are the *intentions* of the agent. Intentions play a vital role in determining the current and future behaviour of an agent, and must be consistent. The process of means–ends reasoning is driven by intentions. In particular, the decisions that the agent makes will be a direct consequence of the intentions of the agent. If the resulting action does not achieve the intention, then the agent will typically attempt a different approach. The intentions of an agent also constrain future deliberation. An agent will not adopt an intention as a result of deliberation that is inconsistent with its existing intentions. Furthermore, deliberation on future actions is founded on the assumption that existing intentions will be met.

An important issue in the adoption of an intention-driven reasoning process is how long the intentions of the agent should persist. That is, how committed should the agent be in achieving a particular intention. There are three popular *commitment strategies* that are used to determine the persistence of the intentions.

1. *Blind commitment*: the agent will retain an intention until it believes that the intention has been achieved.
2. *Single-minded commitment*: the agent will retain an intention until it believes it has achieved the intention, or believes the intention cannot be achieved.
3. *Open-Minded commitment*: An open-minded agent will maintain an intention as long as it is still believed to be achievable.

The choice of commitment strategy raises the issue of how often the agent should check that its intentions can be achieved. This check will require the agent to perform further deliberation, and may be a computationally costly operation. Therefore, we must trade-off between a *bold* strategy, where the agent may be attempting to achieve intentions that cannot be achieved, and a *cautious* strategy where the agent will take a

```
1 Reason(B, D, I)
2   do
3       ρ ← next percept
4       B ← revise(B, ρ)
5       D ← options(B, I)
6       I ← deliberate(B, D, I)
7       P ← plan(B, I, A)
8       execute(P)
9   while true
```

Figure 4.1 *A BDI reasoning algorithm.*

long time to achieve any intention, due to the need for frequent checks. The appropriate strategy is principally determined by the rate of change in the environment of the agent; a high degree of change necessitates a more cautious strategy.

To illustrate how the BDI model is actually used to perform practical reasoning, we outline a pseudocode algorithm for BDI reasoning in Figure 4.1. The sets B, D, and I represent the Beliefs, Desires, and Intentions of the agent respectively. These sets would typically be stored in a knowledge base. The body of the algorithm is a loop, which controls the behaviour of the agent. Changes in the behaviour are triggered by external events, e.g. actions by other agents, and we represent these as percepts ρ. The agents' beliefs are revised in light of these percepts by the function `revise`. The revised beliefs give rise to a number of possible `options` for action, which are desires. From these desires, the agent needs to `deliberate` on competing options and commit to a course of action, resulting in the intentions. The actions A that the agent needs to perform are determined by the planning function `plan`. This function performs a means–ends analysis on the intentions. The resulting actions will typically be operations, such as data retrieval, or communication with other agents. Once a suitable plan (P) has been formed, we `execute` the plan, and the agent returns to the start of the loop. An exemplar of a real agent system, which reasons according to the BDI model, is the Procedural Reasoning System (PRS). Further details on PRS can be found in the Suggested Reading section at the end of the chapter.

4.2 Planning agents

Means–ends reasoning is the process by which we determine the actions that an agent should take (i.e. the means) to achieve its intentions (i.e. the ends). This kind of reasoning is typically performed by AI *planning* techniques. Figure 4.2 illustrates the inputs and outputs of the planning

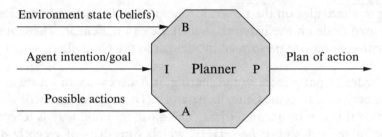

Figure 4.2   *Agent-based planning.*

process. The planner takes as its input the intention that the agent wishes to achieve, the beliefs that the agent has about the environment, and the actions available to the agent. If the planning process is successful, then the output from the planner will be a plan of action. Enacting the plan should lead to the agent achieving its intention. However, this is not guaranteed as conditions in the environment may have changed between planning and enactment. In this case, re-planning will be necessary.

Planning is essentially an automated process that will either succeed or fail. It is beyond the scope of this book to explain the many different approaches to AI planning. Rather, we simply treat the planning process as a black box that performs planning on behalf of the agent. There are many existing off-the-shelf planners that we can utilize for this task, and the majority of these planners take their input in the Planning Domain Definition Language (PDDL). To illustrate the use of these planners in performing means–ends reasoning we now present a detailed example.

Our example scenario is based on a simplified P2P file sharing system. This kind of system has recently gained significant popularity for the decentralized distribution of multimedia files on the Internet, e.g. MP3 music. The key advantage over the centralized client–server approach (e.g. a Web server) is that we do not have a single point on the network acting as a bottleneck in the system. As a result, the system scales as the number of clients increases, and the network bandwidth is effectively utilized as there will only be a limited amount of traffic between any two points. At present, the majority of P2P systems are based on purely algorithmic techniques. However, this kind of system appears ideal for the use of agent-based technology. For example, we can readily anticipate the exchange of files through negotiation between agents.

The model that we describe is loosely based on the Gnutella file sharing protocol. This protocol defines a completely decentralized method of file sharing, and its implementation is very straightforward. The Gnutella system assumes a distributed network of nodes, i.e. computers, that are willing to share files on the network. The protocol is defined with respect to our own node on the network, which we call the client. There are just three main operations performed by a client in the Gnutella protocol:

1. In order to participate in file sharing, it is necessary to locate at least one active node in the Gnutella network. There are a variety of ways in which this can be accomplished. The most common way is to contact one or more *Gwebcache* servers, which store lists of recently active nodes. The Gnutella software is usually configured with the addresses of a large number of these servers. However, it is not enough simply to know about other nodes, as there are no guarantees that these nodes will still be active. Therefore, the client will initiate a ping/pong protocol with each node in the list until a certain quota of active nodes have been located. This protocol simply sends a message (ping) to each node in the list, and waits for a certain period of time until a reply message (pong) is received, indicating that the node is still active.

2. Once a list of active nodes has been obtained, it is possible to perform a search for a particular file. Gnutella uses a *query flooding* protocol to locate files on the network. The client sends the file request (query) to every node on its active list. If one of the nodes has a copy of the requested file, then it sends back a reply message (hit) to the client. If the node does not have the file, then the request is forwarded to all of the active nodes on its own list, and so on. The query will eventually propagate to all of the active nodes that are connected to the network, and the reply will be returned to the client.

3. If the file is successfully located by the query protocol, then client simply contacts the destination node directly and initiates the download. If more than one copy is located, the client may download fragments

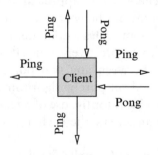 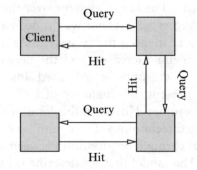

Ping/pong protocol   Query/hit protocol

Figure 4.3 *Query flooding protocols.*

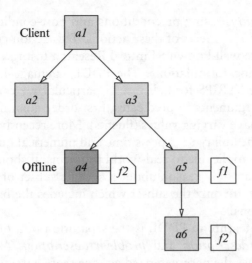

Figure 4.4   *Example P2P network configuration.*

of the file from different locations simultaneously and thereby improve download performance.

The Gnutella *ping/pong* and *query/hit* protocols are illustrated in Figure 4.3. It should be noted that the basic query flooding protocol, as outlined above, is very inefficient in operation and a search will typically take a long time to complete. The number of messages required is exponential in the depth of the search, and rare files may require a large number of queries to locate. This behaviour is tolerated as the network traffic generated by the queries is very small, compared to the bandwidth required to transfer the file itself. A variety of caching strategies have been proposed to improve the speed of the search, though we only consider the basic protocol here.

We can readily express the Gnutella protocol as a planning problem. The planner will determine the actions that must be performed by the client to retrieve a particular file. To illustrate this approach, we define an example file sharing network in Figure 4.4. The network is composed from six individual nodes, labelled $a1$ to $a6$, where $a1$ is the client. Each node is only aware of those directly connected in the graph, for example, $a1$ is aware only of $a2$ and $a3$, and $a5$ is only aware of $a6$. There are two files $f1$ and $f2$, where $f1$ is available on node $a5$, and file $f2$ is available on nodes $a4$ and $a6$. Node $a4$ is currently offline, i.e. unavailable. In this example, the intention of node $a1$ is to retrieve both $f1$ and $f2$ files.

Having now detailed our example P2P scenario, it is necessary to consider the encoding of the example in PDDL; the standard planning language. This will enable us to utilize existing off-the-shelf planning systems to define our planning agents. The PDDL is based around the definition of *actions*, using preconditions and post-conditions to describe the applicability and effects of these actions. This action-centred approach is inspired by the well-known STanford Research Institute Problem Solver (STRIPS) planning formulations. The PDDL language is extensible and goes beyond the STRIPS formalisms. In particular we can include typing constraints on arguments to predicates, first-order quantification in goals, and terms that have varying values (fluents). More recently PDDL has been extended with the ability to express time and numerical quantities in order to make it more applicable to real-world problems. It should be noted that most planners can only reason about a specific subset of PDDL. For our purposes we require only the subset which includes the basic STRIPS and typing conventions.

A key design feature in PDDL is the separation of a *planning problem* into a *domain description* and *problem description*. A PDDL domain description defines the parameterized actions that characterize the domain behaviours. The domain description also defines the predicates, types, constants, and axioms relevant to the domain. We can consider the domain description as an ontology that describes the parts of the domain necessary to accomplish planning. We do not consider the domain description to be a complete ontology as it has no notion of a knowledge hierarchy. However, we note that when we are reasoning about ontological knowledge in a planning agent, it will often be necessary to represent parts of this knowledge in PDDL. A PDDL problem description defines the specific objects, initial conditions, and goals that characterize a particular problem instance. The problem description is paired with the planning domain to create the actual planning problem for the planner. This affords us considerable flexibility in defining planning problems, as the same planning domain can be paired with many different problem descriptions.

To illustrate the key concepts in PDDL, we present an encoding of our example in PDDL syntax. Figure 4.5 contains a PDDL domain description for our scenario, and Figure 4.6 defines the specific file sharing problem. The syntax of PDDL is clearly, inspired by the Lisp programming language, as it imitates the parenthesized expression style. There are currently several proposals for an XML-based PDDL syntax, e.g. PDDXML, but the Lisp-style syntax remains the popular standard. As in previous examples, the line numbers are only for reference purposes, and are not part of the description.

The PDDL domain description in Figure 4.5 specifies our example p2p domain (line 1). The requirements (line 2) list the PDDL extensions that are required in the definition. As stated previously, we restrict our attention to the core `strips` and `typing` conventions. We define two types (line 3) that characterize the objects in our domain: `AGENT` and `FILE`. These

```
1   (define (domain p2p)
2     (:requirements :strips :typing)
3     (:types AGENT FILE)
4     (:predicates
5       (active ?a - AGENT)
6       (hasfile ?a - AGENT ?f - FILE)
7       (knowabout ?a - AGENT ?b - AGENT)
8       (knowactive ?a - AGENT ?b - AGENT))
9     (:action ping
10      :parameters (?agent1 - AGENT ?agent2 - AGENT)
11      :precondition (and (active ?agent1) (active ?agent2)
12                         (knowabout ?agent1 ?agent2))
13      :effect (knowactive ?agent1 ?agent2))
14    (:action query
15      :parameters (?agent1 - AGENT ?agent2 - AGENT ?file - FILE)
16      :precondition (and (knowactive ?agent1 ?agent2)
17                         (hasfile ?agent2 ?file))
18      :effect (hasfile ?agent1 ?file)))
```

Figure 4.5 *P2P domain representation.*

```
1   (define (problem fileshare)
2     (:domain p2p)
3     (:objects a1 - AGENT a2 - AGENT a3 - AGENT a4 - AGENT
4               a5 - AGENT a6 - AGENT f1 - FILE f2 - FILE)
5     (:init (active a1) (active a2) (active a3) (active a5)
6            (active a6) (not(active a4))
7            (knowabout a1 a2) (knowabout a1 a3) (knowabout a3 a4)
8            (knowabout a3 a5) (knowabout a5 a6)
9            (hasfile a4 f2) (hasfile a6 f2) (hasfile a5 f1))
10    (:goal (and (hasfile a1 f1) (hasfile a1 f2))))
```

Figure 4.6 *P2P problem representation.*

types are not strictly necessary, but they help to eliminate a class of errors, i.e. treating a file as an agent and vice versa. Variables in PDDL are indicated with a ? prefix, and assigned a type with -, e.g. ?a - AGENT is a variable a with type AGENT. We define four predicates that have the following meanings:

1. (active ?a - AGENT) implies that agent ?a is active, i.e. able to participate in file sharing.
2. (hasfile ?a - AGENT ?f - FILE) implies that agent ?a currently has a copy of the file ?f.
3. (knowabout ?a - AGENT ?b - AGENT) implies that agent ?a is aware of the existence of agent ?b. However, it does not imply that agent b is aware of agent a.

4. (knowactive ?a - AGENT ?b - AGENT) implies that agent ?a knows that agent ?b is currently active.

It is important to note that we do not specify the semantics of the predicates, as would be required in a typical programming language. For planning it is only necessary to record whether a predicate is true or false. The truth and falsity of the predicates is established by the definition of actions. In our example, we define two actions ping (lines 9–13) and query (lines 14–18). These actions correspond to the Gnutella ping/pong and query/hit protocols respectively. The parameters of each action are a list of variables on which the action operates. For example, the ping action is performed from agent1 to agent2 (line 10). The precondition of an action is an optional goal that must be satisfied before the action is applied. For example, in order to perform a ping operation, it is necessary that both agents are active (line 11), and agent1 knows about agent2 (line 12). If no preconditions are specified, the action can always be applied. The effect of an action defines the changes that the action imposes on the state of the world. For example, the result of a ping action is that agent1 knows that agent2 is active. Although not shown in our example, we can also assert that a predicate is false after an action, e.g. not(active ?a). We briefly note that the precondition can be an arbitrary (function-free) first-order logical sentence, while an effect is restricted, e.g. no disjunction.

Figure 4.6 defines the file sharing problem that we previously presented as a graph in Figure 4.4. The problem is labelled fileshare (line 1) and uses our p2p domain description (line 2). We define six AGENT and two FILE objects to use in our planning problem (lines 3–4). The initial world state, i.e. the values for the domain predicates are also defined (lines 5–6). We specify that all the agents are active, with the exception of agent a4. We then define the topology of the example graph (lines 7–9). Finally, we define the goal for the problem as a first-order formula (line 10). In this case, our goal is to provide agent a1 with a copy of both files f1 and f2.

The pairing of our p2p domain description together with our fileshare problem description gives us the complete specification of the planning problem. This definition can now be given to a PDDL planning system that will attempt to find a solution to the goal. In this case, we used the Blackbox planning system, which yielded the following sequence of actions:

```
(ping a5 a6)(ping a3 a5)(ping a1 a3)(query a3 a5 f1)
(query a5 a6 f2)(query a3 a5 f2)(query a1 a3 f1)(query a1 a3 f2)
```

It should now be apparent that planning is a powerful technique for performing means–ends reasoning. However, the planner requires us to have a complete definition of the problem and the domain in question. If our information was uncertain or incomplete, then the planning task would be considerably more complex. We also note that there are many possible solutions to our example. A planner will generally attempt to find the shortest plan, though this may not always be the most appropriate for our task. For example, the above solution places a copy of the file on every node between the client and the source of the file. If we wish to avoid the creation of these extra copies then it is necessary to tighten our specification.

4.3   Set-theoretic planning

To obtain a better understanding of agent-based planning, it is useful to consider a more formal description of the processes involved. We base our description on a *set-theoretic* representation of classical planning. In this style, the state of the world is captured by a set of propositions. An action is defined as an expression, which specifies the propositions that must belong to the state for the action to be applicable, and the propositions that the action will add or remove from the state of the world. The advantage of this representation, over a purely logic-based approach, is that the definitions are more readable, and there is a clear connection between the representation, and the planning computation.

We begin by defining the *domain description* for an agent in the set-theoretic style. This gives us a representation of various propositions about the world. The language L of the domain is a finite set of proposition symbols p: $L = \{p_1, \ldots, p_n\}$. The planning domain is defined by a restricted state-transition system over L as $\Sigma = (S, A, \gamma)$, where:

1. S is the finite set of *possible world states* for the domain, defined as $S \subseteq 2^L$, i.e. every state $s \in S$ is a subset of L.
2. A is the set of *actions* that can be performed in the domain. Each action $a \in A$ is defined as a triple of propositions (of L): $a = (\textsf{precond}(a), \textsf{effect}^-(a), \textsf{effect}^+(a))$. The set $\textsf{precond}(a)$ are the *preconditions* of a and identify the propositions that must hold in the state for the action to be applied. The action a is applicable to a state s if $\textsf{precond}(a) \subseteq s$. The sets $\textsf{effect}^-(a)$ and $\textsf{effect}^+(a)$ are the *effects* of a, and define the propositions that will be removed and added to the state respectively upon applying the action. The two sets of effects must be disjoint, i.e. $\textsf{effect}^-(a) \cap \textsf{effect}^+(a) = \emptyset$.
3. γ is the *state transition function*: $\gamma(s_1, a) = s_2$, which is defined when $a \in A$ is applicable to $s_1 \in S$, and undefined otherwise. The resulting state s_2 is given by $(s_1 - \textsf{effect}^-(a)) \cup \textsf{effect}^+(a)$. The members of S

must be defined such that if $s_1 \in S$, then for every action a that is applicable to s_1, $((s_1 - \text{effect}^-(a)) \cup \text{effect}^+(a))$ results in a valid state in S.

As in PDDL, we have specified the planning domain separately from the problem description. We now consider the definition of a *planning problem* in the set-theoretic style. This is a specification of the actual problem that the agent will attempt to solve by planning. A planning problem is defined as a triple $\mathcal{P} = (\Sigma,\ s_0,\ g)$, where:

1. Σ is the domain of the planning problem, as defined previously.
2. s_0 is the *initial state*, where $s_0 \in S$. The initial state will typically correspond to the environment state of the planning agent at the commencement of the planning phase.
3. $g \subseteq L$ is a set of *goal propositions* for the agent. These propositions define the requirements that a state must satisfy to be a goal state. The set of possible goal states is defined as $S_g = \{s \in S \mid g \subseteq s\}$.

A (linear) *plan* is any sequence of valid actions $\pi = (a_1,\ \ldots,\ a_k)$. If we apply π to state s, the resulting state is determined by applying the actions of π in the given order. We can express this as an extension of our state-transition function:

$$\gamma(s,\ \pi) = \gamma(\gamma(s,\ a_1),\ \ldots, a_k)$$

A plan π is a *solution* to a planning problem $\mathcal{P}$, if $g \subseteq \gamma(s_0,\ \pi)$. A solution is said to be *redundant* if there is a subsequence of π that is also a solution of $\mathcal{P}$, and *minimal* if there is no such subsequence. We can define the *successor* of a state s in a planning problem as:

$$\Gamma(s) = \{\gamma(s,\ a)\ \text{for all}\ a \in A,\ \text{where}\ a\ \text{is applicable to}\ s\}$$

The set of all *reachable* states from s is defined by the transitive closure:

$$\Gamma'(s) = \Gamma(s)\ \cup\ \Gamma(\Gamma(s))\ \cup\ \cdots$$

Now, we can say that a planning problem is *solvable* iff $S_g \cap \Gamma'(s_0) \neq \emptyset$, i.e. a solution is only possible where a valid goal state can be reached from the initial state s_0.

When defining a planning problem $\mathcal{P}$, it rapidly becomes cumbersome to state all the members of S and γ explicitly. Thus, we may define a *statement* of $\mathcal{P}$ as the triple $P = (A,\ s_0,\ g)$. From this statement, we can obtain the language L, and the members of S can be derived through expansion, i.e. an exhaustive application of $a \in A$ to all states s reachable from s_0, where $\gamma(s,\ a) = (s - \text{effect}^-(a)) \cup \text{effect}^+(a)$. We can consider $\mathcal{P}$ as the

$$P = (A, s_0, g)$$

$$A = \{ping(X, Y), query(X, Y, F)\}$$

$$ping(X, Y) = (\{active(X), active(Y), knowabout(X, Y)\}, \emptyset,$$
$$\{knowactive(X, Y)\})$$

$$query(X, Y, F) = (\{knowactive(X, Y), hasfile(Y, F)\}, \emptyset,$$
$$\{hasfile(X, F)\})$$

$$s_0 = \{active(a1), active(a2), active(a3), \neg active(a4),$$
$$active(a5), active(a6), knowabout(a1, a2),$$
$$knowabout(a1, a3), knowabout(a3, a4),$$
$$knowabout(a3, a5), knowabout(a5, a6),$$
$$hasfile(a4, f2), hasfile(a6, f2), hasfile(a5, f1)\}$$

$$g = \{hasfile(a1, f1), hasfile(a1, f2)\}$$

Figure 4.7   *Statement of the P2P planning problem.*

semantic specification, and *P* as the *syntactic* specification of a planning problem. We illustrate the specification of our P2P example in this notation in Figure 4.7.

To give a flavour of the actual planning process, we present the pseudocode of a simple forward-search planning algorithm in Figure 4.8. The algorithm takes a plan statement as input, and returns with either a plan or a failure condition. The variables *s* and π track the current world state, and the partial plan solution respectively. The body of the algorithm is an iteration of the following steps. A test is performed (line 5) to determine if a valid goal state has been reached, and the plan π is returned if successful. If not, we construct the set $\mathcal{A}$ (line 6) containing all the actions in *A* whose preconditions are satisfied in the current state. If no applicable actions are found, then the algorithm returns a failure condition (line 7). Otherwise, a non-deterministic choice is made between the available actions (line 8), and the new state is calculated from the effects of the action (line 9). Finally, the plan is updated (line 10) with the chosen action. In an actual implementation, we would perform backtracking so that all possible choices (line 8) would be explored before a failure condition occurred.

Our example algorithm illustrates the key steps of a planning algorithm, though it is clearly very inefficient in operation. We can improve the efficiency by searching backward from the goal, as in the classical STRIPS algorithm. There are also a multitude of planning optimizations that have been proposed by the planning community over the past two decades. Hence our recommendations to use off-the-shelf planning tools, rather than attempt to duplicate this effort.

```
1   Plan(A, s₀, g)
2      π ← ∅
3      s ← s₀
4      do
5         if g ⊆ s return π
6         A ← {a ∈ A | precond(a) ⊆ s}
7         if A = ∅ return fail
8         choose a ∈ A
9         s ← γ(s, a)
10        π ← π . a
11     while true
```

Figure 4.8   *Forward planning algorithm.*

4.4   Deductive reasoning agent systems

The third kind of rational agent that we discuss is based on the tradition of *symbolic* AI, which suggests that intelligent behaviour can be generated in a system by defining a symbolic representation of the environment and its behaviour, and syntactically manipulating this representation. Thus, rather than defining specific actions for the agent, as in the practical reasoning agent, we simply equip each agent with a description of the environment in which it is to operate, together with some basic rules, and let the agent deduce the appropriate steps. This is the motivation in the design of a *deductive reasoning* agent.

There are two immediate questions that arise in the design of a deductive agent. First, how do we represent the environment in a way that is adequate and accurate? Second, how can agents reason with this knowledge in an efficient and timely manner? These questions embody the classical *representation* and *reasoning* problems. Thus, in keeping with symbolic AI tradition, we base our representation on *logical formulae*, and our reasoning on deduction, i.e. *theorem-proving*.

To illustrate this approach, we now define a simple deductive agent system based on a logic of beliefs and intentions. In this system, the *environment* is represented by a set of beliefs B, where a single belief is an atomic proposition p. We have yet to define agent communication by message passing, as this is covered in Chapter 6. Thus, we adopt a simpler model of communication by sharing the set of beliefs between all the agents A in our system. Agent communication is captured by the manipulation of beliefs in this shared set. In essence, this is a broadcast, or shared state, mode of communication: the updates to the set are effectively broadcast to every agent in the system. In our definitions, we want to talk about the agent system as a whole, and therefore we define a *configuration* C of the system as the pair $(\mathcal{B}, A)$, where $\mathcal{B}$ is the shared set of beliefs, and A a sequence of all the agents in the system. A deductive step in our agent system is defined as a transformation from one configuration to another: $C \rightsquigarrow C'$.

In order to present a succinct example, our agents do not have any desires, goals, or local beliefs, as we would normally find in such systems. However, we note that it would be straightforward to include these concepts in our model. Instead, our agents are entirely defined by their *intentions*. More formally, the elements of the sequence A (i.e. the agents) are sequences I of intentions, and the elements of the sequence I are individual intentions i. The intentions in our system are defined by partial plans, comprising sequences of actions. Each action a is defined by a set of preconditions $\mathcal{P}$, a set of asserted effects $\mathcal{E}^+$, and a set of retracted effects $\mathcal{E}^-$. The members of these sets are belief propositions. A summary of the syntax of our deductive agent system is presented in Figure 4.9.

Our syntactic definitions make use of *sequences*, which are often called lists. Unlike a set, a sequence preserves the order of its elements, and duplicate elements are permitted. We write $(x_1, \ldots, x_k)$ for a sequence of elements with length k, and () for an empty sequence. To assist our specification, we define a number of basic functions that operate on sequences in Table 4.1. The **cons** function defines the construction of a sequence recursively. The first clause constructs a sequence from a single element and an empty sequence. The second clause adds an element to the front of an existing sequence. The **hd** (head) and **tl** (tail) functions return the first element and remainder of a sequence respectively. Finally, the **select** function returns a pair of a random element from the sequence, and the remaining sequence after the removal of the element. For a sequence of length 2, we return either the first or second element, indicated by the exclusive OR operator $\otimes$.

Representing intentions as partial plans is a common technique in defining agent systems. The underlying intuition in this representation is as follows. In an open agent system, a planning system will often have incomplete information about the domain in question. In particular, we often need to rely upon the actions of another agent in order to satisfy specific intentions. Therefore, planning can only result in partial plans. In

$$C \in \text{Configuration} ::= (\mathcal{B}, A)$$
$$A \in \text{Agents} ::= (I_1, \ldots, I_k)$$
$$I \in \text{Intentions} ::= (i_1, \ldots, i_k)$$
$$i \in \text{Intention} ::= (a_1, \ldots, a_k)$$
$$a \in \text{Action} ::= (\mathcal{P}, \mathcal{E}^+, \mathcal{E}^-)$$

Figure 4.9 *Deductive agent syntax.*

Table 4.1 *Sequence functions.*

Function	Conditions
$\mathsf{cons}(x_1, ()) = (x_1)$	
$\mathsf{cons}(x_1, (x_2, \ldots, x_k)) = (x_1, x_2, \ldots, x_k)$	$k > 1$
$\mathsf{hd}((x_1)) = x_1$	
$\mathsf{hd}((x_1, \ldots, x_k)) = x_1$	$k > 1$
$\mathsf{tl}((x_1)) = ()$	
$\mathsf{tl}((x_1, \ldots, x_k)) = (x_2, \ldots, x_k)$	$k > 1$
$\mathsf{select}((x_1)) = (x_1, ())$	
$\mathsf{select}((x_1, x_2)) = (x_1, (x_2)) \otimes (x_2, (x_1))$	
$\mathsf{select}((x_1, \ldots, x_k)) =$	
$\quad (x_n, (x_1, \ldots, x_{n-1}, x_{n+1}, \ldots, x_k))$	$1 < n < k \quad k > 2$

our deductive system, we assume that the list of partial plans has been generated in advance of the reasoning process, and these plans represent our intentions.

The purpose of the deductive reasoning process in our system is to achieve all of the intentions of every agent. To accomplish this, the actions of each agent must be performed in a suitable order such that all intentions can be satisfied. The appropriate order of the actions is determined by theorem proving. Thus, we reduce the reasoning process to a problem of proof. There are two key operations that must be performed at each stage of the deductive reasoning process:

1. At each step in the reasoning process, we must decide the appropriate intention to apply for a specific agent. To accomplish this, we construct a list of all the intentions that can be applied with respect to our current beliefs. The **options** function, defined below, splits a sequence of intentions I into a pair (I', I''). The first element of the pair I' are the intentions that can be applied, and the second element I'' are the intentions that cannot be applied. We determine the applicability of an intention by the preconditions of the first action in the intention, i.e. an intention $i = ((\mathcal{P}, \mathcal{E}^+, \mathcal{E}^-), \ldots)$ is applicable if $\mathcal{P} \subseteq \mathcal{B}$.

$$\mathsf{options}(\mathcal{B}, I) = ((i \mid i \in I \wedge \mathsf{hd}(i) = (\mathcal{P}, \mathcal{E}^+, \mathcal{E}^-) \wedge \mathcal{P} \subseteq \mathcal{B}),$$
$$(i' \mid i' \in I \wedge \mathsf{hd}(i') = (\mathcal{P}, \mathcal{E}^+, \mathcal{E}^-) \wedge \mathcal{P} \not\subseteq \mathcal{B}))$$

2. After selecting an appropriate intention, from the sequence of applicable intentions, we enact the intention and revise our beliefs. The

$$\begin{array}{c} \mathsf{select}(A) = (I, \ A') \\ \mathsf{options}(\mathcal{B}, \ I) = (I', \ I'') \\ \mathsf{select}(I') = (i, \ I''') \\ \mathsf{enact}(\mathcal{B}, \ i) = (\mathcal{B}', \ i') \\ A'' = \mathsf{cons}(\mathsf{cons}(\mathsf{cons}(i', \ I'''), \ I''), \ A') \\ \hline (\mathcal{B}, \ A) \leadsto (\mathcal{B}', \ A'') \end{array}$$

Figure 4.10 *Transformation rule.*

enactment of an intention corresponds to a removal and application of the first action of the chosen intention, as defined by the **enact** function below. The function returns a pair $(\mathcal{B}', \ i')$ of the revised beliefs, and remaining actions. Our revised beliefs are calculated as: $(\mathcal{B} - \mathcal{E}^-) \cup \mathcal{E}^+$.

$$\mathsf{enact}(\mathcal{B}, \ i) = ((\mathcal{B} - \mathcal{E}^-) \cup \mathcal{E}^+ \mid \mathsf{hd}(i) = (\mathcal{P}, \ \mathcal{E}^+, \ \mathcal{E}^-), \ \mathsf{tl}(i))$$

As stated previously, each deductive step in our system is defined as a transformation from one configuration to another: $C \leadsto C'$. This transformation is specified by a single *proof rule*, shown in Figure 4.10. The premises of this rule appear above the line, and the conclusions appear below the line. To move from the configuration $(\mathcal{B}, \ A)$ to the new configuration $(\mathcal{B}', \ A'')$ we must satisfy each of the premises in turn. If we fail to satisfy any of the premises, then the whole rule will fail. The premises are evaluated as follows. An agent, defined by its intentions I, is selected from the sequence A. We then construct a sequence I' of intentions that can be applied under the current beliefs. A specific intention i is then selected from I''. We enact the first action in i, and update the current beliefs. Finally, we construct a new sequence A', which contains the actions i' composed of the remaining intentions of the agent (I'' and I''').

Deductive reasoning in our system is performed by *theorem-proving*. A theorem prover applies the given proof rules exhaustively until a solution is found, or all possibilities have been explored. This process is called *proof search*, and is very similar to the planning process that we previously presented in Figure 4.8. In our system, we have a single proof rule that has two non-deterministic choices, i.e. the **select** functions. Therefore, the search will attempt to apply the rule for every individual agent, and for every intention of each agent. Typically, a depth-search strategy is adopted for the search, i.e. we pick a particular agent and attempt to satisfy its intentions. If this fails, then we backtrack and begin with another agent, and so on.

To illustrate the theorem-proving process, we now consider an example problem and show how it can be solved using deductive reasoning. Our

$$\mathcal{B}_i = \left\{ \begin{array}{l} has\,filea4\,f2,\quad has\,filea5\,f1,\quad has\,filea6\,f2, \\ active\,a1,\quad active\,a2,\quad active\,a3,\quad active\,a5,\quad active\,a6 \end{array} \right\}$$

$A_1 = (\ \text{query}(a1,\ a3,\ f1),\ \text{query}(a1,\ a3,\ f2)\ )$

$A_3 = (\ \text{query}(a3,\ a5,\ f1),\ \text{query}(a3,\ a5,\ f2)\ )$

$A_5 = (\ \text{query}(a5,\ a6,\ f2)\ )$

Figure 4.11   *Initial beliefs and plans.*

example is based on the P2P scenario described in Section 4.2, and the configuration illustrated in Figure 4.4. As before, the aim of our example is to provide the agent $a1$ with a copy of files $f1$ and $f2$. The initial set of beliefs and actions are defined in Figure 4.11. We do not have variables in our formalism, and so we convert the predicates into atomic propositions. For example the predicate `hasfile` is expanded to a set of propositions such as $has\,filea5\,f1$. The intentions of the system are partial plans, generated in advance by a planning process. For simplicity, the active agents are already identified in our belief set, and so the actions generated by the planning process for each agent are all queries.

We have now defined the initial configuration $(\mathcal{B}_i,\ (A_1,\ A_3,\ A_5))$. By a process of theorem-proving, we can deduce the correct sequence for the actions such that all of the intentions are satisfied. A solution to our example is shown in Table 4.2. Note that the actions are not named, and are simply defined by their preconditions and effects. At each step, we reduce one action and update the set of beliefs, according to our proof rule in Figure 4.10. At the conclusion of the fifth step, we have successfully discharged all of our intentions.

Deductive reasoning is a powerful process that can complement practical reasoning by planning. As we have shown, deductive reasoning can be applied where a choice must be made between multiple competing plans. The decision-making process is encoded as a logical theory, and the selection process is reduced to a problem of proof. An exemplar of this approach is the AgentSpeak(L) language, from which our example system is derived. AgentSpeak(L) includes many concepts that we have omitted from our simplified system, including a full treatment of beliefs, desires, intentions, goals, and events. Further details on AgentSpeak(L) can be found in the Suggested Reading section at the end of the chapter.

4.4.1   Temporal deductive systems

In the system that we have defined, the deductive reasoning process is primarily used to decide the order in which the plans should be applied. The actual actions that are performed are determined in advance by a

Table 4.2 *P2P deduction example.*

Initial	
$\mathcal{B}$	{hasflea4f2, hasflea5f1, hasflea6f2, activea1, activea2, activea3, activea5, activea6}
$\mathcal{A}$	I_1 (({activea3, hasflef1a1}, {hasflef2a1}, ∅), ({activea3, hasflef2a3}, {hasflef2a1}, ∅),
	I_3 (({activea5, hasflef1a5}, {hasflef1a3}, ∅), ({activea5, hasflef2a5}, {hasflef2a3}, ∅),
	I_5 (({activea6, hasflef2a6}, {hasflef2a5}, ∅))
Step 1	**[Reduce I_5]**
$\mathcal{B}$	{hasflef2a5, hasflea4f2, hasflea5f1, hasflea6f2, activea1, activea2, activea3, activea5, activea6}
$\mathcal{A}$	I_1 (({activea3, hasflef1a1}, {hasflef1a3}, ∅), ({activea3, hasflef2a3}, {hasflef2a1}, ∅),
	I_3 (({activea5, hasflef1a5}, {hasflef1a3}, ∅), ({activea5, hasflef2a5}, {hasflef2a3}, ∅))
Step 2	**[Reduce I_3]**
$\mathcal{B}$	{hasflef1a3, hasflef2a5, hasflea4f2, hasflea5f1, hasflea6f2, activea1, activea2, activea3, activea5, activea6}
$\mathcal{A}$	I_1 (({activea3, hasflef1a1}, {hasflef1a3}, ∅), ({activea3, hasflef2a3}, {hasflef2a1}, ∅),
	I_3 (({activea5, hasflef2a5}, {hasflef2a3}, ∅))
Step 3	**[Reduce I_1]**
$\mathcal{B}$	{hasflef1a1, hasflef1a3, hasflef2a5, hasflea4f2, hasflea6f2, activea1, activea2, activea3, activea5, activea6}
$\mathcal{A}$	I_1 (({activea3, hasflef2a3}, {hasflef2a1}, ∅),
	I_3 (({activea5, hasflef2a5}, {hasflef2a3}, ∅))
Step 4	**[Reduce I_3]**
$\mathcal{B}$	{hasflef2a3, hasflef1a1, hasflef1a3, hasflef2a5, hasflea4f2, activea1, activea2, activea3, activea5, activea6}
$\mathcal{A}$	I_1 (({activea3, hasflef2a3}, {hasflef2a1}, ∅))
Step 5	**[Reduce I_1]**
$\mathcal{B}$	{hasflef2a1, hasflef2a3, hasflea5, hasflef1a3, hasflea2a5, hasflea4f2, hasflea5f1, hasflea6f2, activea1, activea2, activea3, activea5, activea6}

separate planning process. However, it is also possible to define *purely deductive* systems, where all of the reasoning is done by deduction. This approach comes very close to the ideal of agents as deductive theorem provers.

An appropriate basis for a purely deductive agent system is an executable logic-based formalism, analogous to the use of executable horn-clauses in logic programming. There are many possible logical formalisms that are appropriate for the definition of agent systems. However, to illustrate this approach, we will define a system based on an LTL, as used previously for the verification of reactive agent systems in Chapter 3. The LTL allows us to define agents that can reason about the future in addition to the present. It should be noted that the use of temporal formulae to define the execution of a system is rather different from our prior use of these formulae to specify properties for model checking. The key difference is that we are now attempting to force the system to bring about the outcome defined by our formulae, while previously we were attempting to find system behaviours that violated our formulae.

Our temporal deductive system is based on a representation of the environment, and an interpretation of the standard temporal operators with respect to this environment. For convenience, we adopt the same formalism for our environment as in our previous deductive system, i.e. the environment is a set B of propositions that collectively represent the beliefs of all the agents. This allows us to abstract away from the details of inter-agent communication. An agent in our system is defined by a sequence of rules, expressed as temporal formulae. The deductive process is performed by repeatedly evaluating these rules. A configuration of the system C is defined by the tuple: $(B, (\Psi_1, \ldots, \Psi_k))$, where Ψ_i defines the rules for agent i. The rules in our definition are not arbitrary temporal formulae, but instead are restricted to a specific *normal form*, shown below:

$$\Psi \in \text{Formula} ::= \Box(r_1 \wedge \cdots \wedge r_k)$$
$$r \in \text{Rule} \quad ::= \phi \Rightarrow \psi$$

The $\Box$ (always) operator in the formula Φ signifies that all the rules r_i will be applied at every step in the execution. Every rule is an implication from ϕ to ψ, where ϕ is a first order formula, and ψ is a temporal formula. The formula ϕ is written in terms of the beliefs B, which are a record of inferences made in the past, and the formula ψ expresses changes that will be made in the future to these beliefs. The intuitive meaning of a rule is as follows:

Premises about the past $\Rightarrow$ *Conclusions about the present and future.*

A rule is analogous to an action, where ϕ are the preconditions, and ψ are the effects. However, there are significant differences between the application (firing) of a rule, and the enactment of an action. The rules are completely independent of one another, and do not collectively form plans. Therefore, the rules are not removed from the agent once they have been fired. As a result, a rule that matches a particular condition will be continuously fired on every step of the execution, until the condition no longer holds. Furthermore, all of the rules that match the current conditions are fired at each execution step, and these rules are fired simultaneously. This is very similar to a reactive agent system, where the agent continually reacts to events in the environment. The deduction process is defined by the execution of the following steps for each agent, and these steps are repeated continually until no more rules can be fired:

1. The premises of each rule are evaluated against the current beliefs to determine the rules that can be fired in the current execution step.
2. The rules are fired, together with any commitments that remain from previous execution cycles. This is done by collecting together the conclusions of each rule, together with previous commitments, into a set of constraints.
3. We attempt to update the set of beliefs while satisfying the constraints in our set. The satisfaction of the constraints is performed by a theorem-proving process. A choice will often have to be made between different execution possibilities. Any constraints that cannot be satisfied in the current step are carried to the next step as commitments.

There are two different kinds of choice that can be made during the deductive process. The first of these arises from the use of the disjunction $\vee$ operator. For example, the formula $A \vee B$ gives us the opportunity to perform either A or B. In many cases, the outcome will be constrained by the state of the environment, but where there are no such constraints, this operator represents a non-deterministic choice. The second kind of choice is a result of the temporal $\diamond$ (eventually) operator. For example, the formula $\diamond A$ states that A must be satisfied at some point in the future. However, it does not define precisely when this should happen. For our purposes, we will attempt to satisfy A as soon as possible, taking into account any other temporal constraints. If there are no such constraints, then A will be satisfied at the end of the current execution step.

To illustrate the deductive process, we now define an example system in this formalism, and show how deduction is performed. Our example is again based on the P2P scenario described in Section 4.2. The use of this scenario allows us to compare the two approaches to deductive agent

Table 4.3 *Temporal specification of P2P example.*

a1

1	$start \Rightarrow \square\neg(query(a1,\ a2,\ Y)$
	$\wedge\ query(a1,\ a3,\ Y))$
2	$ping(a1) \Rightarrow \Diamond(active(a1) \wedge \neg ping(a1))$
3	$\neg active(a2) \Rightarrow \Diamond ping(a2)$
4	$\neg active(a3) \Rightarrow \Diamond ping(a3)$
5	$active(a2) \wedge \neg hasfile(a1,\ f1) \Rightarrow \Diamond query(a1,\ a2,\ f1)$
6	$active(a2) \wedge \neg hasfile(a1,\ f2) \Rightarrow \Diamond query(a1,\ a2,\ f2)$
7	$active(a3) \wedge \neg hasfile(a1,\ f1) \Rightarrow \Diamond query(a1,\ a3,\ f1)$
8	$active(a3) \wedge \neg hasfile(a1,\ f2) \Rightarrow \Diamond query(a1,\ a3,\ f2)$

a2

9	$ping(a2) \Rightarrow \Diamond(active(a2) \wedge \neg ping(a2))$

a3

10	$start \Rightarrow \square\neg(query(a3,\ a4,\ Y)$
	$\wedge\ query(a3,\ a5,\ Y))$
11	$ping(a3) \Rightarrow \Diamond(active(a3) \wedge \neg ping(a3))$
12	$\neg active(a4) \Rightarrow \Diamond ping(a4)$
13	$\neg active(a5) \Rightarrow \Diamond ping(a5)$
14	$query(X,\ a3,\ Y) \wedge hasfile(a3,\ Y) \Rightarrow \Diamond(hasfile(X,\ Y)$
	$\wedge \neg query(X,\ a3,\ Y))$
15	$query(X,\ a3,\ Y) \wedge \neg hasfile(a3,\ Y)$
	$\wedge\ active(a4) \Rightarrow \Diamond query(a3,\ a4,\ Y)$
16	$query(X,\ a3,\ Y) \wedge \neg hasfile(a3,\ Y)$
	$\wedge\ active(a5) \Rightarrow \Diamond query(a3,\ a5,\ Y)$

a5

17	$start \Rightarrow hasfile(a5,\ f1)$
18	$ping(a5) \Rightarrow \Diamond(active(a5) \wedge \neg ping(a5))$
19	$\neg active(a6) \Rightarrow \Diamond ping(a6)$
20	$query(X,\ a5,\ Y) \wedge hasfile(a5,\ Y) \Rightarrow \Diamond(hasfile(X,\ Y)$
	$\wedge \neg query(X,\ a5,\ Y))$
21	$query(X,\ a5,\ Y) \wedge \neg hasfile(a5,\ Y)$
	$\wedge\ active(a6) \Rightarrow \Diamond query(a5,\ a6,\ Y)$

a6

22	$start \Rightarrow hasfile(a6,\ f2)$
23	$ping(a6) \Rightarrow \Diamond(active(a6) \wedge \neg ping(a6))$
24	$query(X,\ a6,\ Y) \wedge hasfile(a6,\ Y) \Rightarrow \Diamond(hasfile(X,\ Y)$
	$\wedge \neg query(X,\ a6,\ Y))$

specification. Table 4.3 defines the temporal rules for each of the agents in the example. As before, each node in Figure 4.4 is represented by a separate agent, and the goal is to provide the agent $a1$ with a copy of files $f1$ and $f2$.

We define the P2P protocol in our example by the predicates *active* and *hasfile*, and the actions *ping* and *query*. We do not represent the predicates *knowabout* and *knowactive*, as these can be inferred from the rules and the shared environment. Both the predicates and actions are represented as assertions in the set of shared beliefs. For example, the predicate (active a1) is represented by the belief *active*($a1$). Similarly, the action (query a1 a2 f1) is represented by asserting the belief *query*($a1, a2, f1$) in the environment. The environment is continually being observed by all the agents, and so a query will be interpreted by the corresponding agent, as if it had been sent directly to the agent.

The majority of the rules have the form $x \Rightarrow \Diamond y$, which are interpreted as: the agent will attempt y as soon as x is true. For example, $\neg active(a2) \Rightarrow \Diamond ping(a2)$ (rule 3) in the definition of agent $a1$ means that if *active*($a2$) is not in the set of beliefs then agent $a1$ will assert *ping*($a2$) as soon as possible. We define a special premise *start* which is true only in the first step. This is used to perform initialization of the environment. For example, $start \Rightarrow hasfile(a5, f1)$ (rule 17) is used to assert the belief that agent $a5$ has a copy of the file $f1$ at the start of the deduction process.

Beliefs are represented by atomic propositions as before. However, we now permit variables in our rules, which can be pattern-matched against belief propositions. For example, $query(X, a3, Y)$ will match a proposition $query(a1, a3, f1)$, and the variables X and Y will be bound to $a1$ and $f1$ respectively. Variables are indicated by the use of upper-case letters. Beliefs persist in the environment until they are retracted by asserting their negation. For example, $ping(a1) \Rightarrow \Diamond(active(a1) \land \neg ping(a1))$ (rule 2) states that agent $a1$ will respond to an assertion $ping(a1)$ by asserting $active(a1)$ and retracting $ping(a1)$ from the environment. Constraints are defined using the $\Box$ (always) operator. For example, agent $a1$ defines the constraint $\Box\neg(query(a1, a2, Y) \land query(a1, a3, Y))$, which should be interpreted as stating that $a1$ will not attempt to query both $a2$ and $a3$ at the same time, i.e. during the same step.

A property of the P2P scenario is that an agent can only communicate with those agents that it knows about. As we do not perform any planning, our agents simply query all of the nodes that they know about. To simplify our model, we explicitly represent the topology in our rules, rather than defining a separate discovery mechanism. For example, agent $a3$ can query $a4$ and $a5$ (rules 15 and 16) as these are the only nodes that it knows about.

Table 4.4 *P2P temporal deduction example.*

Step	Environment (shared beliefs)	Rules fired
1	{*start*}	1, 3, 4, 10, 12, 13, 17, 19, 22
2	{*ping*(*a2*), *ping*(*a3*), *ping*(*a4*), *ping*(*a5*), *ping*(*a6*), *hasfile*(*a5*, *f1*), *hasfile*(*a6*, *f2*)}	3, 4, 9, 11, 12, 13, 18, 23
3	{*active*(*a2*), *active*(*a3*), *active*(*a5*), *active*(*a6*), *ping*(*a4*), *hasfile*(*a5*, *f1*), *hasfile*(*a6*, *f2*)}	7, 8, 12
4	{*query*(*a1*, *a3*, *f1*), *query*(*a1*, *a3*, *f2*), *active*(*a2*), *active*(*a3*), *active*(*a5*), *active*(*a6*), *ping*(*a4*), *hasfile*(*a5*, *f1*), *hasfile*(*a6*, *f2*)}	7, 8, 12, 16
5	{*query*(*a3*, *a5*, *f1*), *query*(*a1*, *a3*, *f1*), *query*(*a1*, *a3*, *f2*), *active*(*a2*), *active*(*a3*), *active*(*a5*), *active*(*a6*), *ping*(*a4*), *hasfile*(*a5*, *f1*), *hasfile*(*a6*, *f2*)}	7, 8, 12, 16, 20
6	{*hasfile*(*a3*, *f1*), *query*(*a3*, *a5*, *f2*), *query*(*a1*, *a3*, *f1*), *query*(*a1*, *a3*, *f2*), *active*(*a2*), *active*(*a3*), *active*(*a5*), *active*(*a6*), *ping*(*a4*), *hasfile*(*a5*, *f1*), *hasfile*(*a6*, *f2*)}	7, 8, 12, 14, 16, 21
7	{*hasfile*(*a1*, *f1*), *query*(*a5*, *a6*, *f2*), *hasfile*(*a3*, *f1*), *query*(*a3*, *a5*, *f2*), *query*(*a1*, *a3*, *f2*), *active*(*a2*), *active*(*a3*), *active*(*a5*), *active*(*a6*), *ping*(*a4*), *hasfile*(*a5*, *f1*), *hasfile*(*a6*, *f2*)}	8, 12, 16, 21
8	{*hasfile*(*a5*, *f2*), *hasfile*(*a1*, *f1*), *hasfile*(*a3*, *f1*), *query*(*a3*, *a5*, *f2*), *query*(*a1*, *a3*, *f2*), *active*(*a2*), *active*(*a3*), *active*(*a5*), *active*(*a6*), *ping*(*a4*), *hasfile*(*a5*, *f1*), *hasfile*(*a6*, *f2*)}	8, 12, 16
9	{*hasfile*(*a3*, *f2*), *hasfile*(*a1*, *f1*), *hasfile*(*a3*, *f1*), *query*(*a1*, *a3*, *f2*), *active*(*a2*), *active*(*a3*), *active*(*a5*), *active*(*a6*), *ping*(*a4*), *hasfile*(*a5*, *f1*), *hasfile*(*a6*, *f2*)}	8, 12
10	{*hasfile*(*a1*, *f2*), *hasfile*(*a3*, *f2*), *hasfile*(*a1*, *f1*), *hasfile*(*a3*, *f1*), *active*(*a2*), *active*(*a3*), *active*(*a5*), *active*(*a6*), *ping*(*a4*), *hasfile*(*a5*, *f1*), *hasfile*(*a6*, *f2*)}	12

We have now presented the rules that define the deduction process. In Table 4.4 we illustrate a possible evaluation of the rules for a number of execution steps. At each step, we list the beliefs that hold at the beginning, and we calculate the rules that can be fired as a result, taking into account any relevant constraints. This task would be performed by theorem-proving in a real implementation. The resulting rules are then fired simultaneously, providing the set of belief for the next step. By the tenth step, agent $a1$ has a copy of both files, and we have satisfied our goal. However, we note that the system will not terminate, as agent $a4$ is undefined and rule 12 will be fired indefinitely.

The use of temporal logic to define the reasoning process is appealing as it provides us with an elegant formalism and a clean logic-based semantics. We have more expressive power than PDDL plans, as we can specify the relationship between beliefs and time, and the precise order in which actions should occur. The system that we have presented is a simplified form of the Concurrent MetateM language. The key difference is that Concurrent MetateM provides a set of operators for reasoning about the past in addition to the future. A full semantics of the Concurrent MetateM language can be found in the Suggested Reading section at the end of the chapter.

The simplicity and expressibility of the executable temporal-logic approach is offset to some extent by the need for a complex theorem-proving process within each agent. Theorem-proving is inevitably a computationally demanding activity, and this makes it questionable whether such an approach is suitable for use in real agent systems. In particular, there is a fundamental assumption that the world will not change in a significant way during the (potentially lengthy) deduction process. Consequently, the majority of real agent systems are based on less computationally demanding formalisms for pragmatic reasons.

There are a large number of alternative approaches to define deductive agent systems. In particular, many different kinds of logical systems have been defined, which include modalities for expressing such concepts as beliefs, locations, actions, commitments. Deductive agent systems have also been defined with alternative semantics based on formalisms such as the situation calculus, and game theory. However, while these approaches are of significant theoretical importance to MASs, the majority are principally specification languages and are not directly executable. For this reason, we do not discuss these approaches further in this book, as we are principally interested in agents that can be straightforwardly implemented. In Chapter 5 we discuss how reasoning on the Semantic Web can be performed by a kind of deductive reasoning process.

4.5 Hybrid agent systems

We have now detailed the main techniques that can be used to define rational agents. It should be clear from our explanation that each of these approaches has certain inherent advantages and disadvantages. The reactive formalisms are relatively straightforward to implement, but they are only capable of reacting to events, and not initiating events of their own accord. The practical reasoning and deductive approaches allow us to define more advanced agent behaviours. However, they require us to have a consistent view of the world and suffer from computational complexity in implementation. Nonetheless, there is no real reason why these approaches should be considered in isolation. We can alleviate the disadvantages of any one approach by considering agents that utilize a combination of different techniques. An agent system that is constructed in this manner is termed a *hybrid* agent system.

In Section 4.4 we hinted at this hybrid approach when we showed how deduction could be used to assist the planning process. In particular, we used deduction to determine the order in which competing plans should be applied. A more popular approach is the combination of reactive and proactive formalisms. When an event in the environment occurs that requires the agent to react, the reactive definitions are employed. Similarly, when conditions dictate that an agent should act, the proactive definitions take control. A natural way to design a hybrid agent is to treat the behaviours of the agent as separate subsystems. This style of design leads to the construction of a hybrid agent as a hierarchy of interacting *layers*.

In the layered agent architecture we will typically have at least a reactive layer and a proactive layer. However, further layers can be included to equip the agent with additional kinds of behaviour. For example, we may include layers for deduction, communication, social interaction, mobility, adaptation, and other common agent properties. There are two main ways to structure the layers of a hybrid agent, illustrated in Figure 4.12:

1. In a *parallel layered* system, each layer takes the input from the environment separately and produces suggestions as to the necessary output action. In effect, each layer acts as a separate agent.
2. In a *sequential layered* system, the input from the environment is passed through all the layers of the system, and handled by at most one layer. The layers act in concert to ensure that the input is handled appropriately.

The parallel layered approach has the advantage of conceptual simplicity, as the layers can be implemented independently. In essence, we can add

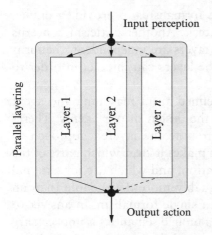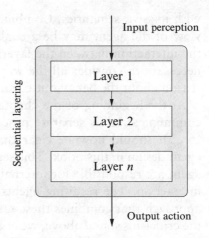

Figure 4.12   *Hybrid agent architectures.*

a new layer for each kind of behaviour that we want the agent to have. However, this simplicity is offset by the need to resolve potential conflicts between the layers, and decide which layer has control of the agent at a given time. These tasks are usually assigned to a separate *mediator* that enforces consistency between the layers. The design of this mediator is non-trivial as it may be required to consider all possible interactions between the different layers. Consequently, the mediator may adversely act as a bottleneck inside the agent.

The difficulties of the parallel layered architecture are addressed to an extent by the sequential layered approach. The environmental input flows between all the layers without the need for a mediator. One layer is responsible for the input, and one layer is responsible for the final output action. However, each of the layers must be explicitly designed to fit with the others. A variant of this approach is a *two-pass* architecture, where the input flows up the layers, and the output flows back down the layers. This variant is analogous to a network protocol stack.

Hybrid agent systems, constructed as layers, are currently the most popular kind of agent architecture. The layered approach is appealing from a pragmatic point of view, as it allows us to define an agent as a composition of different subsystems. These layers can be defined independently, and composed in different ways, affording us considerable flexibility in the design of our agents. For example, we can separate the activities of communication and reasoning, and we can further separate reasoning into reactive and proactive behaviours. The main criticism of the layered approach is that it is inherently difficult to reason about the behaviour of an agent as a whole. Each layer will typically be defined in a different formalism with its own semantics. Combining these formalisms to provide a unified view of the agent may be a challenging task. Another criticism concerns the interaction between the layers. If the layers are independent, then it is necessary to consider all the ways that the layers can interact in order to reason about the behaviour of an agent.

At the beginning of the chapter, we defined agent reasoning and agent communication as separate processes in the design of our agents. Therefore, it should now be clear that we promote the layered approach to agent design in this book. This separation makes it clear which parts of the agent are responsible for internal deliberation, and which are for external interaction. The resulting agents are arguably more dependable than an approach that combines these tasks into a single formalism. In answer to the criticisms stated above, we argue that a unified semantics is unnecessary if we can reason about the individual layers of the system, and we define how the layers interact.

In Figure 4.13 we present a hypothetical hybrid agent for the Semantic Web, which makes use of all the different techniques that we have defined in this chapter. The agent is defined using a two-pass sequentially layered approach. At the lowest level, we have a *knowledge service* layer which is used to combine together different agents into knowledge services for performing specific tasks. Above this layer, we have a *coordination* layer which controls the coordination between the different agents cooperating

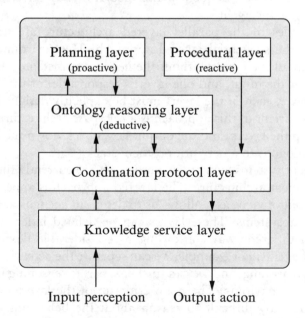

Figure 4.13 *A Semantic Web agent.*

on a task. The actual reasoning of the agent is defined in the higher layers. The *procedural* layer defines the reactive behaviours of the agent in terms of decision procedures. A decision procedure is a deterministic process that returns a choice on some specific input. The reasoning about the knowledge on the Semantic Web is performed deductively in the *ontology reasoning* layer. In this layer, we perform inference about the knowledge that we have available, and attempt to solve the task at hand. This layer is closely connected to the *planning* layer, which provides the proactive agent behaviour. For example, if we do not have enough knowledge available during inference, then we will construct a plan on how this information may be obtained.

We note that the term *hybrid agent* is often used to mean an agent system composed of different kinds of agents, e.g. a system that is defined with both software agents and human agents. This definition is more general than the one that we have presented here, as we are primarily interested in software agents. Nonetheless, while we do not propose to model humans explicitly as agents, it is necessary to consider how humans will interact with the agents that we define. We address this issue in Chapter 6, where we discuss how communication is performed both between different agents, and between humans and agents.

4.6 Summary

In this chapter, we have presented a number of sophisticated techniques for agent reasoning, which attempt to approximate our current understanding of human rational behaviour. We have also shown how different techniques can be combined into layered hybrid systems, where we may simultaneously obtain the key benefits of each approach. A summary of the main features and advantages of the three techniques described in this chapter are given below:

- A *practical reasoning* agent attempts to directly replicate the ways that we understand reasoning to be performed by human beings. This approach gives us a way to specify proactive agent behaviour. Practical reasoning is performed in two phases: deliberation where the agent decides what to do, and means–ends reasoning where the agent decides how to achieve the desired outcome. This process is presented computationally by the BDI model. The beliefs represent the knowledge that the agent has about the state of the world, and the desires are the aims that the agent would like to bring about. The driving force in the BDI model are the intentions, which are the desires that the agent has actually committed to achieving. Reasoning in the BDI model is achieved by the use of AI planning techniques. The planning process takes as its input a specification (typically in PDDL), which comprises a description of the domain, and a representation of the problem that the agent is attempting to solve. The domain description defines the actions that the agent can perform in terms of preconditions and effects. The problem representation defines the state of the world, and the goal (i.e. an intention) that the agent is attempting to achieve. The outcome of the planning process is a sequence of actions that the agent should perform in order to satisfy a particular intention.

- A *deductive reasoning* agent system is based on the notion that intelligent behaviour can be generated by equipping each agent with a symbolic representation of its environment, and its desired behaviour. Reasoning is performed by syntactic manipulation of this representation, which corresponds to deduction by theorem-proving. The representation of the environment is typically defined by logical formulae, and the theorem-proving is defined by proof rules in terms of these formulae. There are many possible approaches to defining deductive agent systems. To illustrate this approach, we defined a system based on a first-order planning formalism, and then presented an alternative based on an executable LTL. Deductive agent systems give us the greatest possible expressive power, but this comes with a significant computational complexity, which limits their applicability in real-world scenarios.

- A *hybrid* agent system attempts to simultaneously realize the benefits of a variety of different reasoning techniques. This is accomplished by defining the agent as a collection of subsystems. For example, a reactive subsystem that responds to changing conditions in the environment, and a proactive subsystem that compels the agent to act when certain conditions are met. The subsystems are typically *layered* in either a sequential or a parallel architecture. In a parallel approach, the subsystems act independently on events triggered in the environment. However, a mediator may be required to ensure coherence. In the sequential approach, the events are passed between layers and handled by at most one subsystem, though the layers must act cooperatively. From a pragmatic perspective, the hybrid approach is appealing as we can engineer the various subsystems independently. However, from a formal perspective, it is difficult to reason about the behaviour of an agent as a whole, given that the subsystems may be specified in different formalisms.

We have now described all of the main techniques that can be used to define individual agents. These techniques are focused on general-purpose reasoning. A summary of the reasoning techniques is presented

Table 4.5 *Summary of agent reasoning techniques.*

Approach	Key technology	Main advantage	Main disadvantage
Equation-based	Simulation	Predictability	Synchronization
State-based	Model-checking	Tableau-based	Verification
Practical	AI Planning	Proactiveness	Consistency
Deductive	Theorem-proving	Expressibility	Complexity
Hybrid	Layered architecture	Unified approach	No formal model

in Table 4.5. However, we do not yet have the ability to define agents specifically for the Semantic Web. We show how this can be accomplished in Chapter 5, where we define reasoning processes for Semantic Web knowledge. Furthermore, in Chapter 6 we show how our individual agents can be made to communicate, and thereby accomplish more sophisticated tasks by working together.

4.7 Exercises

1. Modify the PDDL representation of the Gnutella P2P protocol to include a 'download file' action.
2. Use the Blackbox planning system to verify your modified protocol from Q1. The Blackbox system can be downloaded from:

   `http://www.cs.washington.edu/homes/kautz/satplan/blackbox/`

3. Construct a PDDL representation for the 2PC protocol described in Chapter 3. The goal of the system should be to commit the transaction. Test your implementation using Blackbox.
4. Modify the beliefs in Figure 4.11, so that each agent knows which other agents it is connected to, but not if these agents are active. Also, alter the set of plans to include ping actions that determine active agents.
5. Expand the beliefs and plans from Q4 in the style of Table 4.2 to determine if a solution is possible.
6. Construct a specification for the 2PC protocol from Q3 in LTL. The decisions that the participants make should be included directly in your specification.
7. Exhaustively expand the LTL rules that you defined in Q6 to demonstrate that your protocol terminates correctly.

4.8 Suggested reading

1. J. L. Austin. *How to Do Things With Words*. Oxford University Press, Oxford, UK, 1962.
2. H. Barringer, M. Fisher, D. Gabbay, G. Gough, and R. Owens. MetateM: An Imperative Approach to Temporal Logic Programming. *Formal Aspects of Computing*, 7(E): 111–54, 1995.
3. M. E. Bratman. *Intention, Plans, and Practical Reason*. Harvard University Press, 1987.
4. M. Fisher. Concurrent METATEM—A Language for Modelling Reactive Systems. In *Proceedings of Parallel Architectures and Languages Europe (PARLE'93)*, volume 694 of *Lecture Notes in Computer Science*. Springer-Verlag, June 1993.
5. M. P. Georgeff and F. F. Ingrand. Decision-Making in an Embedded Reasoning System. In *Proceedings of the Eleventh International Joint Conference on Artificial Intelligence (IJCAI'89)*, pp. 972–8, Detroit, USA, 1989.
6. M. Ghallab, D. Nau, and P. Traverso. *Automated Planning: Theory and Practice*. Morgan Kaufmann, 2004.
7. A. Rao. AgentSpeak(L): BDI Agents Speak Out in a Logical Computable Language. In *Proceedings of the Seventh European Workshop on Modelling Autonomous Agents in a Multi-Agent World (MAAMAW'96)*, Eindhoven, The Netherlands, January 1996.
8. J. R. Searle. *Speech Acts: An Essay on the Philosophy of Language*. Cambridge University Press, 1969.

5 Reasoning on the Web

The techniques that we can use to construct rational agents were presented in Chapters 3 and 4. In these chapters, we identified a variety of general-purpose reasoning techniques that can be used by agents to accomplish goal-directed behaviour. In this chapter, we turn our attention to the construction of agent-based reasoning processes that are directed towards the Semantic Web. These processes are based on the general techniques that we described previously, but are tailored specifically for the Semantic Web. In particular, our reasoning processes are designed to operate directly on Semantic Web knowledge expressed in RDF, RDFS, and OWL documents. These reasoning processes are essentially specialized kinds of deductive reasoning systems.

It is important to appreciate that the reasoning processes that we describe in this chapter have certain limitations. For each technique, we will only be able to solve certain classes of problems. These limitations are a direct consequence of the representation that we use. Thus, it is necessary that we understand what kinds of problems we can solve in each approach, as this will determine the kinds of Semantic Web applications that we can construct. In effect, we are seeking to answer two key questions:

1. What kinds of reasoning can we perform with our knowledge?
2. How do we specify the problems that we wish to solve?

The first question concerns the representation of the knowledge. In Chapter 2 we stated that there is a trade-off between expressibility and efficient reasoning. In general, the more features that we have in the representation language, the more difficult it is to reason with the language. The second question concerns the definition of the reasoning process itself. As we show in this chapter, there is a further trade-off between specification complexity and reasoning power. In general, the more complex our specification formalism, the more difficult it is to reason efficiently.

In this chapter, we discuss two main approaches that we can use to define reasoning processes for the Semantic Web: *query languages* and *logic-based formalisms*. The key difference is that logic-based formalisms are more powerful than query languages, but query languages are more efficient and easier to use in a practical setting. Nonetheless, there is a degree of overlap between the approaches. In particular, the query languages can be viewed as an interface onto the more complex logic-based formalisms.

5.1 Query languages

In Chapter 1 we highlighted two steps that were required to represent knowledge on the Semantic Web:

1. The definition of an *ontology* to express the structure of the knowledge.
2. The construction of a *knowledge base* to store the structured knowledge.

When we perform reasoning, we must often take into account the interplay between the ontology and the knowledge base. Typically, in order to answer a question, we first turn to the ontology to find the correct category for the answer, and then to the knowledge base to provide specific instances. For example, we consider the following questions that relate to the camera ontology and knowledge base of Chapter 1:

1. What kinds of camera bodies are available?
2. Are there any medium format cameras with a digital back?
3. Which digital SLR camera has the lowest price at Photomart?

The first question can be answered directly from the ontology, e.g. by listing all the subclasses of **BodyType**. The second question requires us to find all the cameras that are classified as medium format in the knowledge base, and then find the intersection with those cameras that are classified as having a digital back. The final question requires us to find the cameras classified as SLR in one knowledge base, and then combine this with pricing information from another knowledge base. We can readily devise more complex questions that will require us to reason across multiple ontologies and knowledge bases.

The first kind of reasoning strategy that we discuss is designed to answer specific questions, where these questions are restricted to certain standard forms. The questions that we consider in this approach are effectively direct requests for knowledge, called *queries*. In this chapter, we consider queries that operate on knowledge bases that are defined using the RDF.

The inspiration for the query-based style of reasoning comes directly from the widespread proliferation of Relational DataBase Management Systems (RDBMS). A knowledge base can be considered a database of knowledge, and the ontology can be considered to fulfil the same function as a database schema. In an RDBMS, data is extracted from the database by the construction and enactment of Structured Query Language (SQL) queries, which are defined in terms of the database schema. This concept can be adapted by the definition of RDF query languages, which can extract knowledge from a knowledge base with a similar set of operations. However, there are at least six important differences that we must consider when querying knowledge on the Semantic Web:

1. Semantic Web knowledge is *network structured* rather than *relational*. A database defines tables that are sets of logical relations, and a database query composes one or more of these tables using set-based operations. By contrast, an RDF knowledge-base defines a single semantic network of resources. To perform database-style queries in RDF, we must select parts of the network to act as separate tables. This is accomplished by representing a part of the network as a table with a separate column for the subject, predicate, and object of each triple. Once we have defined our tables in this way, we can compose the tables with set-based operations.
2. A Semantic Web knowledge base is generally less structured than a database, i.e. the knowledge is *semi-structured*. In particular, there may be missing information and inconsistencies in the knowledge. If multiple knowledge bases are involved, parts of the knowledge may become unavailable. As a result, the knowledge returned from a query may only be partial, and the size of the result and time to compute the result will be unpredictable.
3. Semantic Web knowledge may be either *asserted* or *inferred*. In general, we do not distinguish between asserted knowledge that is already present in a knowledge base, and inferred knowledge that is calculated only in response to a query. For example, the RDF knowledge base on which we perform a query may be inferred from a constantly changing RSS feed, or a dynamic combination of different RDF sources. As a result, our queries may return different results on subsequent evaluations, and may be unable to return a result if the knowledge provider is unavailable.
4. Semantic Web knowledge may be represented in different syntactic forms. Although we are restricting our attention to knowledge represented in RDF, there are still different ways in which this knowledge can be represented. For example, our RDF may represent an RDFS vocabulary, or an OWL ontology. As a result, our queries must be tailored to the structure of the underlying representation.
5. Queries may not include a specification of the knowledge base on which they are to be applied. In many cases, we will not know in advance which knowledge base will be used to answer a query. This is

analogous to a search on the Web, where we do not know in advance the websites that will be considered. To answer this kind of query, we must typically rely on a service that selects candidate knowledge sources on our behalf.

6. Databases assume a closed-world model, where everything that is not explicitly defined is assumed to be false. By contrast, the Semantic Web has an *open-world* assumption, where things that are false must be explicitly specified, or they are simply undefined. Furthermore, databases assume a finite domain, while the domain of interpretation in the Semantic Web can be infinite.

Before we present the definition of a query language for RDF, it is necessary to discuss querying at the XML level. It may appear that an RDF query language is unnecessary, as there already exist database systems that can store XML data, and evaluate queries on this data, e.g. using the XQuery and XPath languages. However, the fundamental problem with this approach is that it operates at a lower-level of abstraction that can cause problems when dealing with RDF data. In particular, an XML query language will not be aware of the semantics of RDF. For instance, the same knowledge can be represented in several equivalent forms in RDF, and there is no straightforward way to define these equivalences at the XML level, e.g. the following two descriptions can be considered equivalent in RDF:

```
<rdf:Description rdf:about="NikonD70">
<rdf:type rdf:resource="&camera;SLR"/>
<camera:lensMount>NikonF</camera:lensMount>
</rdf:Description>

<camera:SLR rdf:about="NikonD70" camera:lensMount="NikonF"/>
```

However, to extract the `lensMount` information using XQuery, we require two different queries, depending on the representation that we use:

```
/rdf:Description[rdf:type="&camera;SLR"]/camera:lensMount
//camera:SLR/@camera:lensMount
```

The use of an RDF query language is primarily a technique for reasoning about knowledge bases. However, in Chapter 2 we saw that both RDFS vocabularies and OWL ontologies are expressed using RDF syntax. The use of this common syntax allows us to store our ontologies within the knowledge base. As a result, we can perform a limited amount of inference on these ontologies by exploiting the RDF representation, together with a suitable query language. The only real kind of inference that we can perform with a query language is *pattern-matching* on the knowledge base. Nonetheless, complex patterns can be defined to express many different kinds of operations. Pattern-matching does not permit the same kinds of advanced reasoning that we can perform by logic-based methods, e.g. structural subsumption, though the querying mechanism is significantly more computationally efficient.

It is helpful to consider the definition of a query at a formal level before describing the syntax of a specific query language. We can consider a knowledge-base as a set of sentences (i.e. triples) T. Each sentence $t \in T$ is of the form $p(S, O)$, where p is the predicate, S is the subject, and O is the object. A query is specified by a query pattern q, which is a sentence that may contain free variables, i.e. the subject, predicate, and object. For example, the query pattern hasBack(x, DigitalBack) will match all sentences that have the predicate hasBack and the object DigitalBack.

The result of matching a query pattern q against a knowledge base T is a set of sentences Q that satisfy the pattern, such that $Q = match(q, T)$ | $Q \subseteq T$. For each match that is found, the variables in the query pattern are substituted for the terms in the matching sentence. More formally, the variable bindings B are defined as substitution $B = subst(q, t)$ | $t \in T$ of variables in q for terms in t. The bindings B can be considered as answers for the query. For example, the bindings of the variable x in the query hasBack(x, DigitalBack) provide the answers to the query 'Which cameras have a digital back?'.

5.1.1 SPARQL query language

We now describe the SPARQL standard, which is an acronym for: Simple Protocol And RDF Query Language. The standard defines both a network protocol for the exchange of queries, and a language for expressing queries. It is the latter query language that we discuss here. The SPARQL adopts an SQL-like syntax for expressing queries, rather than an XML-based syntax. SPARQL is an attempt to replace a large number of existing RDF query languages, e.g. RQL, RDQL, and RDF Query, with a common standard. For brevity we only present an overview of the main features of the query language here. A reference to the SPARQL standard is provided in the Suggested Reading section at the end of the chapter.

To demonstrate the construction of SPARQL queries, we first define an example RDF knowledge base in Table 5.1. The knowledge base contains information on three different models of camera. We use N3 notation to define our RDF triples, as this style is more compact than an XML-based representation. In this notation, we simply write a triple as a sequence of terms, followed by a period. A blank node is written _:a, where a is the namespace for the node. The prefixes, given at the beginning of

Table 5.1 *Example knowledge base.*

```
@prefix xsd: <http://http://www.w3.org/2001/XMLSchema#>
@prefix camera: <http://www.mycamera.org/photo#>
@prefix canon: <http://www.mycamera.org/canon#>
@prefix nikon: <http://www.mycamera.org/nikon#>
@prefix pentax: <http://www.mycamera.org/pentax#>
canon:CanonEOS300D    camera:manufacturer   canon:CanonInc .
canon:CanonEOS300D    camera:hasBack        camera:DigitalBack .
canon:CanonEOS300D    camera:resolution     "6.3"^^xsd:decimal .
nikon:NikonD70        camera:manufacturer   nikon:NikonCorporation .
nikon:NikonD70        camera:hasBack        camera:DigitalBack .
nikon:NikonD70        camera:resolution     "6.1"^^xsd:decimal .
pentax:PentaxK1000    camera:manufacturer   pentax:PentaxCorporation .
pentax:PentaxK1000    camera:hasBack        camera:35mm .
```

the definition, are syntactic abbreviations, and essentially serve the same purpose as an XML namespace definition.

Queries are defined in SPARQL by specifying a query pattern just as in our formal description. For example, the following SPARQL query selects the cameras in our knowledge base with a digital back:

```
SELECT ?x
WHERE { ?x <http://www.mycamera.org/photo#hasBack>
           <http://www.mycamera.org/photo#DigitalBack> }
```

The query pattern is specified in the WHERE clause of the query as a triple enclosed in braces {}. Each position in the triple can be either a variable, or an RDF term. An RDF term is defined as anything that can be expressed as an RDF resource, i.e. a URI reference, a literal, or a blank node. The URI references are enclosed by <> to distinguish them from literals, and variables are preceded by ?. Any variables are bound to RDF terms during evaluation of the query. The form of the answer to the query is defined in the SELECT statement. In this case, we want the answer to consist of only the first term of any match with the query pattern (?x). If we wished to return the entire triple of any match, we could write SELECT *. In contrast to an SQL query, we do not need to specify a FROM clause, as our knowledge base is not structured into separate tables. The outcome of evaluating the query on our example knowledge base is the following table of answers:

?x
canon:CanonEOS300D
nikon:NikonD70

The use of entire URI references inside query patterns is rather cumbersome, and so the query language includes a PREFIX clause, which has a similar purpose to an XML namespace. A prefix defines an abbreviation for a URI reference, and is expanded during the evaluation of the query. For example, our previous query may be abbreviated as follows:

```
PREFIX camera: <http://www.mycamera.org/photo#>
SELECT ?x
WHERE { ?x camera:hasBack camera:DigitalBack }
```

A SPARQL query can be evaluated against a real, or virtual knowledge base. That is, the knowledge base may already exist, or may be constructed purely for the purpose of answering the query. The following query is performed against a virtual knowledge base, constructed from two independent RDF sources. The RDF sources are specified in the FROM clause of the query. The knowledge base on which the query is evaluated is an aggregate of the separate knowledge sources. We will assume that our example knowledge base is used as the source when we omit the FROM clause.

```
SELECT *
FROM <http://www.myphotomart.co.uk/cameras.rss>
FROM <http://www.myphotomart.com/cameras.rss>
WHERE { ?name ?relation ?value }
```

The query patterns that we have defined are termed *triple patterns* as they match a single triple at a time. SPARQL also permits the definition of *graph patterns* that match multiple triples at the same time. A graph pattern is constructed as a conjunction of triple patterns. An answer to the query must match all of the triple patterns in the graph pattern, with the same binding of values to variables. The following example defines a graph pattern to select all digital cameras manufactured by Nikon. The two patterns in the WHERE clause are logically ANDed together, i.e. a conjunction of patterns. The variable ?x ensures that the matched term is the same in both patterns. Evaluating this query on the knowledge base in Table 5.1 will yield the answer NikonD70.

```
PREFIX camera: <http://www.mycamera.org/photo#>
PREFIX nikon: <http://www.mycamera.org/nikon#>
SELECT ?x
WHERE { ?x camera:hasBack camera:DigitalBack .
        ?x camera:manufacturer nikon:NikonCorporation }
```

The answer to a query is constructed as a set of all matches of the query against the knowledge base. This answer may consist of zero, one, or multiple triples. SPARQL defines three operations that allow us to control

Table 5.2   *Restricted and ordered answer sets.*

?model1	?model2	?model3
canon:CanonEOS300D	canon:CanonEOS300D	canon:CanonEOS300D
canon:CanonEOS300D	canon:CanonEOS300D	nikon:NikonD70
canon:CanonEOS300D	canon:CanonEOS300D	pentax:PentaxK1000
nikon:NikonD70	nikon:NikonD70	
nikon:NikonD70		
nikon:NikonD70		
pentax:PentaxK1000		
pentax:PentaxK1000		
pentax:PentaxK1000		

Table 5.3   *Optional query patterns.*

?model	?resolution
canon:CanonEOS300D	"6.3"^^xsd:decimal
nikon:NikonD70	"6.1"^^xsd:decimal
pentax:PentaxK1000	

the answer set when we have multiple matches. As in SQL, we can specify that the answers to a query must all be unique by the DISTINCT keyword, and we can restrict the number of matches with the LIMIT keyword. We can also control the ordering of the returned results with the ORDER BY keyword. Table 5.2 illustrates the effect of these restrictions on the answer set of a query.

```
SELECT ?model1 WHERE { ?model1 ?x ?y } ORDER BY ?model1
SELECT ?model2 WHERE { ?model2 ?x ?y } LIMIT 4
SELECT DISTINCT ?model3 WHERE { ?model3 ?x ?y }
```

The pattern-matching that we have defined relies on an exact match between the query pattern and the triples in the knowledge base. However, there may often be missing information and inconsistencies in a knowledge base, and this can lead to relevant triples being omitted from our query answer. To work around this problem, SPARQL allows us to define *optional patterns*. These patterns will be included in the answer if a match is found, and ignored if no match is found. Table 5.3 illustrates the use of an optional query pattern, and the results of this query are shown below. If the OPTIONAL keyword was omitted, then the PentaxK1000 model would be excluded from the answer set. Multiple optional patterns can be included in a graph pattern. However, variables cannot be shared between optional patterns, unless they have already been bound in a non-optional pattern.

```
SELECT ?model ?resolution
WHERE { ?model camera:manufacturer ?manufacturer .
        OPTIONAL { ?model camera:resolution ?resolution }}
```

Another method for performing partial matches is to combine separate graph patterns into *alternatives*. This is accomplished with the UNION operator: if more than one of the alternatives is matched, all the possible pattern solutions are found. However, unlike an optional pattern, if none of the alternatives are matched then the graph pattern as a whole will not be matched. The following query uses this technique to return the same results as the previous optional query pattern:

```
SELECT ?model ?resolution
WHERE {{ ?model camera:manufacturer ?manufacturer } UNION
       { ?model camera:resolution ?resolution }}
```

It is possible to perform a limited amount of computation during the execution of SPARQL queries. In some situations this can be more convenient than performing the computation on the results of the query, e.g. to increase the portability of the queries. This computation is accomplished by the definition of *value constraints*. Value constraints are applied with the FILTER operator. These constraints take the form of Boolean-valued expressions, which may include function calls. The SPARQL includes a large number of predefined numerical, date/time, and string functions taken from the XQuery and XPath standards. An example query that uses the greater-or-equal function (>=) to filter the results is shown below:

```
SELECT ?model ?resolution
WHERE { ?model camera:manufacturer ?manufacturer .
        ?model camera:resolution ?resolution .
        FILTER (?resolution >= 6.2) }
```

The final feature of the SPARQL query language that we describe is the ability to perform queries other than the standard SELECT query. There are three alternative kinds of query that can be constructed. These queries are performed by substituting the SELECT keyword with one of the following:

1. An ASK query is simply a test whether or not a query pattern has a solution. The only response is a binary yes/no result; no further information about the query result is given.
2. A CONSTRUCT query is used to extract part or whole graphs from the target RDF knowledge base, rather than simply returning the values of variables. The form of the resulting graph is given by specifying a *graph*

template, which is matched against the target. The syntax of the graph templates is rather cumbersome, and we do not give the details here. However, we note that this kind of query is useful for transforming knowledge from one representation into another.

3. A DESCRIBE query returns a single RDF graph that describes a set of resources. The simplest query of this type simply contains a single URI, e.g.: DESCRIBE <http://www.mycamera.org/>. This kind of query is useful for constructing RDF graphs from data sources that are not already in RDF format.

We have now described the main syntactic constructs SPARQL. It should be readily apparent that this language has been designed with a syntax that should be familiar to SQL programmers using traditional database systems. However, as we discussed at the beginning of the chapter, there are significant conceptual distinctions between databases and knowledge bases. We note that SPARQL can also be used to perform queries on the structure of OWL ontologies. For example, we can perform queries to infer connections between concepts. Nonetheless, these queries can be difficult to construct, and so an alternative query language (OWL-QL) tailored specifically to the expression of queries on OWL ontologies has been proposed. We do not describe this language here as the proposal has yet to be finalized.

Query languages, such as SPARQL, provide a lightweight and efficient approach to reasoning about knowledge, though they are limited in expressivity. As previously stated, query languages are essentially restricted to inferences based on pattern-matching. More advanced inferences can be performed by relating these facts to specific ontologies against which they are classified. In particular, the subsumption inference can determine that one fact is more general or specific than another. To perform these advanced inferences, we must adopt a logic-based approach to the reasoning process, as described in the remainder of the chapter.

5.2   Description logics

In the logic-based approach, knowledge is represented in a variant of first-order predicate calculus, and reasoning is performed by logical consequence, i.e. what we can infer by applying the rules of the logic. The main class of logical systems that we discuss here are DLs. These logics are a subset of first-order logic, tailored to the representation of semantic networks, such as we previously described in RDF. Description logics provide the underlying formalisms in the OWL languages, specifically OWL-DL. Therefore, it is useful to study DLs so that we can understand how reasoning with OWL-based knowledge is performed, and its limitations.

Description logics have a long history of use in knowledge representation. These logics support the common kinds of inference that are required in many different kinds of intelligent information processing systems. They have recently gained significant popularity due to their role in the Semantic Web, though the techniques predate the Semantic Web by several decades. As a result, we can only give a brief overview of DLs here, and the reader is referred to the Suggested Reading section for additional information. In our presentation, we give a brief summary of the main characteristics of DLs, we then show how they can be used to represent knowledge, and finally we illustrate how reasoning with DLs is performed.

To motivate our discussion of DLs, we define an example semantic network in Figure 5.1. This network is a fragment of our camera ontology. We have included **FilmCamera** and **DigitalCamera** as additional concepts. The nodes in the network are used to characterize concepts, and the edges are used to characterize relationships between them. We have two basic relationships: the **subClass** (is–a) relationship, and the **partOf** relationship. In some cases, more complex relationships are also represented as nodes. For example, we have defined a **hasType** relationship from **Camera** to **CameraType** as a node. This relationship is a value restriction, indicated by the $(1, 1)$ annotation. The restriction states that a **Camera** can only have a single **CameraType**, i.e. it is a one-to-one relationship. The **hasLens** relationship is a one-to-many $(1, M)$ restriction, which states that a **Camera** can have many **Lens** objects.

Our example network exhibits three key characteristics that are found in DLs. The first of these is the structuring of concepts into a *subsumption* hierarchy of subconcepts and superconcepts. This hierarchy provides

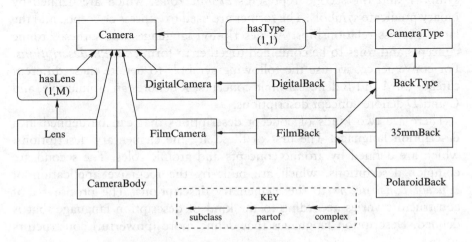

Figure 5.1 *A semantic network.*

information about the connection between concepts, and is key to the inference process. The second characteristic of DLs is that they enable the *classification* of individuals (objects) to determine whether they are an instance of a specific class. For example, if we have an instance of a **Camera** with a **35mmBack**, then we can classify this as a **FilmCamera** with our network. Finally, DLs have the ability to represent *relationships*, beyond simple is–a relations. We can define any desired relationship between concepts, if we can specify appropriate domain and range restrictions. We also note that relationships are inherited from concepts to subconcepts. For example, **BackType** inherits the **hasType** relationship from **CameraType**, i.e. a **Camera** can only have one **BackType**.

Semantic networks are a useful notation for representing concepts and relationships graphically. These networks exhibit the main properties that are found in typical DLs. However, in order to provide a logical definition of a semantic network, we must be more precise about what can be represented in the network, and the kinds of relationships that we allow. This is accomplished by specifying a syntactic representation of the network, which defines precisely the elements in the structure, and provides an interpretation for the labels. The syntactic representation is called a *description language*, and is used as the basis for the logical interpretation.

5.2.1 Description language

Description languages are similar in structure to other logical formalisms such as first-order formulae. However, sentences in a description language do not contain variables. Instead, these languages contain only basic symbols that are defined by two disjoint alphabets. The first of these alphabets represents *atomic concepts*, which are defined by unary predicate symbols, and the second represents *atomic roles*, which are defined by binary predicate symbols. The former are used to express concepts, and the latter express relationships. All description languages allow these atomic concepts and roles to be combined together to form *concept descriptions*. For convenience, we use the following symbols to denote these different categories: A and B denote atomic concepts, R denotes an atomic role, and C and D denote concept descriptions.

There are two kinds of concept descriptions that can be defined in a description language. The first of these are the elementary descriptions, which are defined by atomic concepts and atomic roles. The second are complex descriptions, which are built by the recursive application of *concept constructors* to the elementary descriptions. The precise set of constructors varies according to the kind of description language that is defined. Description languages that define more (powerful) constructors

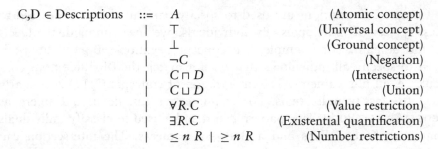

Figure 5.2 *ALCN description language.*

are more expressive in the kinds of semantic networks that they can describe. However, as noted previously there is a trade-off between expressibility and efficient reasoning. In general, the more constructors that we have in the language, the more difficult it is to reason efficiently.

In Figure 5.2 we define the abstract syntax of a description language, called $\mathcal{ALCN}$. This is a reasonably expressive description language that contains most of the key concept constructors found in such languages. Description languages are named according to the constructors that they contain. In this case, the language is founded on the atomic language $\mathcal{AL}$ constructors, which are the basis for most description languages. We also include the complement (negation) constructor $\mathcal{C}$, and number restrictions $\mathcal{N}$. The language $\mathcal{ALC_{R+}}$, which includes transitive roles, is usually abbreviated $\mathcal{S}$. OWL-DL is founded on the $\mathcal{SHOIN(D)}$ DL, which also includes role hierarchies $\mathcal{H}$, nominals $\mathcal{O}$, inverse roles $\mathcal{I}$, unquantified number restrictions $\mathcal{N}$, and datatypes $\mathcal{D}$. Hence, the key additions in $\mathcal{SHOIN(D)}$ over $\mathcal{ALCN}$ are the extra flexibility in describing roles, i.e. relationships. However, the languages are conceptually very similar, and we restrict our attention to the simpler $\mathcal{ALCN}$ language here.

The elementary descriptions in $\mathcal{ALCN}$ are atomic concepts A, the universal concept $\top$, and the ground concept $\bot$. The universal concept is the set of all concepts in the domain, and the ground concept contains no concepts. The atomic concepts are essentially the node labels in a semantic network. For example, the atomic concepts in Figure 5.1 are:

Camera, FilmCamera, DigitalCamera, CameraBody, Lens, CameraType, BackType, FilmBack, DigitalBack, 35mmBack, and PolaroidBack.

The universal and ground concepts are useful when constructing complex descriptions. For example, concept negation can be defined as $\neg C \equiv \top - C$, where $\equiv$ indicates that the two definitions are equivalent.

Complex descriptions are used to specify patterns that will be used to classify sets of individuals. By individuals, we mean individual objects in the domain. For example, the concept negation ¬**DigitalCamera** is used to specify all individuals that do not match the **DigitalCamera** concept, i.e. all film cameras. The intersection of concepts $C \sqcap D$ is similarly used to classify individuals. For example, we can define a Camera as **Lens** $\sqcap$ **CameraBody**. This pattern can then be used to classify individuals that have both a Lens and a Body as Cameras. The intersection can be considered equivalent to the first-order formula $C(x) \wedge D(x)$, where x ranges over all individuals in the domain, and $C(x)$ is true when x matches the concept C. Concept union is equivalent to the first-order formula $C(x) \vee D(x)$. For example, **Camera** can be defined as **DigitalCamera** $\sqcup$ **FilmCamera**. Note that the intersection applies over the **partOf** relationships in our example, while union applies over the **subClass** relationships. Concept union can be derived from the intersection and negation: $C \sqcup D \equiv \neg(\neg C \sqcap \neg D)$.

Relationships between concepts are established by using the quantifiers $\forall$ and $\exists$. The basic kind of relationships are value restrictions $\forall R.C$. A value restriction requires that all individuals, which have a relationship R with C, are included in C. For example, $\forall$**hasType.Camera** states that all individuals which have a **hasType** relationship should be part of the concept **Camera**. Relationships are interpreted as sets of pairs of individuals, while concepts are sets of individuals. Therefore, if we have a relationship **hasType** = {(**NikonD70**, **DigitalBack**), (**PentaxKM**, **FilmBack**)}, then $\forall$**hasType.Camera** means that {**NikonD70**, **PentaxKM**} should be included in the set **Camera**. Existential quantification $\exists R.C$ allows us to isolate specific individuals from relationship R which contains the concept C. For example, $\exists$**hasType.DigitalBack** identifies individuals that are in the **hasType** relationship, with a **DigitalBack** concept. This will be the set {**NikonD70**} in our example. Existential quantification can also be derived from value restriction and negation: $\exists R.C \equiv \neg\forall R.\neg C$.

The final kind of relationships that we can define in $\mathcal{ALCN}$ are number restrictions: $\leq n\ R$ and $\geq n\ R$. These enable us to restrict the number of individuals that participate in a 'many' relationship to specific bounds. For example, the **hasLens** relationship is defined as a one-to-many relation since certain kinds of camera can have multiple lenses, e.g. twin-lens reflex cameras. We can identify individuals with more than 1 lens by the number restriction ≥ 2 **hasLens**. Individuals with exactly 2 lenses can be identified with a pair of number restrictions: $(\geq 2$ **hasLens**$)\sqcap$ $(\leq 2$ **hasLens**$)$.

To further illustrate the $\mathcal{ALCN}$ description language, we now present a definition of the semantic network from Figure 5.1. This definition is

$$
\begin{array}{ll}
\text{Camera} & \equiv \text{Lens} \sqcap \text{CameraBody} \\
\text{Camera} & \equiv \text{DigitalCamera} \sqcup \text{FilmCamera} \\
\text{Camera} & \equiv \forall \text{hasLens.Lens} \\
\text{Camera} & \equiv \forall \text{hasType.CameraType} \\
\text{DigitalCamera} & \equiv \top \sqcap \text{DigitalBack} \\
\text{FilmCamera} & \equiv \top \sqcap \text{FilmBack} \\
\text{CameraType} & \equiv \top \sqcap \text{BackType} \\
\text{BackType} & \equiv \text{DigitalBack} \cup \text{FilmBack} \\
\text{FilmBack} & \equiv \text{35mmBack} \cup \text{PolaroidBack}
\end{array}
$$

Figure 5.3   *Camera terminology in $\mathcal{ALCN}$.*

$$
\begin{array}{lll}
\top & \Rightarrow & \Delta \\
\bot & \Rightarrow & \emptyset \\
\neg C & \Rightarrow & \Delta - A \\
C \sqcap D & \Rightarrow & C \cap D \\
C \sqcup D & \Rightarrow & C \cup D \\
\forall R.C & \Rightarrow & \{a \in \Delta \mid \forall b.(a, b) \in R \rightarrow b \in C\} \\
\exists R.C & \Rightarrow & \{a \in \Delta \mid \exists b.(a, b) \in R \wedge b \in C\} \\
\leq n\, R & \Rightarrow & \{a \in \Delta \mid \|\{(a, b) \in R\}\| \leq n\} \\
\geq n\, R & \Rightarrow & \{a \in \Delta \mid \|\{(a, b) \in R\}\| \geq n\}
\end{array}
$$

Figure 5.4   *Set-theoretic semantics of $\mathcal{ALCN}$.*

shown in Figure 5.3 and expresses all of the relationships shown in the network. We note that this definition will only hold if the domain is finite, and the semantic network remains unchanged. For example, if we were to extend the network with additional subclasses of **FilmBack** then our definition **FilmBack** $\equiv$ **35mmBack** $\cup$ **PolaroidBack** would no longer hold. This restriction is called a *closed-world* assumption, and is not generally a desirable feature. To avoid this restriction, the different kinds of Camera Back should be represented as instances, rather than concepts. This would permit us to extend the set in future without invalidating our definitions.

We conclude our description of the $\mathcal{ALCN}$ description language by presenting a set-theoretic semantics in Figure 5.4. This is an interpretation of the language constructors in classical set theory. The domain of interpretation is defined by the (non-empty) set Δ. Atomic concepts are defined by a set $A \in \Delta$, atomic roles are defined by a binary relation $R \in \Delta \times \Delta$, $\|$ is used to denote set cardinality. As an example, the existential quantifier $\exists R.C$ is defined by $\{a \in \Delta \mid \exists b.(a, b) \in R \wedge b \in C\}$. This should be read as stating that the definition is a set of elements a from the domain Δ, for each (a, b) in the set of relationships R, where b is in the set C. The other constructors are similarly defined.

5.2.2 Knowledge representation

Description languages provide us with a syntactic representation for DLs. We have now shown how description languages can be used to represent concepts and their relationships. We defined the syntax and semantics of the $\mathcal{ALCN}$ description language, and illustrated how it can formally represent a semantic network. We now turn our attention to the more general issues associated with *knowledge representation*. In particular, how can we use DLs to build knowledge bases, and how do we perform reasoning over this represented knowledge?

To answer these questions, it is useful to take a *functional view* of the knowledge representation process. That is, to define an abstract specification of the knowledge base and the inferences that it provides, without reference to the concrete implementation details. This functional view can be specified by viewing the knowledge base through a *tell and ask* interface. This interface facilitates the construction of the knowledge base through tell operations, and the inference process by ask operations. To complete the functional view, we also need to characterize the kinds of knowledge that will pass through this interface.

There are two distinct kinds of knowledge that we will represent: *intensional knowledge* about the problem domain, and *extensional knowledge* about a specific problem. We distinguish between these two kinds of knowledge by the terms *TBox* and *ABox* respectively. The TBox contains the intensional knowledge in the form of a *terminology*, and the ABox contains the extensional knowledge in the form of *assertions*. It should be clear that these two terms are essentially the ontology and knowledge base, as discussed previously. However, the functional view assumes that both are defined together in a unified knowledge base representation. A summary of the functional view is presented in Figure 5.5.

We now define the form of the knowledge that is stored in the TBox and ABox. In keeping with the functional view, we are not directly concerned about the implementation details, and so these definitions are expressed using terms from DLs. The basic form of the declarations in the TBox are *concept definitions*. These definitions express new concepts in terms of existing concepts in the TBox. For example, the following $\mathcal{ALCN}$ definition may be used to define a new concept **Camera** in terms of the existing concepts **Lens** and **CameraBody**:

$$\textbf{Camera} \equiv \textbf{Lens} \sqcap \textbf{CameraBody}.$$

A TBox comprises a set of concept definitions of the above kind that form a concept hierarchy. The construction of a TBox is primarily a process of defining a suitable conceptualization of a part of the world. The rules

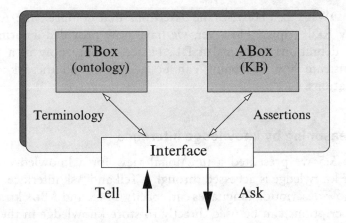

Figure 5.5 *Functional view of knowledge representation.*

that form concept definitions are usually interpreted as logical equivalence, and this imposes two important restrictions on the construction of the TBox. These restrictions ensure that every complex description can be expanded uniquely into an expression containing only atomic concepts:

1. Concept definitions must be acyclic: they cannot refer to themselves, either directly or through other concepts that refer to them.
2. Only one definition of a concept name is permitted.

The knowledge that is represented in the TBox is generally assumed not to change significantly over time. By contrast, ABox knowledge is often dynamic and dependent on circumstances, and therefore liable to change. The basic form of definitions in the ABox are *membership assertions*. These are assertions about individuals, and relate these individuals to concepts and roles in the TBox. For example, consider the following two assertions:

Camera(PENTAXKM)
hasLens(PENTAXKM, 50MMLENS)

The first is a concept assertion, which states that **PENTAXKM** is a **Camera**. The second is a role assertion and states that the individual **PENTAXKM** is related to the individual **50MMLENS** by a hasLens relationship. The important restriction of ABox knowledge is that the assertions should be *consistent*. That is, an individual should not be associated with incompatible concepts, e.g. **Lens**(PENTAXKM).

From our discussion of TBox and ABox knowledge representation, it should be clear that these definitions are equivalent to OWL ontologies and RDF knowledge respectively. The concept definitions that comprise the TBox are similar (though less expressive) to the rules that we can define in OWL-DL. Likewise, the assertions that comprise the ABox are essentially RDF triples. However, we have now provided a formal basis for these definitions in terms of DL. Hence, we are now in a position to demonstrate how reasoning can be performed on these knowledge representations.

5.2.3   Reasoning by knowledge inference

In Figure 5.5 we presented a functional view for a knowledge base, in which the knowledge is accessed through a Tell and Ask interface. We also showed how description languages can specify TBox and ABox knowledge. These descriptions can be used directly to store knowledge in the knowledge base through the Tell part of the interface. However, we have yet to describe how knowledge is retrieved again through the Ask interface. A knowledge base is intended to be more than a simple container for knowledge. To act as a useful tool in knowledge-based applications, the knowledge base should act as an expert system that can answer questions about the knowledge that it contains. These questions are posed through the Ask interface, and answered by reasoning over the represented knowledge.

The DL approach to knowledge representation facilitates certain specific kinds of reasoning. As we have previously shown, a knowledge base is equivalent to a set of axioms in first-order predicate logic. Therefore, just like any set of axioms, it contains implicit knowledge that can be made explicit through inferences. The knowledge that is represented in the TBox and ABox of the knowledge base is different, and therefore, it is reasonable to assume that the kinds of inference that can be performed on these representations also differ. We now describe the kinds of inferences that can be performed with TBox and ABox knowledge, and then outline how these inferences can be automated, which is important if we are to encapsulate them within agents. There are four types of useful inference that can be performed over conceptual knowledge represented in the TBox:

1. The most fundamental kind of inference over concepts is called *subsumption*. We write $T \vdash C \sqsubseteq D$ to denote that the concept D is more general than C in the TBox T. On other words, the set denoted by C is a subset of the set denoted by D. Subsumption is non-trivial when we move beyond simple hierarchies of concepts. For example, when we have to consider multiple relationships and cardinality restrictions. The primary purpose of subsumption is to allow us to infer relationships between individuals that are not obvious from their definitions in the knowledge base.

2. When defining a new concept in a knowledge base, it is important to know that the concept is consistent and does not contradict any concepts that have already been defined. Intuitively, a concept is consistent if it is possible to construct at least one individual that matches the concept. A concept that has this property is said to be *satisfiable* if this can be accomplished, and *unsatisfiable* otherwise. We can express unsatisfiability as the subsumption: $T \vdash C \sqsubseteq \bot$.

3. A further inference that we can perform is a test whether two concepts are *equivalent*. This is useful for removing redundancy and ambiguity of the knowledge base. We write $T \vdash C \equiv D$ if C and D are equivalent in the TBox T. Equivalence can also be expressed in terms of subsumption: $T \vdash (C \sqsubseteq D \wedge D \sqsubseteq C)$.

4. A final useful inference that we can perform is check whether concepts are *disjoint*. That is, there is no relationship that can be inferred between the concepts. Once again, this can be expressed through subsumption: $T \vdash C \sqcap D \sqsubseteq \bot$.

Assertional knowledge about specific individuals is represented in the ABox. There are four important inferences that can be performed over sets of individuals:

1. The basic inference over ABox knowledge is *instance checking*. This is a process of verifying that an individual (i.e. instance) belongs to a specific concept. We write $A \vdash C(a)$ to indicate that the instance a belongs to the concept C in the ABox A. This is important as it indicates that the instance is classified according to the knowledge base terminology.

2. A useful inference in practice is *retrieval*, which finds all of the instances in the knowledge base that are of a specific concept. This can be defined in terms of instance checking: $\{a \in A \mid A \vdash C(a)\}$. Retrieval is essentially the process of *querying* the knowledge base, as we described at the beginning of the chapter. In this case, the description language used to specify the knowledge representation is used directly to define the query patterns.

3. The dual inference to retrieval is *realization*, where the most specific for an individual is obtained. Realization can be defined by instance checking and subsumption: $A \vdash C(a)$ and $T \vdash \bot \sqsubseteq C$.

4. The *consistency* check for the ABox is fundamentally the same as the test for satisfiability of the TBox. That is, every concept in the knowledge base admits at least one individual from the ABox. This can be defined in terms of instance checking: $\forall C \in T. \exists a \in A \mid A \vdash C(a)$.

The eight kinds of inference that we have defined are all useful from a pragmatic point of view as they accomplish different reasoning tasks.

However, when we come to the implementation of an inference engine, the distinction between these different tasks is less useful. Ideally, we would like to implement only a single kind of inference, and obtain the rest as special cases. We have already shown how all of the TBox inferences can be reduced to subsumption, and how all of the ABox inferences can be reduced to instance checking. In fact, all of the inferences can be reduced to the consistency for an ABox. We can reduce the ABox identity check to consistency by noting the following:

$$A \vdash C(a) \text{ iff } A \cup \{\neg C(a)\} \text{ is inconsistent.}$$

This states that adding a to the negated concept $\neg C$ makes the knowledge base inconsistent, i.e. the individual a is already in the knowledge base. As previously noted, ABox consistency is equivalent TBox satisfiability, i.e.

$$C \text{ is satisfiable iff } \{C(a)\} \text{ is consistent.}$$

Finally, all of the TBox inferences can all be reduced to (un)satisfiability as the following statements are all equivalent:

1. C is subsumed by $\bot$.
2. C is unsatisfiable.
3. C and $\bot$ are equivalent.
4. C and $\top$ are disjoint.

The reduction of the DL inferences to the satisfiability problem is important. We have previously stated that DLs are a subset of first-order logic. Hence, with some work we may apply the well-known algorithms for the Boolean satisfiability problem (SAT solvers) to the inference problems in DLs. Nonetheless, this is not a particularly appealing approach. One of the primary reasons for using DLs instead of full first-order logic is that we want to perform more efficient reasoning. Thus, special-purpose reasoning systems have been devised that take advantage of the less expressive nature of DLs to perform more efficient reasoning. We now describe how efficient reasoning can be performed for the $\mathcal{ALCN}$ description language.

5.2.4 Reasoning techniques

We previously stated that less expressivity in DLs enables more efficient reasoning to be performed. However, it has been shown that the subsumption problem is intractable (non-polynomial complexity) in the worst case, even for very inexpressive logics. Nonetheless, this result does not prevent DLs from being useful in practice. In reality, the worst case behaviour does not give a good measure of the performance of a typical reasoning engine. The underlying reasons are too complex to be discussed here. However, it has been repeatedly demonstrated that with suitable optimizations and careful terminology design, the worst-case behaviours can be avoided.

Description Logics are used as a formal foundation in many practical knowledge-based systems. For example, expert systems, recommender systems, and MASs. This practical bias has specific implications for the way that the reasoning system is implemented. In contrast with theorem provers, the reasoner must terminate with a yes/no answer, and should do so in a reasonable time frame so that the user or agent is not unnecessarily delayed. This is generally accomplished by implementing the reasoner as a *decision procedure*. The procedure will be invoked by the external entity and should return an answer as appropriate. Decision procedures are discussed further in Chapters 3 and 6.

We now outline a tableau-based satisfiability algorithm for $\mathcal{ALCN}$. As previously stated, all of the other inferences can be reduced into a test for ABox satisfiability. The algorithm that we present is just for illustrative purposes, and we do not describe in detail the underlying intuitions behind the algorithm. The algorithm defines the satisfiability process in a very straightforward manner. Significantly more efficient algorithms can be constructed by optimizing this technique.

The algorithm requires that the concept description to be tested for satisfiability is described in *negation normal form*. This is obtained by pushing the negation symbols into the description so that negation only occurs directly in front of concepts. For example, C_{NNF} is the negation normalized form of C:

$$
\begin{aligned}
C &= (\exists R.A) \sqcap (\exists R.B) \sqcap \neg(\exists R.(A \sqcap B)) \\
C_{NNF} &= (\exists R.A) \sqcap (\exists R.B) \sqcap \forall R.(\neg A \sqcup \neg B)
\end{aligned}
$$

Satisfiability (i.e. consistency) means that it is possible to construct at least one individual that matches the concept. Therefore, the reasoning algorithm simply attempts to construct an individual a such that $C_{NNF}(a)$. If this individual can be constructed, then the concept C_{NNF} is satisfiable, otherwise the concept is unsatisfiable. In our example, C_{NNF} is a conjunction of three concepts. Therefore, the checking is performed in three stages: $a \in (\exists R.A)$, $a \in (\exists R.B)$, and $a \in \forall R.(\neg A \sqcup \neg B)$.

The checking process is performed by an exhaustive application of the rules in Table 5.4. There is a separate rule for each of the concept constructors in $\mathcal{ALCN}$. Each of these rules preserves the consistency of the knowledge base, and extends the ABox A with new instances that satisfy the concept being checked. For example, from $a \in (\exists R.A)$ we can

Table 5.4 *ALCN satisfiability algorithm.*

⊓ Rule:	
Condition	A contains $(C_1 \sqcap C_2)(x)$, but not both $C_1(x)$ and $C_2(x)$.
Action	$A \cup \{C_1(x), C_2(x)\}$
⊔ Rule:	
Condition	A contains $(C_1 \sqcup C_2)(x)$, but neither $C_1(x)$ nor $C_2(x)$.
Action	$A \cup \{C_1(x)\}$ or $A \cup \{C_2(x)\}$
∃ Rule:	
Condition	A contains $(\exists R.C)(x)$, but not y such that $C(y)$ and $R(x, y)$ are in A.
Action	$A \cup \{C(y),\ R(x,\ y)\}$ where y is not in A.
∀ Rule:	
Condition	A contains $(\forall R.C)(x)$ and $R(x, y)$, but not $C(y)$.
Action	$A \cup \{C(y)\}$
≥ Rule:	
Condition	A contains $(\geq n\ R)(x)$, but not $y_1, \ldots, y_n$ such that $R(x,\ y_i)\ (1 \leq i \leq n)$ and $y_i \neq y_j\ (1 \leq i < j \leq n)$ are in A.
Action	$A \cup \{R(x,\ y_i),\ y_i\}\ (1 \leq i \leq n)$, where distinct $y_1, \ldots, y_n$ are not in A.
≤ Rule:	
Condition	A contains $y_1, \ldots, y_{n+1}$ such that $(\leq n\ R)(x)$ and $R(x,\ y_1), \ldots$ $\ldots, R(x,\ y_{n+1})$ are in A, but $y_i \neq y_j$ is not in A for some $i \neq j$.
Action	For each pair $(x_i,\ y_i)$ such that $i > j$ and $y_i \neq y_j$ is not in A: $A_{i,j} = [y_i/y_j]A$ is obtained by replacing every y_i by y_j.

deduce that there must be another individual b such that $(a, b) \in R$, and $b \in A$. These rules are derived directly from the language definition. At the end of the process, if the ABox A does not contain any clashes between individuals, then it is consistent and C_{NNF} is satisfiable. We note that the rules for ⊔ and ≤ are non-deterministic in that the ABox A is transformed into two or more ABoxes. In this case, the resulting ABox is consistent if one of these ABoxes is consistent.

In general, it is almost certainly not a profitable exercise to construct new reasoner for DLs. Just as with Planning and Model-Checking techniques, highly optimized tools have already been constructed for this tasks. For the Semantic Web, the main ontology description language is OWL-DL, and the main language for knowledge base assertions is RDF. Both of these languages are more expressive than the formalisms that we have described here. The main reasoning systems that have been developed for OWL-DL and RDF are RacerPro and Pellet. Both of these reasoning systems are based on efficient tableau algorithms that have been heavily optimized. These systems can be used as a core component in the construction of hybrid agent systems that can reason about Semantic Web knowledge.

5.3 Beyond ontologies

In this book, we have emphasized the advantages of ontologies for knowledge representation and reasoning on the Semantic Web. We have shown that ontologies are a powerful technique for providing structure to information, and for performing inferences over collections of knowledge. In later chapters, we show that ontologies are also crucial in the creation of knowledge based applications with MASs. These agent-based applications are the key to realizing our goals of automated processing of Web-based knowledge. Nonetheless, while ontologies are a good fit to a large number of knowledge-based applications, we acknowledge that ontologies are not the only means by which we may achieve these goals. In some situations, ontologies may be too expressive, and simpler database-driven methods may be adequate. Conversely, certain kinds of applications may require more expressiveness, and additional reasoning power.

There are a number of different techniques that can provide us with additional expressivity and reasoning power over standard ontologies founded on DLs. We outline two such techniques here, namely *rule languages* and *frame systems*. Both of these techniques are based on formalisms that are well-established in AI. However, they have only recently been explored in the context of the Semantic Web, as the limitations of ontologies have reached in some applications. Nonetheless, we claim that these techniques are only required in certain special cases, and the standard ontological approaches should be adequate for the majority of knowledge based activities.

5.3.1 Rule languages

Ontologies, and the description languages on which they are founded, are principally designed to provide structure to knowledge. As we have shown, this structure enables us to construct knowledge bases, and perform reasoning over this knowledge. This is certainly a non-trivial task, and is very useful in a wide range of situations. However, there are definite restrictions to the kind of representation and reasoning that we can perform with description languages.

When we construct an ontology and a knowledge base, the only information that we have about the knowledge is structural information. In essence, all we have is a set of concepts, the relationships between concepts, and the instances of these concepts. Consequently, the only kinds of inferences that we can perform on this knowledge are structural inferences, e.g. subsumption and identity. What the inference process does not take into account is the precise meaning of the information that we represent.

We can best illustrate the limitations of the reasoning processes by considering a simple example. It is possible to define an ontology for representing probabilistic information, and subsequently construct a knowledge base of probability values. However, the inferences that we can automatically perform over this knowledge will still be limited to structural properties. We will not be able to perform probabilistic calculations over the knowledge, as the reasoning processes do not have any specific information about the knowledge that they are representing. In other words, the reasoning is performed in the same way, regardless of the kind of knowledge that is represented.

To take advantage of the specifics of the knowledge that is represented, we must construct our own applications which are aware of the nature of the knowledge, i.e. its semantics. For example, if we want to perform probability calculations, then we must design our own tools for manipulating probabilities, or adopt a specific ontology that is used by existing probabilistic tools. This is perfectly acceptable in most situations, as it would be unreasonable to expect the inference engine to be able to deal automatically with every possible kind of knowledge that may be represented.

Nonetheless, there are situations where it would be desirable to go beyond the basic structural properties that can be represented, and specify additional properties, which would be handled in a standard manner. If these properties were common to lots of different kinds of knowledge, then there would be an advantage in extending the reasoner to perform inferences over these additional properties. The most obvious candidate for specifying these additional properties would be a variant of first-order logic, since this can be applied to many different situations. For example, if our ontology represents properties of computational services, as in Chapter 7, then first-order formulae can help us to infer appropriate combinations of services. This is precisely the approach taken by rule languages, which extend ontologies with first-order rules.

The SWRL has been proposed specifically to extend OWL-Lite and OWL-DL ontologies with first-order rules. In this proposal, OWL ontologies are augmented with rules specified in the unary and binary Datalog sublanguages of the Rule Markup Language, called RuleML-Lite. The addition of these rules can make the OWL reasoning undecidable. However, the rules are restricted to Horn-like forms, which have been shown to allow useful general-purpose inferences in logical programming languages, e.g. Prolog.

We present the abstract syntax of SWRL in Figure 5.6. This abstract representation is easier to understand than the concrete XML representation. The SWRL extends the OWL notation with the definition of logical

$$
\begin{array}{lll}
X \in \text{Axiom} & ::= & \langle \texttt{uri} \rangle \; R \\
R \in \text{Rule} & ::= & A_1 \wedge \cdots \wedge A_m \Rightarrow B_1 \wedge \cdots \wedge B_n \quad m, n \geq 0 \\
A, B \in \text{Atom} & ::= & C(i) \hfill \text{(Description)} \\
& | & C(d) \hfill \text{(Data range)} \\
& | & P(i_1, \; i_2) \hfill \text{(Object property)} \\
& | & P(i, \; d) \hfill \text{(Datatype property)} \\
& | & \text{sameAs}(i_1, \; i_2) \hfill \text{(Equality)} \\
& | & \text{differentFrom}(i_1, \; i_2) \hfill \text{(Inequality)} \\
& | & \text{builtIn}(r, \; d_1, \ldots, d_k) \quad k \geq 0 \hfill \text{(Function)} \\
i \in \text{Individual} & ::= & v_i \; | \; \text{id} \\
d \in \text{Datatype} & ::= & v_d \; | \; \text{"literal"} \\
v \in \text{Variable}
\end{array}
$$

Figure 5.6 *SWRL abstract syntax.*

axioms X, i.e. statements that should be true under interpretation. Each axiom comprises a rule R, and an optional URI reference $\texttt{uri}$ that can be used to identify the rule. All of the rules in SWRL are logical implications of the form: *antecedent* $\Rightarrow$ *consequent*, where both sides are conjunctions of atoms of the form $a_1 \wedge \cdots \wedge a_i (i \geq 0)$. A rule can be interpreted informally as stating that if the antecedent is true then the consequent must also be true. An empty antecedent is treated as (trivially) true, and an empty consequent is treated as false. Both sides of the rule are conjunctions, which means that all of the atoms must hold, i.e. evaluate to true. Disjunctions can be expressed by the definition of multiple rules.

Individuals (i.e. objects) and Datatypes (i.e. values) are treated separately within SWRL. This distinction is inherited from OWL, where the two kinds are also separated. Individuals i are represented by variables that will be bound to individuals, written v_i, or object identifiers id. Datatypes d are represented by datatype variables v_d that will be bound to values, or directly by literal values. The inclusion of variables v is the primary reason why SWRL is more expressive than OWL.

The SWRL rules are composed from atoms, which have the following informal interpretations: $C(i)$ holds if i is an instance of a class description, and $C(d)$ holds if d is a data value. $P(i_1, \; i_2)$ holds if i_1 is related to i_2 by the property P, and $P(i, \; d)$ holds if i is related to d by property P. Therefore, C and P can be viewed as functions that connect SWRL rules to the OWL ontology in which they are defined. The remaining atoms enable the SWRL rules to perform computations. The sameAs($i_1, \; i_2$) function holds if i_1 and i_2 evaluate to the same individual, and differentFrom($i_1, \; i_2$) holds if i_1 and i_2 evaluate to different individuals. Finally, builtIn($r, \; d_1, \ldots, d_k$) holds if the built-in relation r evaluates to true with the arguments $d_1, \ldots, d_k$. The built-in relations r are taken from the XQuery and XPath standards, just as the functions in SPARQL.

```
<ruleml:imp>
  <ruleml:_rlab ruleml:href="#rule1"/>
  <ruleml:_body>
    <swrlx:individualPropertyAtom swrlx:property="hasFocusType">
      <ruleml:var>x</ruleml:var>
      <owlx:Individual owlx:name="#AutoFocus"/>
    </swrlx:individualPropertyAtom>
    <swrlx:individualPropertyAtom swrlx:property="hasMountType">
      <ruleml:var>x</ruleml:var>
      <owlx:Individual owlx:name="#Fixed"/>
    </swrlx:individualPropertyAtom>
    <swrlx:individualPropertyAtom swrlx:property="hasBodyType">
      <ruleml:var>x</ruleml:var>
      <owlx:Individual owlx:name="#Compact"/>
    </swrlx:individualPropertyAtom>
  </ruleml:_body>
  <ruleml:_head>
    <swrlx:individualPropertyAtom swrlx:property="hasCameraType">
      <ruleml:var>x</ruleml:var>
      <owlx:Individual owlx:name="#PointAndShoot"/>
    </swrlx:individualPropertyAtom>
  </ruleml:_head>
</ruleml:imp>
```

Figure 5.7 *SWRL rule example.*

To illustrate the XML syntax for SWRL, we define an example rule in Figure 5.7. Informally, the rule is an assertion that defines a 'point and shoot' camera as one with an autofocus facility, a fixed lens, and a compact body type. This is represented in the abstract syntax as follows:

hasFocus(i, AutoFocus) ∧ hasMount(i, Fixed) ∧ hasBody(i, Compact) ⇒ hasCamera(i, PointAndShoot)

The XML syntax for SWRL is very straightforward. A rule is defined as a `ruleml:imp` element, which indicates that each rule is a logical implication. A URI reference is specified by the `ruleml:_rlab` (label) element. The antecedent of the rule is defined by a `ruleml:_body` element, and the consequent is defined by a `ruleml:_head` element. Both the antecedent and consequent are lists of SWRL atoms, where the type of atoms is identified by using one of the following elements:

> `classAtom, datarangeAtom, individualPropertyAtom,`
> `datavaluedPropertyAtom, sameIndividualAtom,`
> `differentIndividualsAtom,` and `builtinAtom.`

In our example, all of the atoms are object properties, represented by `individualPropertyAtom` elements. The components of each atom are listed in sequence. Variables are defined by `ruleml:var` elements, and instances are specified by reference to their OWL definitions using `owlx:Individual` and `owlx:DataValue` elements.

It should be clear that SWRL extends the expressivity of OWL through the inclusion of variables, the definition of rules, and the ability to conduct basic kinds of computation. These facilities enable us to perform more advanced reasoning over our ontological knowledge, provided that suitable reasoning processes are available. Using SWRL rules, the knowledge representation task becomes similar to logic programming, and many properties become easier to define by using variables. Nonetheless, the use of SWRL rules means that we are combining DLs with a restricted form of Horn logics. There is currently no theoretical basis for this combination, and this means that our inferences may be unsound. A more natural representation for both knowledge and rules is provided by frame systems that we describe in the following section.

5.3.2 Frame systems

Frame systems are an alternative to semantic networks as a way to characterize the structures of knowledge. The core notions in frame systems are very straightforward. A frame system is constructed from a hierarchy of objects, called *frames*, where each frame represents a single concept. The hierarchy is structured such that more specific concepts appear below more general concepts in the hierarchy. Each frame can be given named attributes, called *slots*. These slots may contain values, which are related to the concept, e.g. specific instances of the concept, or functions that operate on the concept. There is also the notion of *inheritance* in a frame system. Slot values are inherited by the frames that represent specific concepts, from the frames that represent more general concepts. Therefore, *default* slot values can be specified and will propagate down the hierarchy. In essence, a frame system can be viewed as a class hierarchy with multiple inheritance in the object-oriented paradigm.

The structure of a frame system is clearly similar to a semantic network. The frames are structured in a subclass hierarchy, just as the concepts are structured in a semantic network. The key difference is the presence of the slots in the system. Slots can be used to define additional relationships between frames. For example, the **hasLens**(1, M) relationship in Figure 5.1 can be represented by a set-valued slot called **hasLens** in a frame called **Camera**. This means that frame systems can be used to represent all of the information that is present in a semantic network. Furthermore, slot values can be inherited between frames, and slots may contain variables, which makes frame systems more expressive than semantic networks.

Frame systems have been formalized using Frame Logics (F-Logics), just as semantic networks have been formalized with DLs. Frame Logics, usually called F-Logics, are also a first-order formalism for knowledge representation. However, the representation of knowledge in F-Logics is much closer to logic-programming than the specification-based approach of DLs. Similarly, reasoning in F-Logics is similar to program execution, while reasoning in DLs is essentially logical deduction. In general, F-Logics are more expressive than DLs, while permitting the same kinds of knowledge representation, and the same inferences to be performed. However, while reasoning in F-Logics is decidable, the additional expressive power comes with the standard trade-off of efficiency. In general, reasoning with DLs will be more efficient than with F-Logics, and this explains the continuing popularity of ontology-based methods.

To illustrate the application of F-Logics in more detail, we now outline a language that contains the main concepts from frame systems. This language, called frame language (F-Language) permits the representation of knowledge, and provides a framework for performing computation over this knowledge. The abstract syntax of this F-Language is defined in Figure 5.8.

There are just two kinds of core terms in F-Language: constants O, and variables V. Constants are the basic objects in F-Language and are used to represent concepts, individuals, literals, method names, constructor names, etc. We write U to represent the domain containing all of the

$T \in$ Term	::=	O	(Constant)
	|	V	(Variable)
$C, D, E \in$ IdTerm	::=	$O(T_1, \ldots, T_k)$ $k \geq 0$	(Compound)
$M \in$ Molecule	::=	$C : D$	(Membership)
	|	$C :: D$	(Subclass)
	|	$C[ME_1, \ldots, ME_l]$ $l \geq 0$	(Class)
$ME \in$ Method	::=	$NE \mid IE \mid SE$	(Expression)
$NE \in$ Non-inheritable	::=	$C@D_1, \ldots, D_m \to E$ $m \geq 0$	
	|	$C@D_1, \ldots, D_n \twoheadrightarrow \{E_1, \ldots, E_p\}$ $n, p \geq 0$	
$IE \in$ Inheritable	::=	$C@D_1, \ldots, D_q \bullet\!\!\to E$ $q \geq 0$	
	|	$C@D_1, \ldots, D_r \bullet\!\!\twoheadrightarrow \{E_1, \ldots, E_s\}$ $r, s \geq 0$	
$SE \in$ Signature	::=	$C@D_1, \ldots, D_t \Rightarrow (E_1, \ldots, E_v)$ $t, v \geq 0$	
	|	$C@D_1, \ldots, D_w \Rrightarrow (E_1, \ldots, E_x)$ $w, x \geq 0$	
$F, G \in$ Formulae	::=	$M \mid \neg M$	(Literals)
	|	$F \wedge G \mid F \vee G \mid F \leftarrow G \mid \forall V.F \mid \exists V.F$	

Figure 5.8 *F-language abstract syntax.*

basic objects C. Complex objects can be built from these basic terms using IdTerms, e.g. camera(model, price). The initial constant O in the IdTerm acts as the identifier for the object. The variables V can be bound to Terms and IdTerms. The presence of variables is a key distinction between F-Language and description languages. In our examples, we follow the usual F-language conventions and write variables with an initial upper-case letter, and constants with an initial lower-case letter or quotations marks for literals.

Concepts and individuals are not distinguished in F-Language. Hence, objects can be treated as both, depending on their behaviour and relationship to other objects. Relationships between complex objects are created by the definition of molecules M. There are two fundamental relationships: a binary relationship $\in_U$ that defines membership between objects, and a subset relationship $\preceq_U$ that defines a partial ordering between objects. The membership relationship, written $C : D$, states that C is a member of D. For example, pentaxKM : camera means that pentaxKM is a member of camera. The subset relationship, written $C :: D$, states that C is a subclass of D. For example, digitalCamera :: camera.

Methods can be associated with complex objects to turn them into class definitions. Methods are used to define the behaviour of objects, and to provide additional information about objects. The methods are classed into three categories: inheritable, non-inheritable, and signatures. Inheritable methods are propagated down the subclass hierarchy, while non-inheritable objects are specific to a single object. Signatures are always inheritable, and contain assertions about the types that will be returned by the corresponding method. Any method that inherits the signature must have a return type which is a member or subclass of the type specified in the signature. If more than one type is specified, then the output of the corresponding method must be a member or subclass of all of these types. The name of a method is given by an IdTerm C. Methods can also take optional arguments $D_1, \ldots, D_i$. The three kinds of method are all defined with two syntactic forms: single valued (scalar), and set valued. Scalar methods are used when a single output value is required, and set-valued methods for multiple output values. An example that illustrates the different kinds of methods is shown below:

```
    camera [ manufactured ⇒ (year),
             lensMount ⇒ (mount),
             similarTo ⇒» (camera) ]
  pentaxKM [ manufactured → "1977",
             lensmount •→ pentaxKmount,
             similarTo •→» {pentaxK1000, pentaxKX, pentaxK2} ]
```

Our example defines two classes, each containing three methods. The camera class comprises three signature methods. The **manufactured** and **lensMount** methods specify that a single return value is required with the types **year**, and **mount** respectively. We do not define these types further in our example. The **similarTo** signature method specifies a set of values of type **camera** as the return type. The **pentaxKM** class is a subclass of the **camera** class, and inherits the signatures defined in this class. The **manufactured** method returns the year "1977", which is a value corresponding to the **year** type in the signature. This method is defined as non-inheritable as it applies only to a specific instance. The **lensmount** and **similarTo** methods are inheritable as these values will be shared by any subclasses. The **similarTo** method returns a set of values of type **camera**.

It should now be clear that the IdTerms in F-Language are equivalent to the frames that we describe earlier, and the methods are equivalent to the slots. The hierarchy of frames, and the population of the slots is accomplished by the definition of molecules. The final part of the F-Language is the definition of formulae F, G over these molecules. It is these formulae that enable computation to be performed within the F-Language itself. F-Language formulae are essentially first-order expressions, with the usual operators: negation $\neg$, conjunction $\wedge$, disjunction $\vee$, implication $\leftarrow$, and quantification $\forall, \exists$. Two F-Language formulae are illustrated below. The first is a query that returns all cameras A, which were manufactured in 1977. The second is a deduction rule which states that the set of cameras C, which are similar to camera B, are all those with the same **lensMount**.

$$?- \; A : \text{camera} \wedge A[\text{manufactured} \rightarrow \text{``1977''}].$$
$$B[\text{similarTo} \twoheadrightarrow C] \leftarrow B[\text{lensMount} \rightarrow X] \wedge \forall C.C[\text{lensMount} \rightarrow X].$$

We previously stated that F-Logics are more expressive than DLs. Furthermore, F-Logics can represent the same kinds of knowledge as DLs. This means that we can perform a lossless translation of knowledge from description language to F-Language. The actual translation process is beyond the scope of this book. However, we indicate how the main syntactic categories of description languages are translated into F-Language in Table 5.5.

The logic-programming style of definition in F-Language has led to a recent surge in interest over the possibility of using F-Logics as a foundation for the construction of Semantic Web applications. As we have shown, the use of F-Logics would permit the representation of knowledge, and the representation of computation over this knowledge in the same formalism. F-Logics would also allow a body of knowledge to be augmented with additional rule-based semantics, without the need for a separate rule language. However, there are a number of issues that must be resolved before these benefits can be realized, in particular, the construction of efficient

Table 5.5 *Correspondence between DL and F-language.*

DL	F-Language
Concepts	Objects
Roles	Methods
Subsumption	Subclass
Identity	Membership
Constructors	Formulae

reasoning systems for F-Logics. Nonetheless, F-Logics are at the core of the WSMO project, which is attempting to solve these issues. We discuss WSMO in more detail in Chapter 7.

5.4 Summary

In Chapters 3 and 4 we presented a number of techniques for general-purpose reasoning in agent systems. We showed how agents could be constructed to perform reasoning in a similar way to humans, and thereby accomplish specific goals. In this chapter, we narrowed our focus, and considered the particular challenges of reasoning about knowledge on the Semantic Web. In this setting, we have a specific representation of knowledge, and precise goals that we would like to accomplish: we would like to answer questions about knowledge, which is classified according to certain ontologies. We described two key approaches to reasoning about Semantic Web knowledge. A summary of the main features and advantages of these approaches is given below:

1. The first approach is the definition of *query languages*. This approach has its roots in database systems, where SQL queries are used to extract information from relational database tables. However, there are significant conceptual differences when performing queries over Semantic Web knowledge. For example, Semantic Web knowledge is network structured, and dynamic in nature. Query languages are designed to answer questions primarily through a process of pattern-matching. Queries are essentially templates that are matched against a knowledge source. Any knowledge that matches the template will be returned by the query. We can answer relatively complex questions by combining queries together, and using multiple knowledge sources. Nonetheless, there are fundamental limitations in this approach. Specifically, query languages do not take into account the ontologies against which the knowledge is structured. To illustrate the construction of Semantic

Web queries, we outlined the SPARQL standard for performing queries on RDF knowledge bases.

2. The second approach that we presented was the use of *logic-based languages* to perform more advanced kinds of reasoning that is possible with query languages. This approach uses the connection between the ontology and knowledge to perform structural inferences, which are not directly apparent from the knowledge itself. The particular family of logic-based languages that we consider are those based on DLs. These are first-order logics tailored specifically to the description of concepts, and relationships between concepts. Description Logics provide the formal basis for description languages, which in-turn supply the foundations of ontology language such as OWL. We defined the $\mathcal{ALCN}$ description language, which is notionally similar to the $\mathcal{SHOIN(D)}$ description language upon which OWL-DL is based. We showed how $\mathcal{ALCN}$ could be used to define a functional view of knowledge representation, and to perform inferences over this representation. In particular, the key inferences that we identified are instance checking, which determines if an individual is a member of a concept, and subsumption that determines if one concept is more general than another. Finally, we outlined how these inferences could be expressed in terms of satisfiability, and outlined a tableau-based algorithm for efficient satisfiability checking in $\mathcal{ALCN}$.

In the final part of the chapter we noted that there are certain limitations if we adopt a purely ontological approach to knowledge representation and reasoning. These limitations relate to the fact that ontology-based inferences can only operate over the structure of the knowledge, but not on the actual knowledge itself. If we want to reason about the knowledge content, then we must use external representations and techniques. This limitation can be addressed through techniques that extend the expressivity and reasoning power of the ontologies. We identified two such techniques, which are summarized below:

1. The expressivity of ontologies can be enhanced by associating *rules* with the concepts and relationships in the ontology. Rules can express additional properties, such as functional properties that may include variables. In addition, more advanced kinds of reasoning can be performed over these rules. The rules must adhere a standard *rule language*, such as the SWRL which we describe. The SWRL enables first-order Horn-like rules to be defined for OWL ontologies, and permits limited kinds of computation to be expressed. Thus, the use of SWRL is akin to a form of logic-programming for ontologies.

2. Frame Logics provide an alternative to DLs as a formal basis for knowledge representation. F-Logics provide a unified framework that can express concept hierarchies, relationships, instances, and rules within the same model. This framework is derived from frame systems, and is closely connected to the object-oriented paradigm. In this approach knowledge representation is similar to programming, and inference is similar to program execution. We presented the syntax of an F-Language and showed how knowledge representation and inference can be expressed in this language.

5.5 Exercises

1. Consider the knowledge base in Table 5.6. What would the following SPARQL queries return for this knowledge base:
    *   `SELECT ?x WHERE { ?x directedBy Kubrick }`
    *   `SELECT ?x WHERE { ?x writtenBy Clarke .`
        `OPTIONAL ?x directedBy Kubrick }}`

Table 5.6 *Film knowledge base.*

Subject	Predicate	Object
2001	directedBy	Kubrick
2001	writtenBy	Clarke
2001	releaseYear	1968
2010	writtenBy	Clarke
2010	directedBy	Hyams
2010	releaseYear	1984
StarWars	releaseYear	1977
StarWars	directedBy	Lucas
StarWars	writtenBy	Lucas
Trainspotting	directedBy	Boyle
Trainspotting	writtenBy	Welsh
DrStrangelove	directedBy	Kubrick
DrStrangelove	releaseYear	1964
BladeRunner	directedBy	Scott
BladeRunner	writtenBy	Dick
BladeRunner	releaseYear	1982
MinorityReport	directedBy	Spielberg
MinorityReport	writtenBy	Dick
MinorityReport	releaseYear	2002
ClockworkOrange	releaseYear	1971
ClockworkOrange	directedBy	Kubrick
ClockworkOrange	writtenBy	Burgess

- SELECT ?x ?y WHERE { ?x directedBy ?y .
  ?x writtenBy ?y }
- SELECT ?x ?y WHERE { ?x releaseYear ?y .
  FILTER (?y > 1972)} LIMIT 2

2. Construct SPARQL queries to answer the following, for the knowledge base in Table 5.6:
   - All the directors in the knowledge base, without duplicate entries.
   - All the films in the knowledge base, sorted according to the year of release.
   - The writers for the films directed by Kubrick.
   - A list of writers and films, where each writer is responsible for more than one film.

3. Implement the knowledge base from Table 5.6 using the Jena RDF store. The Jena system and documentation can be obtained from:

   http://jena.sourceforge.net/

4. Use the Jena ARQ (SPARQL) module to validate your queries from Q2.

5. Use $\mathcal{ALCN}$ notation to represent the complete camera ontology from Chapter 1 (Figure 1.1).

6. Use the $\mathcal{ALCN}$ tableau algorithm to determine consistency of the following formula:

$$C = (\exists R.(A \sqcup B) \sqcap \forall R.(\neg A \sqcap \neg B)) \sqcup (\exists R.B \sqcap \forall R.\forall R.\neg B)$$

5.6 Suggested reading

1. F. Baader, D. Calvanese, D. McGuinness, D. Nardi, and P. Patel-Schneider, editors. *The Description Logic Handbook: Theory, Implementation and Applications.* Cambridge University Press, 2003.
2. R. Brachman and H. Levesque. *Knowledge Representation and Reasoning.* Morgan Kaufmann, 2004.
3. R. Fikes, P. Hayes, and I. Horrocks. OWL-QL—A Language for Deductive Query Answering on the Semantic Web. Technical Report 03-14, Knowledge Systems Laboratory, Stanford University, 2003.
4. R. Fikes and D. McGuinness. An Axiomatic Semantics for RDF, RDF-S, and DAML+OIL. Available at: http://www.w3.org/TR/daml+oil-axioms, 2001.
5. P. Hayes and B. McBride. RDF Semantics. Available at: http://www.w3.org/TR/rdf-mt/, 2004.
6. I. Horrocks, P. Patel-Schneider, H. Boley, S. Tabet, B. Grosof, and M. Dean. SWRL: A Semantic Web Rule Language Combining OWL and RuleML. Available at: http://www.w3.org/Submission/SWRL/.

7. I. Horrocks, P. Patel-Schneider, and F. van Harmelen. From $\mathcal{SHIQ}$ and RDF to OWL: The making of A Web Ontology Language. *Journal of Web Semantics*, 1(1): 7–26, 2003.

8. I. Horrocks and U. Sattler. A Tableaux Decision Procedure for $\mathcal{SHOIQ}$. In *Proceedings of the 19th International Joint Conference on Artificial Intelligence (IJCAI'05)*, pp. 448–53, Edinburgh, UK, August 2005.

9. M. Kifer, G. Lausen, and J. Wu. Logical-Foundations of Object-Oriented and Frame-Based Languages. *Journal of the Association for Computing Machinery*, 42(4): 741–843, July 1995.

10. M. Minsky. A framework for Representing Knowledge. In P. Winston, editor, *The Psychology of Computer Vision*, pp. 211–77, New York, USA, McGraw-Hill 1975.

11. E. Prud'hommeaux and A. Seaborne. SPARQL Query Language for RDF. Available at: http://www.w3.org/TR/rdf-sparql-query/, 2006.

6 Agent communication

In the preceding chapters, we have described in detail the various techniques that can be used to construct reasoning agents for the Semantic Web. However, as we have repeatedly emphasized, this reasoning capability provides only part of the functionality that will be instrumental in the construction of Semantic Web applications. To supply the remaining functionality, we must also provide a communicative capability to the agents that we construct. This capability will allow our agents to interact and cooperate with other agents on the Semantic Web, and thereby realize more complex tasks than could be accomplished with a single agent in isolation.

The focus of this chapter is on how we can design and build agents which can interact together successfully on the Semantic Web. To address the issues of communication and coordination in this environment, it is useful to take our inspiration from human *social systems*, where these issues are solved in the real world. Following this approach, we treat a group of agents as a *society*, where these agents typically share a common interest, e.g. solving a specific type of problem. To become a member of this society, an agent must agree to observe certain rules and conventions. In return, the agent can itself benefit from the society, e.g. the expertise of other agents. In this societal view, it becomes possible to define conventions for the agents to follow, and the incentives for agents to operate together are made clear. This in turn makes the challenges of agent-based communication and coordination more manageable.

The societal view is a popular approach in the field of MASs, and has important consequences for the way we define our systems. Our discussion is structured around the following five considerations, which must be addressed if we are to design agents that can successfully participate in a society:

1. The ability to communicate with other agents.
2. A basis on which to understand what is being communicated.
3. The ability to structure communication into coherent patterns.

4. The means to act collectively on what is being communicated.
5. A measure of confidence in the outcome of the communication.

6.1 Knowledge and communication

Communication in an MAS is necessary because agents are independent and autonomous entities. By this, we mean that an agent has the freedom to make decisions, and these decisions are not directly controlled by external factors, i.e. the agent should be sufficiently independent to make its own decisions. If the agents were not autonomous, then all of the decisions could be centrally managed, and there would be no need for inter-agent communication.

In order to maintain autonomy and independence, an agent is typically designed with decision-making machinery and knowledge that is local and private to the agent. The local knowledge of the agent will contain such things as the beliefs, desires, and intentions of the agent. This knowledge allows the agent to reason in a way that is independent of the behaviour of any other agent in the system. Nonetheless, an agent will often be unable to complete certain tasks due to insufficient local knowledge or ability. To overcome this limitation, the agent must communicate with other agents in order to convey its requests, and to increase its knowledge. As a result, an autonomous agent must be equipped with a communicative ability in order to interact in a multiagent environment.

To illustrate the importance of local knowledge, we consider a pair of agents who wish to negotiate on the price of an item. In this setting, each agent is seeking to maximize the outcome of the negotiation from their own perspective. However, if the decision-making processes and local knowledge of each agent were freely available, then the negotiation process could be readily subverted. Hence, in this situation, each agent will keep its knowledge private, and only release parts of this knowledge as necessary during the negotiation process.

An example that illustrates the difference between private and public knowledge is shown in Figure 6.1. In this hypothetical scenario, two agents are negotiating over the purchase of a camera. The buyer agent has a maximum value, and an ideal value that they would like to spend. These values are stored in the private knowledge of the agent. Similarly, the seller agent has private knowledge on the minimum and ideal values for the item. The negotiation is a sequence of message exchanges, which comprise an initial offer and a subsequent counteroffer. The knowledge that is exchanged is public, and is used to inform the reasoning process of the agents. At the end of the negotiation, the agents reach a mutually

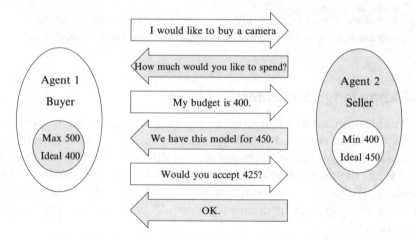

Figure 6.1 *Example negotiation.*

agreeable price for the camera. This negotiation would clearly fail if all of the agents knowledge were made readily available.

6.2 Communication techniques

In providing communicative abilities to agents, we are effectively seeking to mimic the process of (verbal) communication between humans. This is a complex task and so we start from the basic principles, and work towards this goal as the chapter proceeds. We begin by discussing the fundamental mechanisms by which information can be exchanged between two independent agents. At the lowest level, there are two main techniques that are used to facilitate communication:

1. Message passing—the agents communicate by the direct exchange of messages that encapsulate knowledge.
2. Shared state—the agents communicate by asserting and retracting facts in a shared knowledge base.

A message passing approach was assumed in our previous negotiation example. With message passing, one agent sends a message directly to another, without any intermediary becoming involved. This point-to-point method of communication is common on the Web, for example, sending an HTTP request to a Web server. Nonetheless, there is an alternative approach that is popular in MASs. This alternative relies on a shared state, which is accessed simultaneously by a number of agents. The shared state approach is often called a *blackboard architecture*, as it is analogous to the reading and writing of messages on a public blackboard. In this approach, the shared state is managed by an intermediary, and all communication is performed through this entity. The agents never communicate directly. Asserting a fact in the shared stated is analogous to sending a message, and retracting a fact is similar to receiving a message.

6.2.1   The Linda architecture

One of the most popular systems for shared state programming is Linda. This system implements a blackboard architecture by using a shared *tuple space*. Tuples, which are collections of fields of any type, are asserted and retracted from the tuple space. There are just four main operations in Linda that control the tuple space:

1. rd(t) attempts to read the tuple t from the tuple space. This is done non-destructively, so the tuple remains in the tuple space after the operation. If a matching tuple is not found, then the operation will fail. If more than one tuple matches, then a non-deterministic choice is made between the matches.
2. in(t) is a destructive version of rd, such that the matching tuple is removed from the tuple space.
3. out(t) writes the tuple t to the tuple space.
4. eval(expr) writes a tuple to the tuple space after the arguments in the expression have been evaluated.

Table 6.1 illustrates how we can perform agent communication in Linda. The example is based on the negotiation scenario that we outlined previously in Figure 6.1. The example uses variables for pattern-matching, which are preceded by a ? symbol. The functions used in the eval operations are defined simply for illustrative purposes. For example, checkprice(?newprice) is used to evaluate a proposal from the buyer.

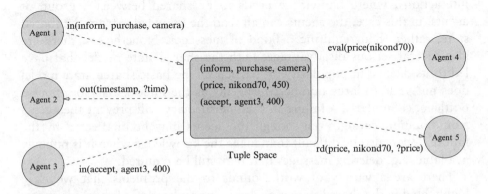

Figure 6.2 *Linda agent communication.*

Table 6.1 *Communication example in Linda.*

Buyer

```
out("inform", "purchase", "camera")
in("request", "camera", "budget")
eval("inform", "camerabudget", mybudget())
in("propose", ?camera, ?value)
eval("propose", ?camera, newvalue(?value))
in("accept", ?camera, ?newvalue)
```

Seller

```
in("inform", "purchase", "camera")
out("request", "camera", "budget")
in("inform", "camerabudget", ?budget)
eval("propose", mycamera(?budget), myprice(?budget))
in("propose", ?camera, ?newprice)
eval("accept", ?camera, checkprice(?newprice))
```

Figure 6.2 illustrates intuitively how inter-agent communication is performed in Linda.

We note that Linda is not itself a programming language, rather the operations of Linda are intended to be added to existing languages. As a result, the capabilities of the `eval` operation are dependent on the target language. The tuple space is provided by a Linda server, which is also independent of the language used to implement the Linda operations. A program containing Linda operations will normally connect to a specific Linda server during initialization. This server would then be used to perform all of the Linda operations.

The shared state approach has certain advantages over message passing. It is generally more straightforward to design agent systems using this approach, as the issues of message loss and communication delays can be easily handled. The shared state is also more convenient in multiparty interactions, where knowledge needs to be shared between a group of agents. In this case, the agents can all read the knowledge from the shared state, rather than requiring a flood of messages. Nonetheless, there are also several serious disadvantages with the shared state model that have led to its decline in popularity. In particular, the basic shared state model does not scale to large numbers of agents as the intermediary becomes a bottleneck. Similarly, a failure in the intermediary will prevent the agents from communicating, even though the agents may be unaffected by the failure. It can also be difficult to manage the knowledge when it is publicly available, e.g. deleting messages that may still be required.

There are a variety of workarounds to the problems that we have highlighted in the shared state model, e.g. the replication of the tuple space. However, for our purposes we concentrate purely on the message passing approach. The key reasons being that message passing is closer to verbal communication between humans, and is a good fit with the large-scale and decentralized organization of the Web. Thus, our agents will communicate entirely by the exchange of messages, and these messages will encapsulate any knowledge that they wish to share.

6.2.2 Message passing in SOAP

To illustrate the message-passing approach to inter-agent communication, we now examine the SOAP standard. SOAP is a key technology for performing communication between nodes on the Web. These nodes may be any kind of distributed computational entity, e.g. services, peers, and agents. SOAP is an XML-based mechanism for exchanging structured and typed information between nodes. The fundamental model of communication in SOAP is one-way stateless message exchange. That is, SOAP provides a means to transmit a single message from one place to another, and no memory (state) of this transmission is retained. It is also possible to build more complex models of communication from these single exchanges, e.g. request/response, dialogues, and broadcasts.

SOAP is essentially a framework in which application-specific data can be transmitted from one place to another. SOAP does not impose any restrictions or interpretation on the contents of the messages, and is independent of the mechanisms used to transport the message from one place to another. A useful analogy that is used in the definition of the standard is that SOAP acts as an *envelope*. This envelope provides a container in which data can be stored, and a standard method of addressing to get the data to its destination. However, the envelope is independent of the content, and does not actually transport this content on its own.

The main concepts in SOAP are illustrated in Figure 6.3. A standard SOAP message is illustrated on the left of this figure. Beginning from the centre of this diagram, a SOAP message is divided into a Header and a Body, both of which can contain arbitrary XML fields. This distinction anticipates that the message will be transmitted along a path from an initial Sender, through a number of intermediaries, to an ultimate receiver. The Header is intended to be interpreted by the intermediaries, while the Body is only intended for the final recipient. Thus, the Header can be viewed as the address details for the message, while the Body contains the content. In some situations, a Header will not be required, and so this part of the message is optional, while the Body is mandatory. The Header and Body are encapsulated by an Envelope that does not contain any message-specific data.

A standard SOAP envelope requires that the message is encoded as XML data. However, this encoding is not always appropriate. For example, it may be necessary to transmit data in a native file format, or the data

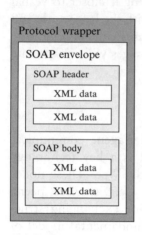

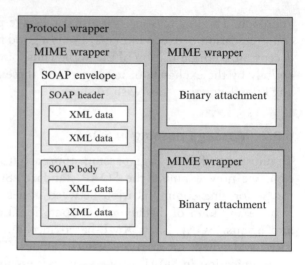

SOAP message   SOAP message with attachments

Figure 6.3 *SOAP message construction.*

may only have a binary representation, e.g. a movie file. Thus, there is an extension to the basic SOAP standard that permits binary files to be attached to standard SOAP messages. This extension is shown on the right of Figure 6.3. The mechanism for binary attachments is identical to that used for attaching binary files to e-mail messages. The SOAP message and binary attachments are all encoded and sent using Multipurpose Internet Mail Extensions (MIME).

We have stated that the SOAP standard does not make any assumptions about the content of the message. While this is generally true, there are a number of exceptions that we will briefly mention here. The SOAP standard recognizes that certain kinds of messages are very common in practice, and so a standardized form for these messages is defined. Two kinds of message for which this is done are error messages, and messages that implement remote procedure calls (RPC). For error messages, this comprises a standard method of expressing the fault, and for RPC, a standard method for the passing of parameters and return values is defined.

In Figure 6.3, the two kinds of SOAP messages are both encapsulated by a protocol-specific wrapper. This wrapper may contain additional information that is required by the underlying protocols during the transportation of the message between sender and receiver. There are many different ways that SOAP messages can be transmitted, e.g. as e-mail messages, as responses from Web servers, and as messages between Web Services. The specification of how SOAP messages are passed from one intermediary to another using an underlying protocol is called a SOAP *binding*. The SOAP

```xml
<?xml version="1.1"?>
<env:Envelope xmlns:env="http://www.w3.org/2003/05/soap-envelope">
  <env:Header>
    <r:request xmlns:r="http://www.mycamera.org/request"
         env:role="http://www.w3.org/2003/05/soap-envelope/role/next"
         env:mustUnderstand="true">
      <r:reference>session_1337</r:reference>
      <r:timestamp>19072006106600</r:timestamp>
    </r:request>
  </env:Header>
  <env:Body>
    <p:pricequery xmlns:p="http://www.mycamera.org/pricequery">
      <camera:manufacturer>Nikon</camera:manufacturer>
      <camera:model>D70</camera:model>
      <camera:type>Digital SLR</camera:type>
    </p:pricequery>
  </env:Body>
</env:Envelope>
```

Figure 6.4 *Example SOAP message.*

bindings currently exist for SMTP, HTTP GET/POST, and WSDL protocols among others.

To illustrate how SOAP can be used for inter-agent communication, we present a brief example in Figure 6.4. It is worth noting that SOAP messages would not generally be constructed by hand in this way. Instead, they would typically be generated automatically by an execution platform. That is, when constructing an agent system, one would normally build the system using high-level primitives and these would be translated into SOAP messages in the underlying architecture. For this reason, we restrict our attention to a single example that illustrates the main messaging features.

Our example SOAP message is intended to convey a query message from one agent to another on the price of a camera. The namespace of the message is env, which is an abbreviation for the following URI:

$$\text{http://www.w3.org/2003/05/soap-envelope.}$$

The env URI references an XML Schema document, which describes all of the elements and types that may comprise a SOAP message. We are not concerned about attachments or bindings here, so the outermost element of the message is a SOAP envelope env:Envelope. Within the envelope we have a SOAP header and SOAP body denoted env:Header and env:Body respectively. As previously noted, both may contain arbitrary XML fields, and their interpretation is left to the applications that interpret the message.

In our example, we follow the normal header conventions, i.e. this part contains information that will assist in processing the message, but does not contain the actual message itself. The header consists of a r:request element, which has an env:role attribute. The role is set to next, which means that every node along the message path should interpret the header. We have also set env:mustUnderstand="true", which means that every intermediate node must also understand the header content before forwarding the message, or it should return an error message. There are two further roles in SOAP: none, which means that the header does not need to be interpreted along the message path and ultimateReceiver, which means that only the last node should interpret the header. In no role is specified for a header field, then the none role is assumed. For the body, the role is always ultimateReceiver. For illustrative purposes, our SOAP header contains a session reference and a timestamp.

The SOAP body contains the actual message that we want to convey to the ultimate recipient. In our example, the body contains a pricequery that specifies a request for a price on a particular camera make and model. The SOAP body must be formatted to one or more fields of XML data. Often this will require conversion from a native data structure into an appropriate XML form; this process is called *serialization*. The recipient will subsequently convert the XML data back into a data structure using a deserialization process. As previously noted, it is possible to attach binary data to SOAP messages, which may be appropriate for certain data types.

We note that SOAP is a one-way protocol, and the sending and receiving of messages are independent. Thus, there is no mechanism in SOAP for ensuring message delivery, and no guarantee that the recipient of our query will reply. If the recipient decides to reply, then they will do so using another SOAP message, which is defined in exactly the same way. There is no distinction in the style of SOAP message between sending and replying. However, this distinction could readily be conveyed inside the message itself if required.

It should be clear that SOAP is an independent language standard, as is Linda. Any programming language that can construct and deconstruct SOAP messages, and pass them across a network, can be used to perform communication. However, with SOAP there is no need for any message storage capability like the Linda server. Instead, messages are passed directly to one or more recipients, and it is the task of these recipients to store or discard these messages. The key advantage of this approach is that it is scalable, as there is no central entity to cause bottlenecks, or act as a point of failure. The SOAP approach can therefore be considered to be a P2P method of communication.

6.2.3 Peer-to-peer architecture

Peer-to-peer communication is an increasingly important technique for the exchange of information over the Web. There are hard limits to the number of clients that can be served effectively from a single server, or cluster of servers. These limits are primarily a function of the available network bandwidth: once the network becomes saturated, the ability to exchange information in a timely manner is lost. The saturation point is reached more quickly as the size of the information grows, e.g. when exchanging large multimedia files.

The network saturation problem can be avoided by adopting a decentralized P2P approach for information exchange. In this approach, information is copied and distributed throughout the network. Thus, when a client wishes to obtain some information it can retrieve it from multiple sources, and thereby avoid overloading any one node. There are a variety of strategies for distributing the information across the network. For example, in a BitTorrent network, any node that makes a copy of a file becomes a server for that file. There are also many strategies for routing queries across a P2P network to find the required information, e.g. distributed hash tables. However, regardless of the specific techniques used, there are several key benefits of adopting a P2P style of communication, for example:

- Large files can be effectively served to multiple clients in a scalable manner.
- The network is robust in the presence of node failures and unreliable nodes.
- A degree of anonymity can be provided as the information provider and consumer may be concealed.

A software system that is built using P2P techniques is said to adopt a P2P architecture. The difference between client/server and P2P architectures is illustrated in Figure 6.5. Multiagent systems that communicate by message passing and have no central control are generally considered to be P2P architectures. Nonetheless, in some systems it is likely that certain agents will become popular, just as certain sites on the Web become popular. Thus, to ensure that the system continues to function, it may necessary to adopt P2P techniques directly in the design and construction of our agent systems.

There are a number of different ways in which P2P techniques can be utilized in the design of MASs. The appropriate approach depends largely on the purpose of the MAS. For example, an MAS whose primary purpose is the manipulation of large video files will likely obtain a significant benefit from adopting an existing P2P file sharing system as the underlying

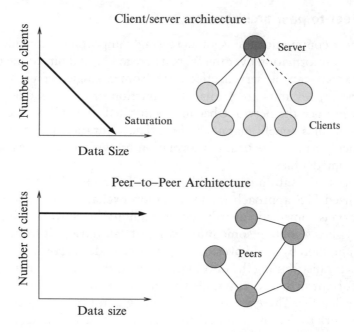

Figure 6.5 *Communication architectures.*

communication platform. Similarly, the content of an existing P2P system may provide a useful information resource for use in an MAS. Finally, a system with a large number of knowledge sharing agents would likely benefit from using a P2P system to make this knowledge available.

The construction of an MAS using a P2P architecture has important design implications for both the communicative and reasoning processes of each agent. The communicative processes must be adapted to work with specific P2P technologies. For example, the agent must be able to construct and interpret messages that are of the correct form for the network. At the reasoning layer, the agent must make decisions on what information to share, and how to retrieve the information that is required for reasoning. In Chapter 4 we presented an example P2P file sharing network, and showed how planning techniques could be used to control the file exchange process between agents.

With the Semantic Web, it is likely that we will design MASs that are responsible for the management of knowledge. This has additional implications when operating in a P2P architecture. The knowledge must be readily available and capable of being widely disseminated. Often this knowledge may be dynamically generated by an agent in response to certain requests, or the knowledge may be local to a particular agent. Therefore, to ensure the smooth running of such systems, we must rely on decidable and practical reasoning techniques that can be straightforwardly utilized. In other words, agent systems that rely on undecidable reasoning, or lengthy theorem-proving operations are unsuitable for use in P2P systems.

6.3   Agent ontologies

The ability for agents to exchange messages does not mean that they will be able to successfully communicate. For this to happen, it is necessary for the agent to interpret and understand the content of the messages that are exchanged. This situation has a direct analogy in human communication. If I attempt to communicate in a language that is unfamiliar to you, then you will be unable to interpret the message, even though you may have heard the message perfectly.

To successfully interpret the content of a message, there must be some form of shared understanding. This does not mean that our agents have a completely shared view of the world, only that there should be some common ground. To understand this, it is helpful to again consider the analogy of human communication. It may be that I wish to communicate some information to you, but you do not understand the terminology that I use. To overcome this problem, I will explain this terminology using concepts that we both understand. For example, I may wish to talk to you about an SLR camera. If I explain that this means a camera where the viewfinder looks directly through the camera lens, then we should be able to proceed with our communication.

A shared understanding between agents means that they have an agreement on the form of the messages that can be exchanged, and a basic vocabulary of concepts with which to interpret the content of the message. It should come as no surprise that this shared conceptualization is usually represented as an ontology. This kind of ontology is called a *common ontology* as it is shared between the participants. A common ontology contains a set of concepts with agreed meanings and is an important requirement for successful communication.

Common ontologies for agent communication are constructed according to the techniques that we have previously discussed in Chapter 2. To ensure that the concepts have well-defined meanings, the common ontology may be augmented with axioms that precisely define the meanings of the concepts. Common ontologies for agents have traditionally been defined in the Knowledge Interchange Format (KIF). This is an ontology description language, which includes the ability to specify axioms in first order logic. For the Semantic Web, we generally assume our ontologies are constructed in OWL. OWL ontologies can be augmented with axioms using SWRL, which we briefly outlined in Chapter 5.

6.3.1 Performative verbs

Having established the need for a common ontology, as the basis for a shared understanding between agents, it is necessary to consider which concepts should be present in this ontology. These concepts should be unambiguously defined and sufficient to allow the agents to interact in meaningful ways. We discuss a classification of interactions types in Section 6.4. However, for now we simply state that a library of performative verbs is a good basis for such an ontology.

The use of performative verbs to express agent interactions is a popular technique in MASs. This approach comes from the theory of speech acts, which we outlined in Chapter 1. The theory identifies certain verbs, called performatives, as having characteristics similar to real-world actions. In effect, by saying the verb we cause some change to the state of the world. A popular example is the phrase 'I now declare you husband and wife', which has real-world consequences as a result of a spoken act. Other common examples of speech acts include requests, orders, promises, and apologies. The performative verbs can be grouped into five distinct categories:

1. Assertives commit the speaker to the truth of what is asserted, e.g. inform.
2. Commissives commit the speaker to a course of action, e.g. promise.
3. Declaratives effect some change on the state of affairs, e.g. declare war.
4. Directives attempt to get the listener to do something, e.g. propose.
5. Expressives express a mental state, e.g. prefer.

In this approach, inter-agent communication is performed by exchanging messages, where each message has an associated performatives that expresses the intended meaning of the message. An example ontology that contains a common set of performatives is shown in Figure 6.6. The concepts in the ontology are the five categories of performatives that we previously highlighted. The actual performatives are defined as instances of these concepts. The particular set of performatives in this example are taken from the FIPA-ACL.

In many agent systems, the common concepts relating to the communication process are not defined in an ontology, rather they are encapsulated in a separate ACL. The advantages and disadvantages of the two approaches are summarized below.

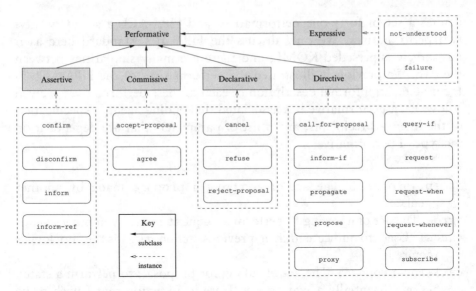

Figure 6.6 *FIPA-ACL performative ontology.*

1. The use of a common ontology for both communication and internal agent reasoning allows the concepts to be defined in a common formalism, and permits the same reasoning techniques to be applied over the communication process. However, it may be cumbersome to represent some communicative processes in this way, e.g. due to the lack of variables in the underlying DL.
2. A common ACL can be tailored specifically to the needs of the communication process. The semantics of this language can be defined in a richer and more expressive formalism (e.g. full first-order logic), though the reasoning process becomes more complex (or undecidable) as a result.

At the present time, ACL is the most popular technique for defining inter-agent communication. However, this is slowly changing as the popularity of the Semantic Web increases. Common ontologies, such as OWL-S that we describe in Chapter 7, may be considered as a partial replacement for ACL. Nonetheless, given the current popularity of ACL, we explore them in detail in the following section.

6.3.2 The FIPA agent communication language

Agent Communication Languages define common sets of performatives, which are message types, to be used for inter-agent communication. The two popular ACLs in MASs are the KQML and the FIPA-ACL. KQML defines a set of forty-one performatives and FIPA-ACL a set of twenty-two performatives. We only discuss the FIPA-ACL standard here as it has largely superseded KQML, and there are many similarities between the two. We previously illustrated the performatives of the FIPA-ACL in Figure 6.6. An informal description of each of these performatives is given below. Each performative has associated the sending agent, a specification of the intended recipients, and a list of parameters that are dependent on the type of performative:

accept-proposal The act of accepting a propose made by another agent.

agree The act of agreeing to perform a request made by another agent.

cancel Used to indicate that a previous action request is no longer required.

call-for-proposal The act of calling for proposals to perform a stated action. Essentially a way to say 'Here is an action that I wish to be performed, and these are the conditions under which it should be applied'. This act is typically used to initiate a negotiation between agents.

confirm An act used to inform another agent of the truth of the content, where the sender believes that the recipient is unsure of the truth.

disconfirm An act used to inform another agent that the content is false, where the sender believes that the recipient believes that the content is true.

failure Used to tell another agent that an action could not be performed, typically an action that was made by a previous request.

inform An act used to inform the recipient about the truth of the content.

inform-if An act used to request that the recipient informs the sender if they believe the content or not.

inform-ref An act used to request the actual value that corresponds to the content, e.g. a fact.

not-understood Used to inform another agent that the action performed by this agent was not understood, e.g. to indicate that a received message could not be interpreted, together with a reason why the action was not understood.

propagate An act that requests that the recipient sends the content to a specified set of agents.

propose The act of submitting a proposal for some action, e.g. a response to a previous call-for-proposal.

proxy An act that requests the recipient to forward to the content to a set of agents that match a particular specification. This action is typically used for brokering between agents.

query-if An act used to request that the recipient informs the sender of their belief on the content of the message.

query-ref An act used to request the value of the message content.

refuse Used to indicate that an agent refuses to perform an action, together with a reason why the action was not performed.

reject-proposal The act of rejecting a propose made by another agent during negotiation.

request An act used to request that another agent performs some specific action.

request-when An act used to request that another agent performs some action when a supplied statement becomes true.

request-whenever An act used to request that another agent performs some action when a statement becomes true, and each time after when the statement becomes true again.

subscribe An act used to request that the recipient informs the sender whenever something referenced by the content changes.

The inform and request performatives are the most important in the FIPA-ACL. They provide the fundamental mechanisms for an agent to send and request information. These performatives are often called *tell* and *ask* respectively. It is important to note that there is no mechanism to force another agent to perform an action. To obtain some information from another agent it is necessary to ask for the information from the agent, and then wait for the agent to tell this information in return. However, the agent may not reply, or may refuse to supply the requested information. This approach is necessary to retain the autonomy and independence of the individual agents, and is rather different from the typical send and receive operations found in distributed systems.

In addition to the sending and requesting of information, the FIPA-ACL also has a mechanism for soliciting proposals from a group of agents. This mechanism is best demonstrated by the FIPA Contract-Net protocol, which is illustrated by the AUML-style diagram in Figure 6.7. This protocol defines the negotiation process between a single initiator agent and a group of participants. The protocol begins with the initiator sending a call-for-proposal message to the group. The group of participants will then wither refuse, after which they are simply ignored, or a propose message. The responses are collected up to some deadline, after which the initiator will reply with with either an accept-proposal or reject-proposal message to each of the remaining participants. A participant who receives an accept-proposal should perform the accepted action and return either a failure message, or an inform(result) message upon completion, where result is the outcome of the action.

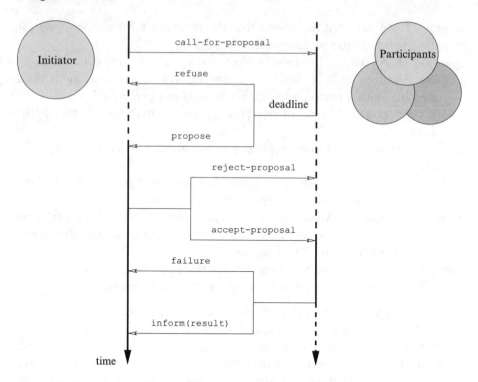

Figure 6.7 *FIPA ContractNet protocol.*

The remaining performatives in the FIPA-ACL are special cases of the ask/tell operations, or they are used for error handling. For example, a `query-if` is a request that the message content should be directly evaluated, typically on a database or knowledge base, and a `subscribe` message is a kind of persistent request. The kind of error handling message is dependent on the kind of error that has occurred. For example, a `not-understood` message means that an action could not be comprehended by an agent, while a `refuse` message means that the agent will not perform an action for some specified reason. The `cancel` message is used to retract a previous action. For example, Figure 6.8 shows how a `cancel` message may be used during the ContractNet protocol. In some cases it may not be possible to cancel a message, e.g. the action has already been performed, and so a `failure` is returned.

6.3.3   FIPA-ACL formal model

The popularity of the performative-based approach to agent communication can largely be attributed to the theory of rational action by Cohen and Levesque. This is a unified theory that combines the theory of intentional

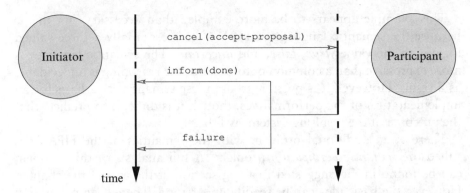

Figure 6.8 *Cancel protocol.*

Table 6.2 *FIPA-ACL* inform *performative.*

$\langle i, \mathbf{inform}(j, p)\rangle$	p is a propositional formula
Feasibility precondition:	$B_i\ p \wedge \neg B_i(Bif_j\ p \vee Uif_j\ p)$
Rational effect:	$B_j\ p$

reasoning that we outlined in Chapter 4 with the theory of speech acts. In other words, this provides us with an appealing theoretical model of both agent reasoning and agent communication. The key to the theory is that we can express the semantics of each performative in terms of mental states. For each performative, we define preconditions over the states of the agent that must hold before the performative is sent, and post-conditions on the states that hold after sending the performative. For example, we may insist that the agent has a certain set of beliefs before performing some communicative act. In this way, the two theories are combined, such that the internal state of the agent is directly related to the interaction that it performs.

The formal theory of rational action is too complex to present here, but we can understand the key concepts by considering an example. Table 6.2 is taken from the FIPA-ACL specification and defines the semantics of the inform performative in a BDI-like logic. The semantics uses three connectives: $B_i\ p$ is used to express that agent i believes p, $Bif_i\ p$ states that agent i has a definite opinion on the truth of p, and $Uif_i\ p$ states that agent i is uncertain about p. Therefore, the precondition of agent i informing agent j of the p is that agent i must believe p, and also it is not the case that i believes that j already has a belief about p, or that j is uncertain about p. The post-condition of the performative is that agent j will believe p.

This example appears to be more complex than necessary, but this is because the semantic language of FIPA-ACL is essentially a three-valued logic with the values *true, false,* and *uncertain.* The semantic language is more expressive than a common ontology, but the reasoning is undecidable as a result. However, it is possible to use these semantics as a basis for an implementation of the performatives, though it is difficult to predict what the outcome of the resulting systems will be.

There is an additional problem with the semantics of the FIPA-ACL called the *semantic verification* problem. A full analysis of this problem can be found in the Suggested Reading section at the end of the chapter. However, the basic idea can be readily understood. There is an underlying *sincerity assumption* in the semantic definitions, which demands that an agent always acts in accordance with their intentions. That is, if an agent states that they believe a fact then this statement is genuine. If an agent supplies incorrect information the system will break. This assumption is considered too restrictive in an open environment, such as the Web, as it will always be possible for an insincere agent to simulate compliance, and we cannot verify the sincerity of an agent as we have no access to its mental states. This issue also precludes interactions that are not fully cooperative, for example, negotiation or persuasion.

Despite the issues with the formal semantics, the FIPA-ACL standard has remained popular. This is principally because the formal model is rarely adhered to in practice. Instead, the performatives are simply treated as a library to identify different types of message. This approach is adopted in the popular Java Agent DEvelopment Framework (JADE) multiagent platform. Performatives are used to facilitate the exchange of messages, but compliance with the formal model is not enforced.

6.3.4 FIPA-ACL messages

The FIPA-ACL is just one of many standards promoted by the FIPA organization, though it is arguably the most well known. There are also standards for the implementation of agent architectures, the management of groups of agents, and the transportation of messages between agents. Consequently, there is a degree of overlap between the FIPA standards and the Semantic Web standards, which are defined by the World-Wide-Web Consortium (W3C). For example, the FIPA 'Agent Message Transport Envelope' standard fulfils a similar role in agent communication to SOAP. To resolve this ambiguity, we primarily focus on the W3C standards as they are more widely adopted, and more relevant to the Semantic Web. In addition, the FIPA standards were not

```
<?xml version="1.1"?>
<fipa-message act="inform">
  <sender>
    <agent-identifier>
      <name>photomart</name>
    </agent-identifier>
  </sender>
  <receiver>
    <agent-identifier>
      <name>customer42</name>
    </agent-identifier>
  </receiver>
  <content>(price nikonD70 450)</content>
  <language>sl</language>
  <encoding>utf8</encoding>
  <ontology href="http://www.mycamera.org/photo"/>
  <conversation-id>session1337</conversation-id>
  <in-reply-to>message1881</in-reply-to>
</fipa-message>
```

Figure 6.9 *Example FIPA-ACL message.*

originally designed for the Web environment. However, one further exception is the standard for representing FIPA-ACL messages that we now describe.

Figure 6.9 illustrates the representation of FIPA-ACL messages in XML. The example is a message from `agent1` informing `agent2` that the price of `nikonD70` is 450. The message also specifies the content language of the message, in this case the FIPA Semantic Language (`sl`). The message specifies the ontology relevant to the communication, which is defined as `http://www.mycamera.org/photo`. For convenience, most of the other message fields can also be defined using `href` attributes, which allows the use of URI within messages. The final fields are the `conversation-id` and `in-reply-to`, which allow agents to reference specific messages and define relationships between messages.

The FIPA-ACL message specification gives us a straightforward way to construct and deconstruct messages for transmission between agents. The messages are constructed using a standard set of XML tags, and can be processed by any agent with an XML parser. To transport these messages between agents it is necessary to encapsulate them with a message envelope, such as provided by SOAP. As with SOAP envelopes, FIPA-ACL messages would not normally be constructed by hand, but would be automatically generated by an agent execution platform.

6.4 Dialogues

In the preceding sections, we have described at length how messages can be constructed and exchanged between agents. We have outlined the technologies that are used for message transportation, and the standards that are used to encapsulate and represent these messages. We now shift our focus to the content of the messages, and the underlying reasons why agents want to exchange these messages.

We have consistently presented a view of agents as an abstraction for humans, and the exchange of messages as an analogue to verbal communication between humans. In keeping with this view, we now consider the various different kinds of communication that occur between humans, and their analogies in the field of MASs. Our first observation is that spoken communication rarely consists of a single act of speech in isolation. This kind of communication is only used for special purposes, such as orders or exclamations. Instead, human communication typically consists of a sequence of exchanges between participants, such as a conversation. This kind of communication is termed a *dialogue*.

A study of dialogue, or dialectic, is important in many different fields, including philosophy, sociology, and AI. There are many interesting properties that dialogues can conform to. For example, a dialogue is typically initiated for a specific purpose, which is the *focus* of the dialogue. Similarly, *coherence* of a dialogue means that the dialogue is internally consistent, and does not contain any contradictions. More importantly, dialogues can assume certain patterns, which correspond to the purpose of the communication. The philosophers Walton and Krabbe have classified human dialogues into six top-level categories, which we recap in Table 6.3.

The six types of dialogue are categorized according to two main factors, which are also shown in the table. The first of these is the *initial situation* that states the purpose of the dialogue. This is chiefly the presence or absence of conflict between the parties. The second factor is the *goal* of

Table 6.3   *Dialogue types.*

Dialogue type	Initial situation	Goal
Persuasion	Conflicting point of view	Conflict resolution
Negotiation	Conflict of interest	Making a deal
Deliberation	Need for action	Reach a decision
Information seeking	Personal ignorance	Spreading knowledge
Enquiry	General ignorance	Growth of knowledge
Eristic	Antagonism	Humiliation

the dialogue, which corresponds to the goals of the participants. These aims can be private aims of an individual participant, or joint aims to which both participants implicitly subscribe. The eristic dialogue type is essentially the breakdown of communication and is representative of physical fighting. This kind of dialogue is not generally applicable to agent systems and therefore will not be explored further here. We briefly describe the remaining five types below:

1. A *persuasion* dialogue arises in response to a recognized conflict of beliefs between the participants. Typically, this occurs when one participant believes a fact to be true, and the other participant believes the same fact to be false. The goal of the dialogue is to resolve the conflict, and this will typically be accomplished by each participant exhibiting evidence as to how they came to believe the fact. There is an implicit assumption that both of the participants are willing to alter their beliefs in light of this evidence, otherwise the dialogue would be futile.

2. A *negotiation* dialogue is initiated over a conflict of interest between participants. Typically, a negotiation will be over a limited resource, such as money or time. The goal of the dialogue is to reach a deal that is satisfactory to both participants, though each participant will seek to maximize their share. This is typically accomplished through a sequence of bids in the form of proposals and counterproposals. There is an underlying assumption that both of the participants are seeking to reach a deal, though often a satisfactory outcome may not be possible.

3. The goal of a *deliberation* dialogue is similar to that of a negotiation. That is, both are aimed at reaching an agreement and the aim of the individual participants is to influence the agreement in their favour. However, the initial situation in a deliberation is the recognition of a need for action, rather than a particular conflict. As a result, deliberation dialogues are typically more cooperative in nature than negotiations.

4. An *information seeking* dialogue is initiated when one participant wishes to obtain information that is possessed by another participant. There is no assumed conflict in this kind of dialogue, and therefore it is simply a decision as to whether the keeper of the information wishes to share it with the other participant. This is the only kind of dialogue where one of the participants has a distinct advantage over the other.

5. An *enquiry* dialogue is initiated so that the participants can collectively prove or disprove a proposition. A real-world example would be an enquiry into an air disaster. The aims of the participants are assumed to be similar and not in conflict. The enquiry is intended to be a cumulative process, from established information that does not require

further discussion. Thus, the enquiry should progress linearly towards the outcome.

The six categories of dialogue that we have discussed can be broken down into further subcategories. For example, according to particular kinds of negotiation strategy. However, these top-level categories are sufficient for our discussion here. We have repeatedly stated that communication in MASs is intended to be an abstraction for human communication. Therefore, we now discuss how this categorization of human dialogue can be related to communication between computational agents.

6.4.1 Dialogue frames

A dialogue is a useful concept in MASs when we want to define communication at a level above the exchange of single messages. Dialogues give us a way to express relationships between messages, and the overall purpose of the communication. In essence, dialogues provide structure to the communication beyond what we can achieve with performatives. Walton and Krabbe have further defined human dialogue as 'an exchange of speech acts between two speech partners in turn-taking sequence aimed at a collective goal'. Translating this into a multiagent view, we obtain the definition of a dialogue as a sequence of message exchanges between agents where the agents are acting towards a specific goal.

There are many proposals for implementing dialogues in MASs. To illustrate the key concepts in these proposals, we focus our attention on a specific technique called *dialogue frames*. This approach attempts to specify the Walton and Krabbe model directly in a manner that is suitable for use in MASs. The result is a formal model of dialogue, which can be implemented by a pair of agents.

A key construct in the dialogue frame approach is the specification of the *dialogue type*. This type identifies the five classes of dialogues, and the kind of values over which these dialogues operate. For the persuasion, enquiry, and infoseek dialogues these values are beliefs B, while negotiation dialogues operate on contracts C, and deliberation dialogues work over plans P. A dialogue type D has five possible values and is defined formally as follows:

$$D = \{\langle \text{persuade}, B \rangle, \langle \text{negotiate}, C \rangle, \langle \text{deliberate}, P \rangle, \langle \text{infoseek}, B \rangle, \langle \text{enquire}, B \rangle\}$$

In this approach, beliefs, contracts, and plans are somewhat simplified over their usual meanings. Beliefs B are represented as a set of values, which includes facts and evaluation results. Contracts C are defined as a set of $\langle issue, value \rangle$ pairs, e.g. $(\langle Price, 15 \rangle, \langle Quantity, 100 \rangle)$. A contract can also be considered as a conjunction of beliefs. Finally, plans P are defined as an ordered set of contracts. During plan construction, these contracts may contain variables and be underspecified.

We now define the dialogue frame, which is at the centre of this approach. A dialogue frame F is formally expressed as a tuple with four elements as follows:

$$F = \langle \langle t, \Delta \rangle \in D, \ \tau \in \Delta, \ \{u^0_{x_0 \to y_0}, \ \ldots, \ u^n_{x_n \to y_n}\} \rangle$$

The first element t identifies the kind of dialogue, and the second element Δ defines the values over which the dialogue operates. These elements are taken from a specific dialogue type D as previously discussed. The third element τ identifies the topic of the dialogue and is taken from Δ. The final component is a list of utterances $\{u^0, \ldots, u^n\}$, which define the actual dialogue steps between the two participants x and y. This is a turn-taking sequence, where $x_i \to y_i$ denotes an exchange from participant x to participant y at step i of the dialogue. An utterance u is defined by a pair $\langle s, \{\delta_0, \ldots, \delta_k\} \rangle$, where s is a statement and $\delta_i \in B$ is a list of beliefs in support of the statement. Statements are defined in terms of a communication language that is shared between the participants, e.g. FIPA-ACL.

A dialogue frame defines a dialogue of a particular type t and focused on a particular topic τ. The dialogue is initiated with a propose/accept sequence, and terminates with an acceptance or concession by one of the participants. These final utterances contain no supports. We now present an example that illustrates how a dialogue frame is used to formalize a dialogue between two participants. Figure 6.10 defines a negotiation over the price of a camera. This example can be viewed as a formalization of the scenario previously outlined in Figure 6.1.

$F = \langle\langle negotiate, \{\langle buy(b, \ Camera)\rangle\}\rangle, \langle buy(b, \ Camera)\rangle$
$u^0_{a \to b} : \langle\langle propose(negotiate, \{\langle buy(b, \ Camera)\rangle\})\rangle, \{\emptyset\}\rangle$
$u^1_{b \to a} : \langle\langle accept(negotiate, \{\langle buy(b, \ Camera)\rangle\})\rangle, \{\emptyset\}\rangle$
$u^2_{a \to b} : \langle\langle propose(\{\langle buy(b, \ Camera)\rangle, \langle Price, \ 400\rangle\})\rangle, \{\emptyset\}\rangle$
$u^3_{b \to a} : \langle\langle propose(\{\langle buy(b, \ Camera)\rangle, \langle Price, \ 450\rangle, \langle Model, \ D70\rangle\})\rangle, \{\emptyset\}\rangle$
$u^4_{a \to b} : \langle\langle propose(\{\langle buy(b, \ Camera)\rangle, \langle Price, \ 425\rangle, \langle Model, \ D70\rangle\})\rangle,$
$\qquad\qquad \{selling(BigPhoto, \ D70, \ 430)\}\rangle$
$u^5_{b \to a} : \langle\langle accept(\{\langle buy(b, \ Camera)\rangle, \langle Price, \ 425\rangle, \langle Model, \ D70\rangle\})\rangle, \{\emptyset\}\rangle \ \rangle$

Figure 6.10 *Example negotiation dialogue.*

Our example has the dialogue type $\langle negotiate, \{\langle buy(b, \text{Camera})\rangle\}\rangle$. This defines the dialogue to be a negotiation, and sets the topic to be the purchase of a camera from participant b. Recall that the purpose of a negotiation dialogue is the construction of a contract. Thus, the topic τ is specified as a contract with a single entry. As the dialogue progresses, this contract is extended with additional entries. The dialogue is defined between two participants a and b, and comprises a sequence of six utterances. The utterances are expressed using *propose* and *accept* performatives, where the parameters of the performative are the current contract. We assume that the concepts used in the dialogue are defined externally in an ontology that is common to the participants.

The first two utterances u^0 and u^1 in the example are used to initiate the dialogue, and establish that both a and b are willing to negotiate over the purchase of a camera. Subsequently, the contract is extended with the pair $\langle \text{Price, } 400 \rangle$, which is a proposal from a to purchase a camera with a cost of 400. A counterproposal is then made by b with a price of 450 and the contract is extended with a specific camera model: $\langle \text{Model, D70} \rangle$. A further counterproposal is made by a with a price of 425, and this is supported by the statement *selling*(BigPhoto, D70, 430), i.e. BigPhoto is selling this camera model for 435. In the final step, b accepts the proposal from a with a price of 425.

We have now shown how a dialogue frame can be used to express a dialogue between a pair of agents. All of the dialogue categories in the Walton and Krabbe categorization can be readily expressed in this manner. The purpose of the dialogue frame was to move beyond the exchange of single messages, and to talk about groups of messages with a specific purpose. It should be readily apparent that this is accomplished: the utterances are defined by sequences of performatives, and the purpose is identified by the dialogue type and topic.

There are many proposals for extending the basic dialogue frame approach. The Walton and Krabbe analysis permits dialogues to shift between topic. For example, when negotiating over a specific item, it may be necessary to have another dialogue about payment methods before concluding the negotiation process. This can be captured by embedding dialogue frames within one another. A dialogue frame can also serve as the basis for dialogue generation. In particular *dialogue games* have been used to generate frame-based dialogues between agents.

In a dialogue game, the participants (agents) make moves according to a defined set of rules. The moves that they make correspond to utterances, and the resulting sequence of utterances provides the dialogue. The rules of the game can be tailored to specific dialogue types. We note that dialogue games are effectively an interactive process of *argumentation*.

This is because each move is essentially an argument put forward by an agent to support its point of view. Further details on the extensions to dialogue frames can be found in the Suggested Reading section at the end of the chapter.

6.5   Artificial social systems

Agent dialogues are a useful concept that enables us to move from simple message exchanges to the definition of *conversations* between agents. Dialogues provide a purpose to agent-based communication, and define the meaning of individual messages within a wider context. However, the techniques that we have presented thus far only consider exchanges between two agents. We now consider the implications of broadening our scope to include conversations between multiple agents. This will be necessary as we are principally interested in the construction of MASs for the Semantic Web, which may contain large numbers of agents.

A naive approach to dealing with large numbers of agents is to reduce the complexity of the system to pairwise interactions between agents. That is, we consider communication in an MAS as comprising lots of simultaneous dialogues between pairs of agents. This view enables the previous definitions to be trivially extended into a multiagent context. Nonetheless, while this approach is useful from a theoretical perspective, there are obvious practical limitations when we attempt to construct MASs in this manner. For example, broadcast and multi-cast communications cannot easily be expressed through pairwise interaction.

While it is possible to extend agent dialogues to cover more than two agents, the real issues involved in multiagent communication do not directly involve the communication process itself. When we scale up to include large numbers of agents in our systems, there are a multitude of other pragmatic concerns that must be addressed before the actual communication can take place. In small agent systems, these issues can either be trivially solved, or safely ignored. However, in large agent systems, the same issues become dominant and threaten to derail the entire communication process. Three of these issues are outlined below:

1. One of the key features of an MAS is that the agents have different *capabilities*. In particular, agents will typically have access to different kinds of resources, e.g. knowledge, computational power, and physical devices. If all of the agents were required to have identical capabilities, then this would exclude a large class of agent-based applications. In a large MAS, it is no longer feasible for each agent to retain a list of all

the other agents and their capabilities. Therefore, we need to consider how an agent can describe and advertise their capabilities, and how other agents can find suitable agents to perform specific tasks.

2. As the size of the MAS increases, the ability to communicate reliably deteriorates. In particular, an MAS that operates over the Web will be affected by all of the problems that affect Web-based applications. For example, message passing may take time to complete, messages may be lost during communication, and agents may become unavailable. Therefore, it is necessary to perform multiagent communication in an *asynchronous* style. An agent must not wait indefinitely for a reply to a message, and the agent should be able to continue when other agents are unavailable.

3. An open MASs is designed to enable interoperability between agents from many different sources. However, by opening up an MAS in this way, we introduce a wide range of potential problems. For example, unreliable, untrustworthy, and malicious agents may be present in the system, just as viruses and worms are present on the Web. Therefore, it is necessary to consider how we can *trust* particular agents, and how we can prevent interference with our interactions by malicious agents.

To address the issues that arise in large MASs, we return to an idea that we outlined at the beginning of the chapter. Instead of treating an MAS as simply a collection of agents, we can view these agents as members of a society. In this view, agents are designed to act individually, but their actions are constrained in ways that make them mutually compatible. When we design an MAS in this way, we equip our agents with both the ability to communicate, and the ability to act as a member of a society. If our society is well designed, then we can lessen or completely avoid many potential issues that arise in such systems.

The society-based approach to MAS construction is again inspired by the study of human interaction. Human societies rely on rules and conventions to ensure that they run smoothly. Many kinds of animals have also been observed to obey conventions that reduce friction in their societies. We can provide similar benefits for MASs through the explicit definition of *artificial social systems*. To become a member of a society, an agent must agree to adhere to the constraints of the system, and in return the agent can benefit from the other members of the society, e.g. their knowledge or services.

In a human society, the underlying rules and conventions are termed *social norms*. These norms may be explicitly defined, e.g. a legal system, but are often implicit in the society, e.g. traditions. It is these norms that ensure the smooth running of the society, and often it is very apparent to the members of the society when the norms have been violated. For example, at a conference there is an implicit norm that the speaker does the talking while the audience listens. If everyone were to talk at the same time then the conference would rapidly break down.

Returning to MASs, we can readily define a system of social norms for a group of agents to follow. These norms must be explicit, and will often have implications in the way that agents are designed. The norms should be defined in such a way to facilitate the successful interaction between agents, but should not be overly restrictive in that they affect the autonomy of the agents. There are many proposed approaches for implementing norms in MASs. However, we now discuss one of the most popular approaches, which is termed 'Electronic Institutions' (EI).

6.5.1 Electronic institutions

The Electronic Institution framework is a formal approach to specifying norms for large MASs. The underlying concept of this framework is that human interactions are never completely unconstrained, instead they are always guided by formal and informal notions, i.e. social norms. Examples of these norms include conventions, traditions, customs, etiquette, and laws. An EI is a means to apply similar kinds of social norms to groups of agents.

To make the specification of norms for agents more manageable, the EI framework introduces two levels of abstraction. The first of these is the *institution* abstraction, from which the framework derives its name. This abstraction has a very similar meaning to its real-world counterpart. An institution is a collection of norms that are connected to particular kinds of interactions. For example, a shop institution will contain norms relevant to buying and selling, and an auction institution will contain norms relevant to the bidding process. This abstraction makes clear the kinds of norms that we need to define. It is also used as an administrative boundary, e.g. agents that have no connection to buying and selling will not be permitted to participate in a shop institution.

The second level of abstraction is a *scene*, which is a part of an institution relevant to a particular task. For example, a payment scene as part of a shop institution. A useful analogy, from which the scene abstraction takes its name, is to consider an institution as a theatre production. The individual agents are analogous to the *actors*, and each agent takes one (or more) *roles*. The interactions are articulated through the use of *scenes* in which groups of agents directly interact. Scenes are composed as a network called a *performative structure*. Agents move through the production (i.e. institution), participating in different scenes, with the possibility of assuming different roles in each. Within a scene, all the participating agents follow a single *script* (modelled as a finite-state system) that guides their interactions.

It is important to note that the agents only interact directly within scenes, and not at the higher institution level. Because the actors are agents and not real humans, some additional terminology is also required. The agents interact through the use of speech acts. Institutions define the acceptable vocabulary (i.e. ontology) through the use of a *dialogic framework*. The actions of an agent in the context of an institution may have consequences that either limit or enlarge its subsequent acting possibilities. The possible paths for an agent within the performative structure are thus defined by a set of *normative rules* containing obligations and commitments.

To obtain a better understanding of the EI framework, we now present an example institution for a typical shop. Figure 6.11 shows this example at the institution level, where a group of scenes are composed together to form the actual institution. The rectangles represent scenes, and the hexagons between scenes represent the performative structure. We do not show the normative rules that control the movement of the agents from one scene to another as they are externally defined in a logical language. However, we note that these rules are enforced by a separate governor process, which is a part of the framework.

There are five scenes in our example, which correspond to the different stages that an agent will go through when purchasing an item. The first of these is the enquiry scene, where details about the items for sale can be obtained. This is followed by the negotiation scene, where the buyer and seller will reach a mutually acceptable price for the items. The following scene is either a payment scene where the agent has sufficient

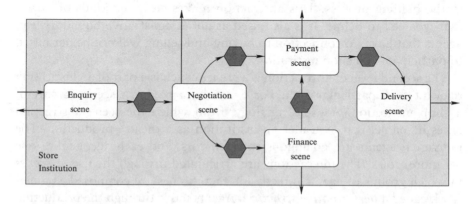

Figure 6.11 *Shop institution.*

funds, or a finance scene where suitable funds are obtained. The final scene is the delivery of the items to the buyer. Each scene has an arrow that extends outside the institution. This indicates that the agent can leave the institution at this point, e.g. if the agent decides not to proceed with the purchase.

We continue our example in Figure 6.12 where we define the actual negotiation scene in our institution. There are two roles in this scene: buyer and seller. Any number of agents (i.e. actors) satisfying these roles are permitted. For convenience we assume that all agents use the same dialogic framework, i.e. ontology. In this example, the vocabulary consists of OFFER, PROPOSE, ACCEPT, and REJECT messages. A scene is defined as a finite-state system, with a start state and one or more final states. All of the agents in the scene move simultaneously between the states, and the transitions between states are controlled through message exchanges. The states represent decisions that the agents must make, e.g. deliberation over the price of an item.

Our negotiation scene is an attempt to simulate a standard bargaining process between two parties (a buyer and a seller). We do not impose artificial constraints, such as turns or rounds, on the participants in the scene. The negotiation begins with an offer from the seller to the buyer, which we denote with the message OFFER(S, B). Upon receipt of the initial offer, the buyer enters a deliberative state, in which a decision is

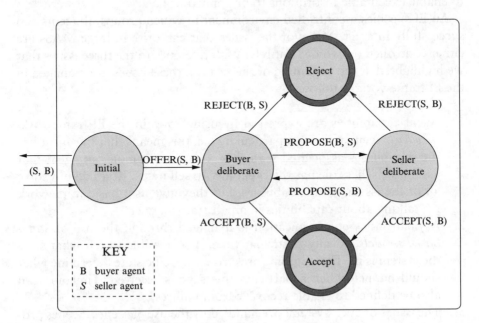

Figure 6.12   *Example negotiation scene.*

made. The buyer can accept or reject the offer in which case the scene terminates. The buyer can also make a proposal to the seller PROPOSE(B, S), e.g. an offer at a lower price. If a proposal is made to the seller, then the seller enters a deliberative state. The seller can in turn accept or reject the proposal, or make a counterproposal. If a counterproposal is made, the buyer deliberates further. Thus, the negotiation is effectively captured by a sequence of proposals and counterproposals between the buyer and the seller until an agreement is reached, or the proposals are rejected.

We have simplified our negotiation scene for the purposes of explanation. A complete negotiation would typically involve many more steps. Nonetheless, this example adequately demonstrates the specification of interactions within the EI framework. We note that EI are defined as instances of *state-charts*. Further details on the formal definition of EI can be found in the Suggested Reading section at the end of the chapter.

The EI framework is principally a system for specifying interactions between agents. It does not make any attempt to define how the agents reach the decisions that are required to guide these interactions. Thus, a process of refinement is necessary to translate an institution into an implementation. The ISLANDER tool has been developed to assist in the construction of sound institutions, and the AMELI system has been created to enable executable institutions to be defined in Java.

An EI specifies a controlled environment in which groups of agents can successfully interact. Many of the issues that can arise in large MASs are either controlled or avoided entirely. With reference to the three issues that we highlighted at the beginning of the section, these issues are managed in the EI framework as follows:

1. Agent capabilities are expressed by using *roles* in the EI framework. When an agent assumes a particular role, this means that the agent has the capabilities associated with that role. For example, an agent that assumes a seller role has the capability to sell items. Roles do not solve all of the issues with capabilities, but they give us a basic framework for talking about capabilities in an abstract manner.
2. Asynchronous communication is managed through the use of *state-based models*. At any particular time, it is possible to tell what state the system is in. The outgoing arcs from a specific state determine what should happen when a particular message is received. Timeouts can also be defined to enable recovery from failures.
3. The issues of open systems are handled by the use of scenes. Scenes provide a partially closed environment in which the issues are controlled.

Only agents that are relevant to a particular task are admitted into a specific scene by the performative structure. Normative rules define the obligations and commitments for agents, and governor agents within the scenes enforce these rules.

6.5.2   Protocol languages

We now present one further formal technique for defining interactions in MASs. This approach is an improvement over the EI framework, as it avoids the need for a refinement step between an abstract specification of interaction and an agent-based implementation. In this approach, we define *executable specifications* for agent interactions, which may be used directly to construct real MASs. These executable specifications are defined in an executable *protocol language*.

We present one multiagent protocol language here, which is called the Lightweight Coordination Calculus (LCC). LCC is founded on process calculus, which is an algebraic technique for defining the semantics of concurrent systems. In particular, LCC can be considered a sugared variant of the π-calculus, with an asynchronous semantics. The important feature of LCC is that it enables us to define precisely the interactions that should occur between agents in a scene, i.e. the script as presented in our theatre analogy (Section 6.5.1). We present LCC in more detail than the previous approaches, as we revisit the language in Chapter 7 when we discuss Semantic Web agents.

The key concepts in LCC are *scenes*, and *roles*. A protocol in LCC is considered to be broadly equivalent to an institution. As in the EI framework, a scene is a bounded space in which a group of agents interact on a single task. The use of scenes divides a large protocol into manageable parts. For example, a bidding scene may be part of a larger auction room protocol. In LCC, a scene places barrier conditions on the agents, such that a scene cannot begin until all the agents are present, and the agents cannot leave the scene until the dialogue is complete. This is different from EI, where agents could potentially join and leave a scene at any time. Agents entering a scene assume a role that they maintain until the end of the scene. For example, a bidding scene may involve agents with the roles of *bidder* and *auctioneer*.

An LCC protocol defines one or more scenes, which are sequence of protocol steps parameterized on a specific role. That is, the protocol steps that the agent follows in a scene are directly dependent on their role. This differs from the EI approach, where all the agents followed the same protocol steps. The role also identifies *capabilities* that the agent must provide. It is important to note that a protocol only contains operations that are specific to the mechanisms of communication and coordination between agents. This makes it straightforward to understand the operation of the protocol without extraneous details, and makes it possible to verify the protocols using automated means, e.g. model checking. All of the other agent facilities, e.g. the reasoning processes, are encapsulated by *decision procedures* that are external to the protocol. In effect, the decision procedures provide an interface between the communicative and the rational process of the agent.

Interaction between the agents in a scene is performed by the exchange of messages. Messages can be sent or received and this exchange happens in a non-blocking manner. Every message has an associated *performative*, which is used to indicate the type of the message and parameters. LCC does not assign any fixed semantics to these performatives. However, individual agents can agree on a semantics for a particular scene. In this way, LCC can readily represent FIPA-style agent communication, e.g. the ContractNet protocol.

A Backus-Naur-Form (BNF-style) abstract syntax for LCC is defined in Figure 6.13. For brevity, we only present the syntax for the scene level, and not the institution level. There are five key syntactic categories in the definition, namely: Protocols P, Methods M, Operations op, Terms ϕ, and Types τ. These categories have the following meanings. A protocol P, which corresponds to a single scene in our simplified definition, is uniquely

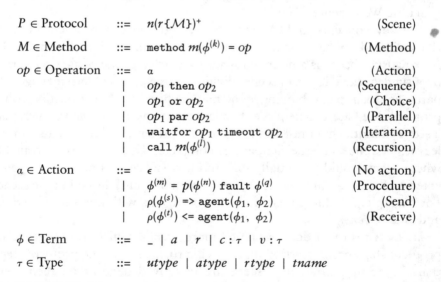

$P \in$ Protocol	::=	$n(r\{\mathcal{M}\})^+$	(Scene)
$M \in$ Method	::=	$\texttt{method } m(\phi^{(k)}) = op$	(Method)
$op \in$ Operation	::=	α	(Action)
	|	$op_1 \texttt{ then } op_2$	(Sequence)
	|	$op_1 \texttt{ or } op_2$	(Choice)
	|	$op_1 \texttt{ par } op_2$	(Parallel)
	|	$\texttt{waitfor } op_1 \texttt{ timeout } op_2$	(Iteration)
	|	$\texttt{call } m(\phi^{(l)})$	(Recursion)
$\alpha \in$ Action	::=	ϵ	(No action)
	|	$\phi^{(m)} = p(\phi^{(n)}) \texttt{ fault } \phi^{(q)}$	(Procedure)
	|	$p(\phi^{(s)}) \texttt{ => agent}(\phi_1, \phi_2)$	(Send)
	|	$p(\phi^{(t)}) \texttt{ <= agent}(\phi_1, \phi_2)$	(Receive)
$\phi \in$ Term	::=	$\_ \mid a \mid r \mid c : \tau \mid v : \tau$	
$\tau \in$ Type	::=	$utype \mid atype \mid rtype \mid tname$	

Figure 6.13 *LCC abstract syntax.*

named n and defined as a set of roles r, each of which defines a set of methods $\mathcal{M}$. A method m takes a list of terms $\phi^{(k)}$ as arguments, where $k \geq 0$ is the arity, i.e. list length. The initial method in a protocol is named main. Agents have a fixed role r for the duration of the protocol, and are individually identified by unique names a. Protocols are constructed from operations op that control the flow of the protocol, and actions α that have side effects and can fail. Failure of actions causes backtracking in the protocol.

The interface between the protocol and the service that defines its behaviour, is achieved through the invocation of procedures p. A procedure is parameterized by three sequences of terms. The input terms $\phi^{(n)}$ are the input parameters to the procedure, and the output terms $\phi^{(m)}$ are the output parameters, i.e. results, from the procedure. A procedure may also raise an exception in which case the fault terms $\phi^{(q)}$ are bound to the exception parameters, and backtracking occurs in the protocol. Interaction between agents is performed by the exchange of messages that are defined by performatives ρ, i.e. message types. The parameters to procedures and performatives are terms ϕ, which are either variables v, agent names a, role names r, constants c, or wild cards _. Literal data is represented by constants c, which can be complex datatypes, e.g. currency, flat-file data, or XML documents. Variables are bound to terms by unification that occurs in the invocation of procedures, the receipt of messages, or through recursive method invocations. Constants and variables are assigned explicit types τ to ensure that they are treated consistently.

To illustrate the LCC protocol language, we now specify the EI negotiation scene from Figure 6.12 in LCC syntax. The LCC definition of the negotiation protocol is presented in Figure 6.14. For convenience, we distinguish between the different types of terms by prefixing variables names with $, and role names with %. We define two roles: %buyer and %seller. Each of these roles has three associated methods that define the protocol states for the roles: main, wait, and deliberate.

When exchanging messages through send and receive actions, a unification of terms in the definition agent(ϕ_1, ϕ_2) is performed, where ϕ_1 is matched against the agent name, and ϕ_2 against the agent role. For example, when the buyer receives the initial offer, in line 5 of the protocol, the terms will match any agent whose role is a %seller, and $seller will be bound to the name of the seller.

The semantics of message passing corresponds to reliable, buffered, non-blocking communication. Sending a message will succeed immediately if an agent matches the definition, and the message M will be stored in a buffer on the recipient. Receiving a message involves an additional unification

```
1    negotiate_scene[
2      %buyer{
3        method(main) =
4          waitfor
5            (offer($value) <= agent($seller, %seller) then
6              call(deliberate, $value, $seller))
7        method(deliberate, $value, $seller) =
8              ($newvalue = acceptOffer($value, $seller) then
9                accept($value) => agent($seller, %seller))
10         or ($newvalue = counterPropose($value, $seller) then
11              propose($newvalue) => agent($seller, %seller) then
12              call(wait, $newvalue))
13         or  reject($value) => agent($seller, %seller)
14       method(wait, $value) =
15         waitfor
16             (accept($sellvalue) <= agent($seller, %seller)
17           or reject($oldvalue) <= agent($seller, %seller)
18           or (propose($newvalue) <= agent($seller, %seller) then
19                 call(deliberate, $newvalue, $seller)))
20         timeout (call(wait, $value))}
21     %seller{
22       method(main) =
23         $value = getValue() then
24         offer($value) => agent(_, %buyer) then
25         call(wait, $value)
26       method(wait, $value) =
27         waitfor
28             (accept($sellvalue) <= agent($buyer, %buyer)
29           or reject($oldvalue) <= agent($buyer, %buyer)
30           or (propose($newvalue) <= agent($buyer, %buyer) then
31                 call(deliberate, $newvalue, $buyer)))
32         timeout (call(wait, $value))
33       method(deliberate, $value, $buyer) =
34             ($newvalue = acceptOffer($value, $buyer) then
35               accept($value) => agent($buyer, %buyer))
36         or ($newvalue = counterPropose($value, $buyer) then
37              propose($newvalue) => agent($buyer, %buyer) then
38              call(wait, $newvalue))
39         or reject($value) => agent($buyer, %buyer)} ]
```

Figure 6.14 *LCC negotiation protocol.*

step. The message *M* supplied in the definition is treated as a template to be matched against any message in the buffer. For example, in line 5 of the protocol, a message must match offer($value), and the variable $value will be bound to the content of the messageif the match is successful.

Sending a message will fail if no agent matches the supplied terms, and receiving a message will fail if no message matches the message template.

The send and receive actions complete immediately and do not delay the agent. For this reason, all of the receive actions are wrapped by `waitfor` loops to avoid race conditions. For example, in line 15 the agent will loop until a message is received. If this loop was not present the agent may fail to find a response and the protocol would terminate prematurely. The advantage of non-blocking communication is that we can check for the receipt of a number of different messages. For example, in lines 16, 17, and 18, of the protocol, the agent waits for either an `accept`, `reject`, or `propose` message respectively. The `waitfor` loop includes a `timeout` condition that is triggered after a certain interval has elapsed. The timeout is defined to restart the loop (in lines 20 and 32), though we could define an alternative behaviour, such as withdrawing from the negotiation. Timeouts give us a measure of fault tolerance in the presence of delays or failures.

At various points in the protocol, an agent is required to perform various tasks, e.g., making a decision, or retrieving some information. This is achieved through the use of decision procedures. As stated earlier, a decision procedure provides an interface between the dialogue protocol and the rational processes of the agent. A decision procedure p takes a number of terms as arguments and returns a single result in a variable v. The actual implementation of the decision procedure is external to the dialogue protocol. For example, the `acceptOffer` decision procedure in line 34 of the dialogue refers to an external decision procedure, which can be arbitrarily complex, e.g. based on reputation, or according to some negotiation strategy.

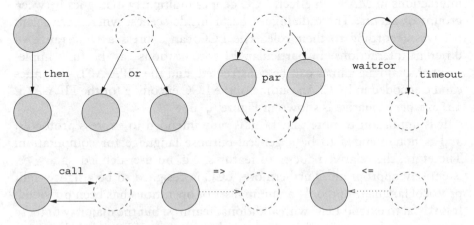

Figure 6.15 *LCC operations.*

FIPA semantics:

$< i, \ \texttt{inform}(j, \ \Phi) >$

$FP: \quad B_i \Phi \ \wedge \ \neg B_i (Bif_j \Phi \ \vee \ Uif_j \Phi)$

$RE: \quad B_j \Phi$

LCC encoding:

```
method(inform, $p, $i, $j) =
  believe($i, $p) then
  not(believe($i, bif($j, $p))) then
  not(believe($i, uif($j, $p))) then
  inform(p) => agent($j, _) then
  assert(believe, $j, $p)
```

Figure 6.16 *LCC encoding of FIPA-ACL inform.*

The operations in the protocol are sequenced by the then operator that evaluates op_1 followed by op_2, unless op_1 involved an action that failed. The failure of actions is handled by the or operator. This operator is defined such that if op_1 fails, then op_2 is evaluated, otherwise op_2 is ignored. External data is represented by constants c in the language. LCC does not attempt to assign types to this data, rather the interpretation of this data is left entirely to the decision procedures. For example, in line 23 the starting value is returned by the getValue procedure, and interpreted by the acceptOffer procedure in line 8.

A state-based interpretation of the LCC language constructs is shown in Figure 6.15. The solid arrows are used to indicate control flow, and the dashed arrows indicate message passing. However, LCC is asynchronous in nature, and so the state of the system at any particular time cannot be directly determined as in the EI approach.

It should now be clear that LCC is a powerful language for expressing interactions in MASs. In effect, LCC defines multiparty dialogues between groups of agents. These dialogues occur inside scenes, where each agent behaves according to their role. The LCC can express a wide range of different interactions. In particular, EI specifications can be fully implemented, dialogue games can be constructed, and the FIPA-ACL semantics can be encoded in LCC. An outline of the LCC encoding for the FIPA-ACL inform performative is shown in Figure 6.16.

It is important to note that LCC is only intended to express protocols, and is not intended to be a general-purpose language for computation. Therefore, the relative paucity of features, e.g. no user-defined datatypes, is entirely appropriate. Furthermore, LCC is designed to be a lightweight protocol language and only a minimal set of operations has been provided. It is trivial to extend LCC with additional features, but the majority of these features can be expressed in the basic language. It is intended that LCC protocols will be generated from higher-level languages, or automatically from EI specifications.

6.6 Summary

In this chapter, we have presented an overview of the main techniques and technologies for defining and implementing communicative behaviours in MASs. These techniques define agent communication from low-level message passing through to high-level application construction from distributed services. We have specifically emphasized the approaches that are of relevance to the construction of Semantic Web applications. A summary of these approaches, and their relationships are shown in Figure 6.17.

It is important to note that the various techniques for agent communication are designed to work together, rather than compete with one another. For example, agent dialogues are constructed from performatives, which rely on message passing. Outfigure attempts to show how the various techniques can be combined. A technique that appears directly above another can be combined directly with this technique. For example, dialogues appear directly above both performatives and message passing. This means that dialogues can be constructed either from performatives, or directly

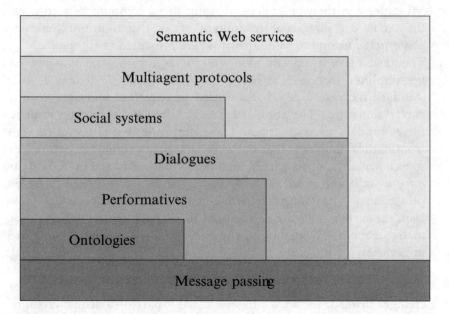

Figure 6.17 *Agent communication techniques.*

using message passing. A summary of the seven layers in our diagram is given below:

1. The lowest layer of agent communication that we consider is message passing. This is the ability for one agent to send a message to another agent. At this level we are not concerned with the content of the message, only that a message can be passed in a standard way and with a reasonable degree of reliability. Message passing can be performed directly between agents, or through a *shared state*. The shared state is a central repository to which messages are asserted and retracted. This approach is implemented in the Linda architecture, and has the advantage of simplicity for small agent systems. However, direct message passing is generally used for large agent systems as it does not impose a bottleneck on the communication process. The SOAP standard defines a one-way stateless message exchange method, which is based on the analogy of an envelope being transferred from one place to another. Finally, we noted that P2P techniques are a useful alternative to direct message passing when large messages are required.

2. When agents exchange messages they need some basis for interpreting the content of the messages. Without this, the messages would simply appear to the agents as a set of unintelligible binary data. A shared understanding of the messages can be obtained by defining a common ontology of concepts, which are understood by both participants. Messages can then be expressed using these common concepts, and the agents can interact in meaningful ways. Common ontologies are constructed using the techniques that we presented in Chapter 2.

3. The task of creating common ontologies for message passing can be simplified through the use of an ACL. An ACL defines a set of standard message types that are used to construct messages with an agreed semantics. The popular FIPA-ACL uses performatives to define these standard message types. These performatives are a set of verbs from natural language that have characteristics similar to actions, i.e. speech acts. The most widely used performatives in the FIPA-ACL are *inform* (tell) and *request* (ask). The semantics of FIPA-ACL are expressed in a logical language, which is similar to the BDI model. However, these semantics are rarely used in practice due to various pragmatic concerns. Nonetheless, the FIPA-ACL performatives are used in a variety of multiagent architectures, including the popular JADE platform.

4. Communication between agents rarely involves a single message exchange. Instead, each exchange is usually part of a sequence that is aimed at accomplishing a specific task, or resolving an issue. We can

understand this sequence of messages as a *dialogue* between a pair of agents. The study of human dialogues has identified six main categories of dialogue that are in common use. Five of these categories are of particular relevance in agent systems, and can be used to provide a formal basis for agent dialogues. In particular, a *dialogue frame* captures the type of dialogue, the topic (i.e. goal) of the dialogue, and the sequence of message exchanges. This provides us with a basis for the generation of agent dialogues that adhere to specific rules, such as in formal dialogue games.

5. When we attempt to move from dialogues between pairs to agents to complex interactions between multiple agents, there are a wide range of auxiliary issues that we must consider. These issues include the location of agents with appropriate capabilities, reliability problems that are magnified by the increase in scale, and the potential for untrustworthy or subversive agents in an open environment. These issues can be addressed by the definition of artificial social systems to which agents subscribe. To become a member of a society, an agent must agree to observe certain rules and conventions (social norms). EI are a popular technique for defining artificial social systems. An EI comprises a set of definitions that specify a society with a common purpose.

6. The construction of MASs that adhere to specific artificial social systems is a challenging task. In the EI approach, agents must be manually synthesized from the institution specification. Furthermore, if the institution definition is modified, then these agents must be re-engineered. The limitations of EI can be avoided by adopting an executable specification to express an artificial social system, called a protocol language. In this approach, an institution is defined in a document, which is distributed among groups of agents. The protocol expressed in the document is executed directly by these agents, and can be independently modified and verified. An exemplar of this approach is the LCC, which defines multiagent protocols in an asynchronous process calculus.

6.7 Exercises

1. Use the ContractNet protocol to express the purchase of a camera with a single buyer and multiple sellers.
2. Design EI for the following:
   (a) An online book store.
   (b) A digital photo library.

(c) A supply chain, as described in Chapter 3.

(d) Part of a multi-player adventure game.

3. Implement and validate your institutions from Q2 using the IS-LANDER tool. ISLANDER is part of the Electronic Institutions Development Environment (EIDE), which can be downloaded from:

```
http://e-institutor.iiia.csic.es/islander/islander.html
```

4. Figure 6.18 outlines a protocol that simulates a simple English-style auction room. The protocol assumes a single auctioneer agent and a variable number of bidder agents. The auction begins with the auctioneer sending out the starting value for a particular auction item. Each bidder then makes an internal decision whether to bid at the current value, and makes a bid if appropriate. When the auctioneer receives a valid bid, the bid value is incremented and the new value is sent to all of the bidders. The bidders then make a decision to bid at the new value. The auction continues until no further bids are received by the auctioneer and a timeout occurs, analogous to the 'going, going, gone' ritual. At this point the winning bidder is notified and the auction concludes. Define an LCC protocol that implements this auction protocol. You should define two roles in this protocol: the bidder, and the auctioneer.

5. We defined the basic Gnutella protocol for P2P file sharing in Chapter 4. This protocol uses a query flooding approach, where the search query is forwarded to all connected nodes. By contrast, the Gnutella2 protocol uses a *query walk* approach, which lowers the network utilization. In the query walk technique, the search query is forwarded to only one connected node at a time. The query is only forwarded to

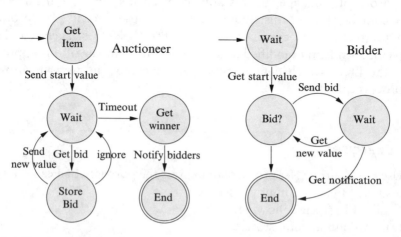

Figure 6.18 *Auction protocol.*

another connected node if this initial query was unsuccessful, or a time-out occurred. Design LCC protocols for the Gnutella and Gnutella2 protocols. You should only require one 'node' role in each protocol.

6.8 Suggested reading

1. F. Bellifemine, A. Poggi, and G. Rimassa. JADE: A FIPA-Compliant Agent Framework. In *Proceedings of the 1999 Conference on Practical Application of Intelligent Agents and Multi-Agent Technology (PAAM'99)*, pp. 97–108, London, April 1999.
2. P. R. Cohen and H. J. Levesque. Rational Interaction as the Basis for Communication. *Intentions in Communication*, pp. 221–56, 1990.
3. M. Esteva, D. de la Cruz, and C. Sierra. ISLANDER: An Electronic Institutions Editor. In *Proceedings of the First International Joint Conference on Autonomous Agents & Multiagent Systems (AAMAS'02)*, pp. 1045–52, Bologna, Italy, ACM press, July 2002.
4. M. Esteva, J. A. Rodríguez, C. Sierra, P. Garcia, and J. L. Arcos. On the Formal Specification of Electronic Institutions. In *Agent-mediated Electronic Commerce (The European AgentLink Perspective)*, volume 1991 of *Lecture Notes in Artificial Intelligence*, pp. 126–47, 2001.
5. M. Esteva, B. Rosell, J. A. Rodríguez, and J. Arcos. AMELI: An Agent-Based Middleware for Electronic Institutions. In *Proceedings of the Third International Joint Conference on Autonomous Agents and Multiagent Systems (AAMAS'04)*, volume 1, pp. 236–43, New York, 2004.
6. R. A. Flores and R. C. Kremer. Bringing Coherence to Agent Conversations. In *Proceedings of Agent-Oriented Software Engineering (AOSE'01)*, volume 2222 of *Lecture Notes in Computer Science*, pp. 50–67, Montreal, Canada, Springer-Verlag, January 2002.
7. Foundation for Intelligent Physical Agents. FIPA Specification Part 2—Agent Communication Language. Available at: http://www.fipa.org, April 1999.
8. M. Genesereth and R. Fikes. Knowledge Interchange Format (KIF) Version 3.0 Reference Manual. Available at: http://logic.stanford.edu/kif/Hypertext/kif-manual.html.
9. M. Greaves, H. Holmback, and J. Bradshaw. What is a Conversation Policy? In *Proceedings of the Workshop on Specifying and Implementing Conversation Policies, Autonomous Agents '99*, Seattle, USA, May 1999.
10. N. Maudet and B. Chaib-draa. Commitment-based and Dialogue-game based Protocols—New Trends in Agent Communication Language. *The Knowledge Engineering Review*, 17(2): 157–79, 2002.
11. J. McGinnis and D. Robertson. Realising Agent Dialogues with Distributed Protocols. In *Developments in Agent Communication: Proceedings of the Autonomous Agents & Multiagent Systems Workshop on Agent Communication (AC'05)*, volume 3396 of *Lecture Notes in Artificial Intelligence*. Springer-Verlag, 2004.
12. R. Milner, J. Parrow, and D. Walker. A Calculus of Mobile Processes (Part 1/2). *Information and Computation*, 100(1): 1–77, September 1992.
13. J. Odell, H. Van Dyke Parunak, and B. Bauer. Representing Agent Interaction Protocols in UML. In *Proceedings of the 2nd International Workshop on*

Agent-Oriented Software Engineering (AOSE01), volume 2222 of *Lecture Notes in Computer Science*, pp. 121–40, Montreal, Canada, Springer-Verlag, January 2002.

14. J. Pitt. *Open Agent Societies*. Wiley, 2004.

15. C. Reed. Dialogue Frames in Agent Communication. In *Proceedings of the 3rd International Conference on Multi Agent Systems (ICMAS'98)*, pp. 246–53, Paris, 1998.

16. J. A. Rodríguez, F. J. Martín, P. Noriega, P. Garcia, and C. Sierra. Towards a Formal Specification of Complex Social Structures in Multi-Agent Systems. In J. Padget, editor, *Collaboration between Human and Artificial Societies*, volume 1624 of *Lecture Notes in Artificial Intelligence*, pp. 284–300. Springer-Verlag, 2000.

17. M. P. Singh. Agent Communication Languages: Rethinking the Principles. *IEEE Computer*, pp. 40–7, December 1998.

18. D. N. Walton and E. C. W. Krabbe. *Commitment in Dialogue: Basic Concepts of Interpersonal Reasoning*. SUNY Press, 1995.

7 Semantic Web services

In this book we have been consistently directed by the vision of the Semantic Web. This vision can be summarized as the ability for computers to automatically use information on the Web in a similar way to humans. In particular, we want to be able to retrieve, comprehend, and exchange knowledge using automated techniques. At this point we have defined all of the main techniques that can be used to realize these goals. A summary of the four key techniques that we now have at our disposal is presented below:

1. We have the ability to represent knowledge in a form suitable for automated processing. This ability is provided by the definition of *ontologies*, which provide structure to knowledge.
2. We can construct entities, called agents, which act on behalf of humans and solve specific goals. We have presented many different techniques that can be used to construct these agents, dependent on the purpose for that the agents to be applied.
3. We can reason about the knowledge that we represent to answer specific questions. This can be accomplished by *query answering* techniques, or by *complex inferences* over the knowledge, guided by the ontology.
4. Our agents can *communicate* with other agents, and form *societies* based on common interests. Within these societies, agents can collaborate towards the resolution of common goals, which could not be accomplished by individual agents alone.

The purpose of this penultimate chapter is to show how we can harness and combine these four key techniques to build systems and applications for the Semantic Web. As stated in Chapter 1, Semantic Web applications are not constructed statically in the traditional manner. Instead, these applications are constructed dynamically, at run-time, from combinations of services, termed *knowledge services*. Our presentation is designed to answer the two key questions below:

1. How can we construct knowledge services that encompass the various capabilities that we have available?
2. How do we compose knowledge services into applications that can accomplish specific tasks?

To address these questions, we first outline how software systems are constructed on the Semantic Web, and then describe how agents and knowledge fit into the picture. We note that the core technologies that we describe in the first half of the chapter are not specific to the Semantic Web, but are also used in other areas such as Distributed Computing, Grid Computation, and Web-based programming. This overlap of technologies is important as it facilitates interoperation and means that we are not creating proprietary architectures for the Semantic Web. In the latter half of the chapter, we show how these core technologies are specialized and utilized specifically to realize Semantic Web applications.

7.1 Service-oriented architecture

The primary notion underlying the construction of software systems on the Semantic Web is that of a *Service-Oriented Architecture* (SOA). In an SOA, nodes on a network make resources available to other nodes as independent services that are accessed through a published interface. This is comparable to the way that Web servers make information available on the Internet. However, the concept has been generalized to include generic resources made accessible by independent application services. In other words, an SOA comprises a collection of loosely coupled, highly interoperable services. There is no central control in an SOA, and therefore it can be considered as a P2P architecture that operates at the level of applications.

An SOA is a generic set of concepts for building software systems, and there are many different ways in which SOA can be implemented. This is comparable to a multiagent architecture, which can be implemented using many different techniques. There are four key concepts that define an SOA: *services, service invocation, service discovery,* and *service composition.* These concepts and their relationships are illustrated in Figure 7.1. The core concepts are generally understood to have the following meanings:

1. Services are naturally the most important concept in SOA as they underpin the entire architecture. A service can be considered as a computational wrapper around some set of resources. The resources that are managed by a service will typically be abstract, e.g. money, information, or algorithms. However, services may also manage resources in the real world, e.g. telescopes, printing presses, or banking systems. A

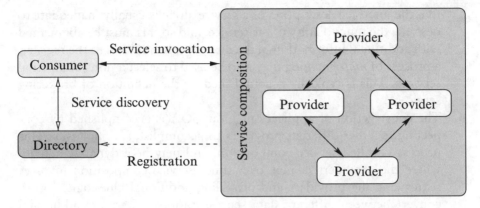

Figure 7.1   *A service-oriented architecture.*

service is able to manage these different kinds of resources by providing a well-defined *interface* to the resources. Any set of resources that can be represented and controlled through a standard electronic interface can be considered as a service. Nonetheless, a service must be self-contained and not reliant on external resources, or control mechanisms outside the interface. Services are usually described as *stateless*. However, this term is slightly misleading as a service can maintain internal state, only that it should not be reliant on external state information.

2. Service invocation describes the way that a service is actually used through its interface. The interface to a service partitions the service into a set of separate *operations*. These operations can be individually invoked and will usually return results. The entity that performs the invocation is termed the *consumer*, and the service that is invoked is termed the *provider*. In many cases, the consumer will also be defined as a service. The entire invocation process is accomplished by the exchange of messages between the consumer and provider. Services, and their operations, are generally intended to be platform independent and programming language neutral. Invocation is generally accomplished through standard RPC mechanisms.

3. To invoke a service, the consumer must know how to find the provider. This process of service discovery can be a non-trivial task in an open environment, where the issues are similar to those faced when attempting to find suitable information on the Web. The SOA assume that services can be located through *dynamic discovery*, rather than being known in advance. This is essential as services may change location and functionality, or become unavailable. The discovery issue can be addressed by the presence of *directory services*, which store the location of services provider and their features. Directory services can be queried by consumers to locate candidate providers. We note

that the interface description of a service alone is usually inadequate to describe the functionality of the service, and so this must be augmented with additional information in the directory. In addition to the registry, a process of *matchmaking* may also be used to select among competing services. This is typically accomplished by the definition of brokering services.

4. The construction of applications in an SOA is accomplished by connecting together different providers to accomplish specific tasks. This process is called service composition, and may be a dynamic activity where the providers change over time. Service composition involves sequencing the providers and providing additional glue-logic, e.g. to convert between different data representations. There are additional issues concerning the presentation of the results back to the end consumer. For example, the details of the composition process should normally be hidden from the consumer. Service composition is inherently dependent on the kind of application being constructed, and different solutions have been proposed that depend on the kind of services being composed. The provision of flexible yet transparent composition of services is currently one of the least understood aspects of SOA.

We now present an example SOA that illustrates the construction of an application from individual services. We return to this example later in the chapter when defining specific techniques for service composition. Our example is an application for processing digital photographs and is illustrated in Figure 7.2. The application is constructed by composing together four services. The composed services appear externally as a single

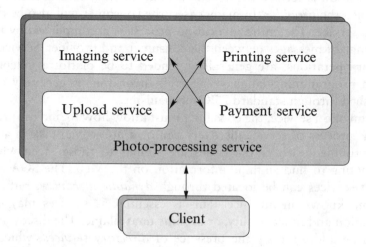

Figure 7.2 *Digital photo-processing application.*

photo-processing service that is invoked by a client. The four services at the core of the application perform the following tasks:

1. The upload service is used to transfer the images from the client.
2. The payment service is used to obtain payment from the client for specific processing options.
3. The imaging service performs preprocessing on the uploaded images, e.g. resizing them correctly for printing.
4. The printing service is a real-world service for printing and dispatching photographs.

7.2   Web services architecture

The concept of a generic SOA has been around in a variety of guises for some time, and certainly predates the Semantic Web. However, SOA have recently come to prominence as they provide the underlying context for *Web Services*. Web Services are essentially a family of middle-ware technologies that facilitate the implementation of service-based applications on the Web. All of the concepts that we previously described for a generic SOA still hold when we consider Web Services. The key difference with Web Services is that specific technologies are prescribed for each of the SOA concepts that we outlined previously. We outline below the various Web Services technologies which satisfy the four key SOA categories:

1. An individual service in the Web Services architecture is called a *web service*. A web service is effectively nothing more than a software component accessible through an interface at a particular Web location, i.e. a web service has a specific URL. This software component can perform any task, but should not depend on external state information. A web service will often reside within a *container* on a Web Server, where the container provides a managed execution environment for the service. For example, a Java-based web service located in a container on an Apache Tomcat server. However, web services can be defined in any programming language and on any platform provided that they are accessed through a standard web service interface. This interface is specified using the XML-based WSDL.
2. A WSDL interface document specifies the location of a web service, the operations that comprise the service, and their input and output types. From this, we can obtain the appropriate information to invoke the web service, and interpret the results. The invocation of a web service is performed by message passing: the input arguments to the service

are packaged as a message and sent to the service. The web service should then respond with a message containing the output arguments, or an error message. Invoking a web service is essentially the same as invoking a procedure, thus RPC mechanisms are generally used. WSDL permits messages to be sent in a variety of different formats, which are called *bindings*. Typically, the messages are sent using either SOAP or HTTP bindings. We previously discussed the SOAP message-passing standard in Chapter 6.

3. Web services can be made available to the world by registering them with specific directory services. This registration process is usually done manually, though automatic registration is possible. A registry entry can be created by filling in a web form with a description of the service, according to certain categories, and a link to the WSDL interface document. These entries can then be used by others to invoke the service, and to perform dynamic service discovery. Web service registries are implemented as web services. Thus, a registry has a WSDL interface and can be invoked by other services, e.g. to perform automated registration, or to answer discovery queries. There are currently a number of competing registry standards with different WSDL interfaces. Two of the most popular interfaces are the Universal Description, Discovery and Integration language (UDDI) and Electronic Business eXtensible Markup Language (ebXML).

4. The construction of applications by composing separate web services is less well defined. There are a variety of standards and technologies that are tailored to specific application areas. The main techniques are *workflow* composition, *structural* composition, and *semantic* composition. Workflow-based composition is employed in the Open Grid Services Architecture (OGSA), and the Web Services Business Process Execution Language (WS-BPEL). Structural composition is used in the Web Services Choreography Description Language (WS-CDL) that is aimed at e-business, and the WS-Coordination specification for generic web services. Finally, semantic composition is adopted in the OWL-S, and WSMO. Semantic composition is targeted specifically towards Semantic Web applications. We describe these two approaches further in Section 7.2.

The core Web Services technologies are summarized in Figure 7.3. Individual web services are managed by Web Servers that provide an environment in which services can be stored and invoked. A Web Server may manage a collection of web services inside a Service Container, as illustrated on the left of the diagram. Alternatively, a Web Server may manage only a single service as shown on the right. Every web service has an associated

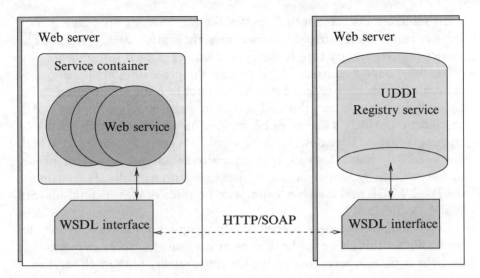

Figure 7.3 *Web services technologies.*

WSDL interface that specifies the types and operations of the service. The WSDL interface, together with a service description, can be stored in a UDDI registry. This is a special kind of service that can be used to locate services for specific tasks. Finally, web services are invoked remotely by message passing, typically using the SOAP and/or HTTP standards.

We note that the Web Services architecture is intended to be independent of any specific platform or programming language. In particular, web services can be defined in any programming language, provided that they can be invoked through a WSDL interface. A popular approach to constructing web services is the Java Web Services Development Pack (JWSDP) APIs. However, similar APIs have been defined for a wide variety of other programming languages.

7.3 Web service description language

From our discussion of Web Services technology, it should be apparent that the WSDL plays a critical role in many different activities. It is through this language that services are exposed to the network, and their internal implementation details are concealed. The WSDL document enables services to be invoked by external entities, and the WSDL document is central to the registration and discovery process. The WSDL also plays a major role in the different approaches to service composition. Consequently, we now examine this specification language in more detail.

To motivate our description of WSDL, we consider an example web service, taken from our photo-processing application in Figure 7.2. The service that we specify here is the upload service, which is responsible for uploading image files from the client into the processing application. For convenience, we have reduced this web service to a single operation called UploadFile. Nonetheless, this still results in a reasonably complex WSDL specification, which is shown in Figure 7.4. As with the other XML-based languages that we have described, we would not generally construct WSDL documents by hand. Instead, it is generally easier, and less error prone, to use tools to generate these specifications automatically. For example, the Java2WSDL tool converts from Java interface or class definitions into WSDL documents.

Every WSDL document is enclosed by a top-level <description> element. Within this element, the document contains four core elements that describe various aspects concerning the functionality of the web service:

1. `types` describes the format of the messages that the service will send and receive.
2. `interface` describes the operations that comprise the web service, and their argument types.
3. `binding` describes how the service will be accessed, e.g. using SOAP messages.
4. `service` describes the location of the service on the Web.

With WSDL documents, *namespaces* are particularly important as they are used to locate the web service itself, and to construct messages for service invocation. Therefore, our example contains a number of namespace definitions at the start of the document. In general, these namespaces should refer to real locations on the Web, i.e. they should be dereferenceable. We previously discussed the purpose of namespaces in Chapter 2. As before, we use the dummy www.mycamera.org domain for illustrative purposes.

The first namespace declaration xmlns defines the namespace for the WSDL standard itself: http://www.w3.org/2005/08/wsdl. This namespace will be used for elements in the document that do not have an explicit namespace prefix. The wsoap namespace references the SOAP bindings for WSDL, and the soap namespace references the main SOAP elements. We define these namespaces as our web service will be accessed using SOAP messages. The targetNamespace should reference the origin of the WSDL document. This is useful as the document may be copied to different locations. Finally, tns is a reference to the target namespace, and msgns is the namespace for the message types.

```
<?xml version="1.1"?>
<description xmlns="http://www.w3.org/2005/08/wsdl"
    xmlns:wsoap="http://www.w3.org/2005/08/wsdl/soap"
    xmlns:soap="http://www.w3.org/2003/05/soap-envelope"
    targetNamespace="http://www.mycamera.org/wsdl/uploadSvc"
    xmlns:tns="http://www.mycamera.org/wsdl/uploadSvc"
    xmlns:msgns="http://www.mycamera.org/schemas/uploadSvc">
  <types>
    <xsd:schema xmlns="http://www.mycamera.org/schemas/uploadSvc"
        xmlns:xsd="http://www.w3.org/2001/XMLSchema"
        targetNamespace="http://www.mycamera.org/schemas/uploadSvc">
      <xsd:element name="Upload" type="UploadType"/>
      <xsd:complexType name="UploadType">
        <xsd:sequence>
          <xsd:element name="fileLocation" type="xsd:anyURI"/>
          <xsd:element name="fileName" type="xsd:string"/>
          <xsd:element name="fileType" type="xsd:string"/>
        </xsd:sequence>
      </xsd:complexType>
      <xsd:element name="UploadResponse" type="xsd:boolean"/>
      <xsd:element name="InvalidFileError" type="xsd:string"/>
    </xsd:schema>
  </types>
  <interface name="UploadInterface">
    <fault name="InvalidFileFault" element="msgns:InvalidFileError"/>
    <operation name="UploadFile"
        pattern="http://www.w3.org/2005/08/wsdl/in-out"
        style="http://www.w3.org/2005/08/wsdl/style/iri">
      <input messageLabel="In" element="msgns:Upload"/>
      <output messageLabel="Out" element="msgns:UploadResponse"/>
      <outfault ref="tns:InvalidFileFault" messageLabel="Out"/>
    </operation>
  </interface>
  <binding name="UploadSOAPBinding" interface="tns:UploadInterface"
      type="http://www.w3.org/2005/08/wsdl/soap"
      wsoap:protocol="http://www.w3.org/2003/05/soap/bindings/HTTP">
    <fault ref="tns:InvalidFileFault" wsoap:code="soap:Sender"/>
    <operation ref="tns:UploadFile"
        wsoap:mep="http://www.w3.org/2003/05/soap/mep/soap-response"/>
  </binding>
  <service name="UploadService" interface="tns:UploadInterface">
    <endpoint name="UploadEndpoint" binding="tns:UploadSOAPBinding"
        address ="http://www.mycamera.org:8080/upload"/>
  </service>
</description>
```

Figure 7.4 *WSDL upload interface.*

XML Schema types are generally used to specify the input and output types of web services. However, there is nothing precluding the use of an alternative types language. The types language is indicated by the declaration of additional namespaces within the types element. The xsd namespace references the XML Schema language definitions, and the `targetNamespace` is the namespace for the types that we define. These types could be defined in an external document that is imported. However, we have chosen to include these type definitions directly in our specification.

Three separate message `types` are defined in our example. The `Upload` type is used for sending messages to the service. This type defines the input arguments, which are `fileLocation`, `fileName`, and `fileType`. The file location is given as a URI, while the file name and file type are supplied as strings. The `UploadResponse` type and `InvalidFileError` type are used by messages that are returned from the service. The former is a Boolean type indicating success or failure of the service, while the latter is a string type that can be used to return an error message indicating a specific problem with the file upload process.

The `interface` element is central to the WSDL specification, as it defines the abstract interface of a web service. This interface is specified as a set of operations that represent simple interactions between the client and the service. Operations are functionally equivalent to methods or procedures in other languages. Each `operation` in the interface specifies a message exchange *pattern*, which indicates the sequence that the messages are to be transmitted between the service and the client. The interface also specifies fault messages that will be used to indicate errors in the service, similar to exceptions in Java. All fault messages that can be generated by an operation must be explicitly specified.

We define an `UploadInterface` to describe our web service. This interface specifies a fault `InvalidFileFault`, and an `UploadFile` operation. A fault declaration comprises a name and an optional message type, and we use the `InvalidFileError` type that we previously defined. An operation is declared by stating a particular message style, and then providing elements that match this pattern. The `pattern` for our operation is defined as `in-out`, which is a standard request/response interaction. Other patterns are possible, e.g. `in-only`, but these are less commonly used. The `in-out` pattern has a single input and a single output with the labels `In` and `Out` respectively. Patterns may be defined with multiple inputs and outputs, and so the labels are used to disambiguate between these. Our operation is defined with the `iri` style, which ensures that the messages can be mapped to Internationalized Resource Identifiers (IRIs). Other common message styles are `rpc` and `multipart`. To complete the interface we simply specify the message types for the inputs and outputs, and reference any faults that may occur during the operation.

The purpose of the `binding` is to specify how messages will be exchanged with the service, i.e. what protocols should be used. This is distinct from the interface, which specifies what the messages should contain.

As previously noted, our service will be accessed by sending and receiving SOAP messages, and therefore we require a SOAP binding. A binding is defined for a specific interface and should specify the message details for every operation and fault in the interface.

In our example, we create a binding called `UploadSOAPBinding` that refers to the `UploadInterface`. Interfaces can have different or multiple bindings, though we do not use this feature here. The `type` parameter specifies that SOAP messages should be used, and the `protocol` parameter states that HTTP should be used as the underlying transmission protocol. Our fault message is given a `soap:Sender` error code, and our upload operation is given a `soap-response` message exchange pattern (`mep`) that corresponds to a request/response interaction. These specifications are rather cryptic, but will be the same in most WSDL documents.

The `service` element completes the WSDL specification by stating where to find the web service for which the document was created. It combines all of the information that has previously been specified together with a list of *endpoints* where the service can be accessed. A service can only have one interface. However, multiple endpoints can be defined, each of which must declare a binding to indicate the necessary transmission protocols. In our example, there is a single endpoint, and this references a dummy web location and port.

7.4 Knowledge services

In our discussion of the Web Services architecture, we have now described all of the main technologies. However, we have yet to detail how these technologies relate directly to the Semantic Web, and the kinds of problems that we are trying to solve. In our overview of SOA, we stated that this style of architecture is key to the construction of applications on the Semantic Web. In the remainder of the chapter, we take a more detailed look at how these applications may be constructed.

The use of a Web Services architecture is an important step towards the construction of a computer-oriented Web. This architecture enables information to be accessed through standard procedure-based mechanisms, rather than through screen-scraping of websites. Although this is still a long way from the full Semantic Web vision, this is an important step as it provides a context for the Web-based information, and allows this information to be automatically processed.

The relationship between Web Services and the Semantic Web is very straightforward. In essence, web services are used directly to encapsulate knowledge-based components, such as problem solving methods, reasoning systems, and agents. A web service that is used in this way is termed a *knowledge service*, or a Semantic Web Service. As stated in Chapter 1, there are essentially two different kinds of knowledge services: those that *provide* knowledge, and those that *transform* knowledge. The first kind of service is used to obtain knowledge, e.g. to access a resource such as a knowledge base. The second kind of service performs computation on the knowledge, e.g. to perform a particular kind of inference on a collection of knowledge. Some knowledge services may be both knowledge providers and transformers, e.g. agents.

Semantic Web *applications* are constructed by composing together knowledge services. We can view our example application in Figure 7.2 from a knowledge-based perspective. The client can be viewed as a knowledge provider, as they provide the initial photo file and processing options. The remaining photo-processing services can be viewed as knowledge transformers as they apply various transformations over the photo and options, which eventually result in the printed image. In the remainder of this chapter, we focus on two key questions:

1.   How can we encapsulate rational and communicative agents as knowledge services?
2.   How do we actually compose together knowledge services to construct Semantic Web applications?

7.4.1   Web services and agents

At an intuitive level, the Web Services architecture would appear to be an ideal platform on which to support executable MASs. If we can represent agents, or groups of agents, as web services, then we will obtain an environment in which MAS can be rapidly constructed and deployed in a Web environment using existing off-the-shelf technologies. This has certain advantages over specialized agent deployment architectures such as FIPA-OS and JADE. For example, direct compatibility between agents and existing web services. Moreover, the representation of agents as web services may in turn lead to a more widespread adoption of multiagent techniques on the Web in general. To illustrate how Web Services may be used as a platform for the deployment of MAS, Figure 7.5 outlines the key multiagent techniques, and their approximate Web Services equivalents.

Despite the apparent similarities between multiagent techniques and Web Services technologies, there are some important challenges that must be addressed if we are to successfully unite the two. An agent is generally designed to be a computational abstraction for a human entity and as such is assumed to encompass complex behaviours such as autonomy,

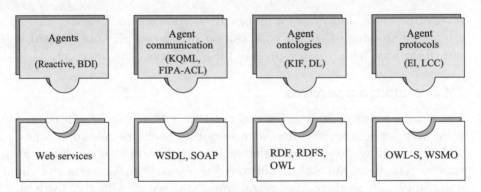

Figure 7.5 *Conceptual similarities between MAS and WS.*

rationality, and independence. By contrast, a web service is typically assumed to comprise straightforward computational procedures, with passive and predictable behaviours.

From an engineering perspective, it is relatively straightforward to construct a web service that encapsulates the behaviour of a single rational agent. For example, we can readily engineer a web service that contains decision procedures, or a planning system, as found in a typical reactive-style agent. However, it is important that these behaviours are appropriately tailored for execution on the Web. In particular, web services should not have long execution times, or make excessive resource demands, as they may be invoked many times from many different locations. This may preclude the representation of certain kinds of agents as web services, e.g. deductive theorem-proving agents.

The key challenges of constructing a MAS with Web Services technology are encountered when we attempt to combine together individual web services. At this point, the inflexible nature of the Web Services architecture becomes apparent, primarily due to the requirements of the agents communicative processes. Interaction between web services is accomplished by the invocation of one service by another. By contrast, in a MAS we often need to define long-lived communications, or complex communication patterns such as broadcast and multicast. These behaviours are difficult to support within the current Web Services architecture.

In a Web Services architecture, we must normally define the topology of the system in advance. Every service needs to know precisely which other services it will communicate with, and this information will be statically encoded into the service itself. There is currently no standard mechanism for informing a service, at run time, about other services with which it should communicate. By contrast, MASs typically have a dynamic topology, where agents gather together into groups or societies to cooperate on specific tasks, and these groupings are not known in advance. This is essentially an issue of service composition, which we previously noted is one of the least understood aspects of the Web Services architecture.

7.4.2 Multiagent services

There are a number of different ways in which MAS can be constructed using Web Services architecture. We now outline three possible approaches, and discuss how they address the various challenges that we have described. The first approach is illustrated in Figure 7.6. We term this the *naive approach* as there are several important issues with this method, which mean that no real systems are constructed in this way. Nonetheless, it is instructive to examine this approach as a motivation for the alternatives that we present.

We can summarize the key challenges by stating that the Web Services architecture does not provide a sufficiently rich model of communication and coordination for the construction of MASs. The naive approach attempts to address this deficiency directly, by equipping each web service with some extra functionality for communication and coordination. We term this extra functionality the *agent stub*, as it provides agent-like communicative behaviours to each web service. We do not go into details on the internals of this stub here as this is orthogonal to our discussion. However, we note that there are two significant issues that relate to the use of stubs:

1. Agent stubs necessitate the direct modification of the web services. We are in essence converting web services into a kind of agent and thereby breaking compatibility with existing web services, and Web Service

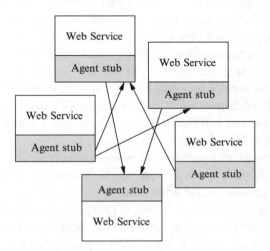

Figure 7.6 *Multiagent Web services.*

architecture. Any web service wishing to participate in the MAS must be extended with the agent stub. However, a key advantage of both MAS and the Web Services architecture is that they permit interoperation between external entities that are not under direct control. It is infeasible for any new approach to require the modification of third-party services before interaction can be performed. By requiring that all of the services be modified for a specific technique, we are in effect returning to a specialized agent architecture. Ideally, we would like an approach to coordination that does not require modification of all the web services involved.

2. In general, agent stubs provide a common set of functionality to the web services, and are essentially identical in implementation. However, web services may be created in a variety of different languages and on different operating platforms. Consequently, the agent stub may need to be repeatedly re-implemented in the language of the web service. Ensuring that the agent stubs implemented in different languages provide the same functionality and are completely compatible is a non-trivial task. Again, it is clear that the modification of the web services will create significant issues in this approach.

An alternative to the naive approach is presented in Figure 7.7. We term this the *gateway approach* as the central feature in this model is a gateway between the agents and the web services. The rationale in this approach is to keep the agents and web services as separate entities: the agents continue to be executed using a traditional agent architecture, and the web services use an unmodified Web Services architecture. A gateway is defined that permits communication between systems defined using either approach. From

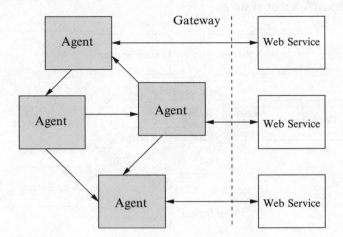

Figure 7.7 *Web service integration gateway.*

the web services perspective, the gateway appears as just another service, and from the agents perspective, the gateway is just another agent. This permits web services to access the agent system, and for agents to access web services. An exemplar of this approach is the Web Services Integration Gateway (WSIG), which has been defined for the JADE agent platform. The AgentScape system also has a similar notion of a web service gateway.

The gateway approach avoids the need to alter the Web Services architecture, which was the key issue in the naive approach. This enables third-party web services to be readily incorporated into the agent systems. Similarly, existing agent systems can be adapted to use web services with a minimum of effort. Nonetheless, the use of a gateway is effectively a centralized solution, which runs contrary to the principles of multiagent construction. For example, a failure in the gateway may prevent messages from being exchanged. Similarly, the gateway may itself become a communication bottleneck, particularly if our systems are constructed from large numbers of agents or services.

The final approach, which we term the *service approach*, is illustrated in Figure 7.8. This approach has a similar structure to the gateway approach, but removes the communication bottleneck, and the need for a specialized agent architecture. The service approach is based entirely on existing Web Services technology. This permits different agent reasoning techniques to be used, and third-party services can be readily incorporated. This approach is founded on the notion of an artificial social system, as described in Chapter 6. Agents are grouped together into societies, and communication only occurs within a society. The use of a society enables large agent systems to be constructed, and provides a controlled environment for agent interaction in a web services environment. The exemplar of this approach is the MagentA agent system.

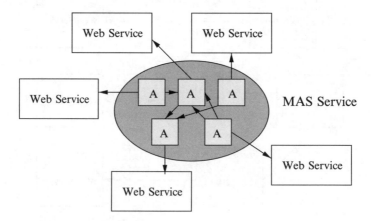

Figure 7.8 *Multiagent Web services.*

Each agent in the service approach is represented by a web service, and one or more *proxies*, which are marked A in our diagram. These proxies are responsible for the communicative processes of the agent. Each web service encapsulates the knowledge and reasoning capabilities of a specific agent, which are expressed as decision procedures. At the core of the approach are *MAS Services*, which enable the proxies to interact. MAS services are regular web services that internally contain an agent communication environment. These services can be considered as institutions, which define rules that govern the agent interactions. All of the complex agent interaction happens within the MAS Service, while the external web services containing the decision procedures are accessed using standard RPC.

Although the MAS services impose some central control on the MAS, the approach is still scalable. This is because an institution will typically only contain a small number of agents that directly interact, even in a large MAS. Figure 7.9 shows how large systems can be constructed from multiple MAS services. These services may define different institutions, or separate instances of the same institution. Furthermore, a single agent can participate in multiple institutions at the same time. That is, the proxies for a web service can reside inside different MAS services. Consequently, the service approach can be considered as a P2P model for implementing MASs in a Web Services architecture.

7.4.3 Agent-based service composition

We have now presented a high-level description of the service approach to MASs construction. This approach enables agents to be constructed from web services, and integrated into social systems by means of MAS services. However, we note that this approach can be extended beyond

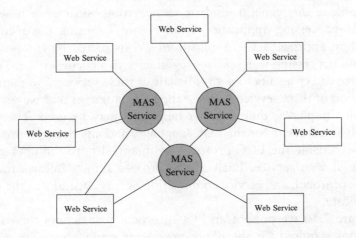

Figure 7.9 *Multiagent Web service systems.*

MASs construction, and used to provide a general solution for web service composition. We term this technique *agent-based* service composition as it is founded on methods from MASs. The agent-based approach is a useful alternative to workflow and structural composition techniques, and is complementary to the semantic style of service composition that we discuss in Section 7.2. The agent-based approach is directly relevant to the construction of Semantic Web applications that include both agents and knowledge services. Hence, we now provide a more detailed account of this approach to service composition.

To recap, the core of the service approach to multiagent construction is the provision of MAS Services. MAS Services define institutions, and these institutions provide a social framework in which proxy agents can cooperate on specific tasks. The proxy agents act on behalf of external agents, and these external agents are defined as web services. Each web service contains a set of decision procedures that supply the agents' behaviour. A key advantage of this approach is that it does not mandate any particular model of agency. For example, the decision procedures of one agent may be implemented using the BDI approach, while another agent may be purely reactive.

The key observation that allows us to define general-purpose service composition is that there is nothing in the architecture which mandates that the external services are actually agents. All that required is that the external services supply the proxies with a set of procedures. All web services are constructed as a set of procedures (i.e. operations), and therefore the proxies can interact with any kind of service. In this general approach, the proxies are simply responsible for passing the correct arguments to the external services, and service composition is accomplished through the pattern of interaction between the proxies.

To illustrate this general kind of service composition, we now define our photo-processing application from Figure 7.2 using the agent-based composition approach. The application is constructed by composing the four photo-processing web services together with a client service. Thus, we require five proxy agents to act on behalf of these services. To express the composition of these services, we use the LCC language that we previously defined in Chapter 6, though other languages may be used. The proxies are simply interpreters for the LCC language, and any decision procedures that appear inside the LCC protocol are mapped onto the operations in the external web service. Each of the proxies simply follows their role inside the protocol, and service composition occurs naturally as the proxies communicate.

In Figure 7.10 we present an LCC protocol that defines the roles and interactions required for the photo-processing application. The protocol

```
1  imaging_scene[
2    %client{
3      method(main) =
4        $file = getFile() then $opts = getOptions()
5        then request(upload, $file, $opts) => agent(_, %upload)
6        then waitfor(inform(uploaded, $id) <= agent($up, %upload))
7        then waitfor(request(fee, $id, $value) <= agent($pay, %payment))
8        then $money = getMoney($value)
9        then inform(pay, $id, $money) => agent($pay, %payment)
10       then waitfor(inform(paid, $id) <= agent($pay, %payment))
11       then waitfor(inform(complete, $id, $out) <= agent($up, %upload))}
12   %upload{
13     method(main) =
14       waitfor (request(upload, $file, $opts) <= agent($client, %client))
15       then $id = uploadFile($file, $opts)
16       then inform(uploaded, $id) => agent($client, %client)
17       then request(fee, $id, $opts, $client) => agent(_, %payment)
18       then waitfor (inform(paid, $id, $client) <= agent(_, %payment))
19       then $img = getImage($id)
20       then request(process, $id, $img, $opts) => agent(_, %imaging)
21       then waitfor (inform(image, $id, $newimage) <= agent(_, %imaging))
22       then request (print, $id, $newimage, $opts) => agent(_, %printing)
23       then waitfor (inform(printed, $id, $out) <= agent(_, %printing))
24       then inform(complete, $id, $out) => agent($client, %client)}
25   %payment{
26     method(main) =
27       waitfor(request(fee, $id, $opts, $client) <= agent($up, %upload))
28       then $value = getPrice($opts)
29       then request(fee, $id, $opts, $value) => agent($client, %client)
30       then waitfor (inform(pay, $id, $money) <= agent($client, %client))
31       then setPaid($id, $client, $opts, $money)
32       then inform(paid, $id) => agent($client, %client)
33       then inform(paid, $id, $client) => agent($up, %upload)}
34   %imaging{
35     method(main) =
36       waitfor(request(process, $id, $img, $opts) <= agent($up, %upload))
37       then $newimage = processImage($id, $img, $opts)
38       then inform(image, $id, $newimage) => agent($up, %upload)}
39   %printing{
40     method(main) =
41       waitfor(request(print, $id, $img, $opts) <= agent($up, %upload))
42       then $out = printImage($img, $opts)
43       then inform(printed, $id, $out) => agent($up, %upload)}]
```

Figure 7.10 *LCC service composition.*

assumes the existence of five external web services, whose interfaces are shown in Table 7.1. Each interface is defined by a list of operations and their types. To make our example more readable, we present these interfaces at an abstract level, rather than defining a lengthy WSDL document for each service. Consequently, the types in this table are assigned descriptive names, rather than XML Schema types. For example,

Table 7.1 *Service interfaces and operations.*

Service	Operation	Argument Types
Client	getFile	unit → file
	getOptions	unit → options
	getMoney	price → money
Upload	uploadFile	file × options → id
	getImage	id → image
Payment	getPrice	options → price
	setPaid	id × client × options × money → unit
Imaging	processImage	id × image × options → image
Printing	printImage	image × options → output

we use price instead of xsd:decimal. In this abstract representation, the input and output types are separated by →, multiple arguments are separated with ×, and the unit type is used to indicate that there are no arguments.

Our interface definitions are intended to represent the minimum functionality that each of the five services would provide. These operations are clearly simpler than we would require in a real implementation. For example, we have defined an options type that encapsulates all of the image processing options. In a real implementation there would likely be a collection of operations for setting all of the different image parameters. Similarly, we treat money as a simple value that can be transferred from one place to another. However, in reality the exchange of money from one service to another would generally require complex authentications mechanisms. Nonetheless, our example is intended to represent a plausible service composition scenario.

The interfaces in Table 7.1 contain nine operations that have the following informal meanings. The Client service provides a getFile operation to represent the retrieval of an image file for upload, and a getOptions operation as a means to retrieve the options that will be applied to the image. The getMoney operation is used to retrieve a particular quantity of money. The upload service provides an uploadFile operation to represent the upload of an image file, and a getImage operation for subsequent retrieval of the uploaded image. The Payment service provides a getPrice operation that calculates the price for a specific set of options. The setPaid operation is used to record the payment by a specific client for a particular job. The Imaging service defines a processImage operation, which performs preprocessing on an image according to the options and returns the processed image. Finally, the printing service defines a printImage operation that represents the actual printing process.

The LCC protocol for the photo-processing application defines a single scene, called `imaging_scene`, inside which the proxy agents will interact. Each of the five proxy agents will be assigned the appropriate role from the protocol. There are five roles defined in our protocol: `%client`, `%upload`, `%payment`, `%imaging`, and `%printing`. Each of these roles is defined by a single main method, which comprises a sequence of protocol steps. To make the protocol readable, we have removed the steps for handling errors. We note that the services are stateless, and the protocol may be enacted simultaneously by many clients. Therefore, we use a unique job identifier `id` to identify the client at each stage of the process. The protocol steps in each of the five roles are described informally below:

1. The `client` role defines a sequence of actions that the client must perform in order to interact successfully with the photo-processing application. The order of these actions must be observed, or the interaction will be unsuccessful. Before an upload can be performed, the client must obtain the photo file, and decide on the processing options. These actions are represented by the invocation of the `getPhoto` and `getOptions` operations in line 4. The client should then upload the file and options to the upload service, which is accomplished by the transmission of a request message to the service in line 5. The protocol states that the upload service will inform the client once the upload has been completed. Therefore, the client waits for this acknowledgement in line 6. Before image processing and printing can be performed, the client must make a payment. Therefore, the client waits for a message from the payment service in line 7, which contains the required payment amount. A payment is made by invoking the `getMoney` operation in line 8, and sending the result to the payment service in line 9. The client waits for an acknowledgement of the payment in line 10, and then waits for an acknowledgement that the photo has been printed in line 11. At this point the photo processing is finished, and the client protocol terminates.

2. The majority of interactions in the application occur between the client and the upload service. Thus, the protocol for the upload role defines the core of the application. The application begins by the receipt of a message from the client in line 14. This message contains the image file, and the processing options. The upload service acts as an image storage database for the application, and the image is stored by the `uploadFile` operation, which is invoked in line 15. An `id` is assigned to the image to enable later retrieval, and to identify the image in subsequent interactions. The client is informed of a successful upload in line 16, and a `fee` message is sent to the payment service in line 17

to request a payment from the client. The upload service waits in line 18 until notified that the client has paid. The image is then retrieved by the getImage operation in line 19, and sent to the imaging service for processing in line 20. The processed image is returned to the upload service by a message in line 21, and then forwarded in another message to the printing service in line 22. Once the image has been printed, a printed message is returned to the upload service in line 23, and finally a completed message is sent back to the client.

3. The payment role is defined in lines 25 to 33. The payment service begins in line 27 by the receipt of a fee message from the upload service. This message contains the image processing options, $opts, which are used by the getPrice operation in line 28 to determine the transaction value. In line 29, a fee message is sent to the client informing them of the required payment. As previously noted, we represent the payment process simply by the passing of a value. Thus, the client returns the required value in line 30 using a pay message. The payment is checked and recorded in line 31 by the setPaid operation, and the client is informed that they have paid in line 32. Finally, a paid message is sent back to the upload service in line 33, so that the image processing and printing can be initiated.

4. The imaging and printing roles are very straightforward. In both cases, these roles are initiated by the receipt of a message from the upload service containing the image file and the image options. In the former case, the image is processed by the processImage oper-ation, and in the latter case the image is printed by the printImage operation. A message is subsequently sent back to the upload service indicating the successful completion of the task.

As we have previously stated, Semantic Web applications are constructed through a process of service composition. We have now shown how this composition process can be specified by the definition of LCC protocols, and realized through MAS services. LCC protocols can be considered as pre-prepared *plans* for achieving service composition. MAS services can be configured in advance with LCC protocols and will then perform specific tasks. Alternative approaches to agent-based composition are also possible, e.g. the conversion of AUML protocols into WS-BPEL definitions. However, these approaches are primarily a manual activities as the relevant services must be identified directly, and the initial protocols must be con-structed by hand.

In the remainder of this chapter we describe two approaches that provide a framework for automated service composition. Both of these approaches are based on the definition ontologies which classify knowledge services.

The intention is that service composition can be automatically realized by reasoning over these ontologies. We term this approach semantic composition, as it is tailored specifically towards Semantic Web application construction.

7.5 Service ontologies

In the semantic composition approach, every knowledge service is classified according to a standard ontology, which is called a *service ontology*. The knowledge that is defined in this classification is used to supplement the WSDL interface definition of the service. This is necessary, as the WSDL interface only specifies the input and output types of a service; it does not ascribe meanings to these types, or describe the functionality of the service itself. For example, the WSDL input to a service will be of the form xsd:string, and not **FirstName**. Additional knowledge is required if we are to perform any meaningful automated service composition. In particular, if we were simply to compose services by type name, this would be unlikely to result in useful applications. Consequently, a service ontology is used to classify each service into meaningful categories based on the functionality of the service. We note that this additional knowledge is also intended to support the invocation and discovery of knowledge services, principally through automated methods that are termed *semantic matchmaking*.

We describe two different kinds of service ontology in this chapter. The first of these is the OWL-S. This is a service ontology for classifying knowledge services, defined using the OWL standard. However, there are a number of important facets of knowledge services that cannot readily be defined in OWL. For example, the preconditions and effects of services are expressed using logical formulae. Thus, the knowledge that is expressed in OWL-S ontologies cannot be fully utilized by standard OWL reasoning tools, and additional techniques are required to support fully automated service composition. The second approach that we describe is the WSMO. This is also an ontology for classifying knowledge services. However, WSMO avoids the representational issues of the OWL-S approach by defining the ontology using an F-Logic. The F-Logic provides a natural representation for both ontological notions and logical rules. We previously presented an overview of F-Logic in Chapter 5. Nonetheless, as discussed previously, tools to support efficient reasoning in F-Logic are still in their infancy.

It is important to emphasize that the ontological approaches that we describe here are complementary to the service-based techniques that we have defined previously. For example, OWL-S descriptions are directly grounded on WSDL interface definitions, and assume that services are invoked with SOAP messages. Similarly, both techniques can be used in conjunction with MAS services and LCC protocols to provide agents with additional knowledge about the services with which they are interacting.

7.5.1 OWL service ontology

In Chapter 1, we briefly outlined the concepts at the top-level of the OWL-S ontology, which are illustrated in Figure 7.11. To recap, OWL-S defines four top-level concepts. A *service* is classified by the ontology into three key categories: the profile, the model, and the grounding. The profile describes what the service does in order to advertise the service. The model details how the service works so that we can perform composition. Finally, the grounding specifies how to access the service so that invocation can be performed. There are two cardinality restrictions associated with these concepts. A service can be described by at most one model, and a single grounding is required for each service. No such restrictions are placed on the profile. A service may be described by multiple profiles, which tailor the service to particular application areas. For example, our example photo-processing service may be described as both a printing service, and a photo storage facility.

In the following presentation of OWL-S, we provide a broad overview of the key features of the language. A complete description of the language can be found in the Suggested Reading at the end of the chapter. Our overview is motivated by the provision of an OWL-S specification for the photo upload service. This specification is intended to match the WSDL interface that we defined previously in Figure 7.4.

The first part of the specification that we define is the top-level service description for our upload service. This description is shown in Figure 7.12. The majority of this description is occupied by the namespace declarations that we will use when constructing our OWL-S description. These

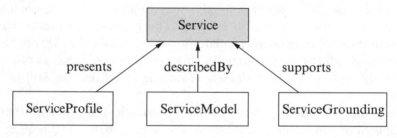

Figure 7.11   *OWL-S top-level ontology.*

```
<?xml version="1.1"?>
<!DOCTYPE uridef[
  <!ENTITY rdf "http://www.w3.org/1999/02/22-rdf-syntax-ns">
  <!ENTITY rdfs "http://www.w3.org/2000/01/rdf-schema">
  <!ENTITY owl "http://www.w3.org/2002/07/owl">
  <!ENTITY xsd "http://www.w3.org/2001/XMLSchema">
  <!ENTITY service "http://www.daml.org/services/owl-s/1.1/Service.owl">
  <!ENTITY profile "http://www.daml.org/services/owl-s/1.1/Profile.owl">
  <!ENTITY process "http://www.daml.org/services/owl-s/1.1/Process.owl">
  <!ENTITY grounding "http://www.daml.org/services/owl-s/1.1/Grounding.owl">
  <!ENTITY actor "http://www.daml.org/services/owl-s/1.1/ActorDefault.owl">
  <!ENTITY up_service "http://www.mycamera.org/owl-s/UpService.owl">
  <!ENTITY up_profile "http://www.mycamera.org/owl-s/UpProfile.owl">
  <!ENTITY up_process "http://www.mycamera.org/owl-s/UpProcess.owl">
  <!ENTITY up_grounding "http://www.mycamera.org/owl-s/UpGrounding.owl">
  <!ENTITY up_wsdl "http://www.mycamera.org/wsdl/UploadSvc.wsdl">
  <!ENTITY camera "http://www.mycamera.org/photo">]>

<rdf:RDF xmlns:rdf="&rdf;" xmlns:rdfs="&rdfs;" xmlns:owl="&owl;"
         xmlns:xsd="&xsd;" xmlns:service="&service;" xmlns:profile="&profile;"
         xmlns:process="&process;" xmlns:grounding="&grounding;"
         xmlns:actor="&actor;" xmlns:up_service="&up_service;"
         xmlns:up_process="&up_process;" xmlns:up_profile="&profile;"
         xmlns:up_grounding="&up_grounding;" xmlns:up_wsdl="&up_wsdl;"
         xmlns:camera="&camera;" xmls="&service;" xmlsn:base="&service;">

  <owl:Ontology rdf:about="">
    <owl:imports rdf:resource="&service;"/>
    <owl:imports rdf:resource="&up_profile;"/>
    <owl:imports rdf:resource="&up_process;"/>
    <owl:imports rdf:resource="&up_grounding;"/>
  </owl:Ontology>

  <service:Service rdf:ID="UploadAgent">
    <service:presents rdf:resource="&up_profile;#UploadProfile"/>
    <service:describedBy rdf:resource="&up_process;#UploadProcess"/>
    <service:supports rdf:resource="&up_grounding;#UploadGrounding"/>
  </service:Service>

</rdf:RDF>
```

Figure 7.12 *OWL-S service description.*

declarations are assumed to be included in all of the OWL-S definitions that we subsequently define. The OWL-S ontology itself requires four separate namespace definitions: service, profile, process, and grounding. The namespaces preceded by up are specific instances of these concepts for our upload service. The remaining namespace declarations have been explained previously.

The actual service description in Figure 7.12 is defined by the Service element. We describe our service as an UploadAgent, and link this description to the three core parts by the presents, describedBy, and supports elements. We present a detailed description of these three parts in the remainder of this section.

7.5.2 OWL-S profile description

The primary purpose of a service profile is to advertise the service to external entities. These entities may be either human, or computational. Therefore, a service profile can contain both human-readable, and machine-readable descriptions of a service. There is an implicit assumption in OWL-S that a registry model is used to advertise the service, such as the UDDI registry for web services. Thus, the profile is effectively a self-contained document that can be copied and exchanged. As previously noted, a service can be described by different profiles, which may advertise different capabilities of the service.

OWL-S is intended to facilitate the automatic discovery of services, though it does not mandate how this automated discovery should be performed. Therefore, the machine-readable part of the service profile can specify the functionality of the service at varying levels of detail. This is intended to allow various different discovery methods to be used, e.g. matchmaking, planning, and reasoning. A profile is principally a *black box* description of a service. That is, the service is described in terms of its external behaviour, rather than its internal implementation.

The external behaviour of a service is defined in the profile by a functional description of the service. This is expressed firstly by an *information transformation* from inputs to outputs. That is, the profile specifies the inputs required by the service, and the outputs generated from the service. These inputs and outputs are specified by ontological concepts, rather than types as in the WSDL interface. Secondly, the *state change* of the service can be expressed by defining conditions that must be met before the service is invoked, and the effect on the state of invoking the service. Specifically, the profile specifies the preconditions and effects of the service. The functional description of a service in terms of its inputs, outputs, preconditions, and effects is called the IOPE description of a service.

In addition to the functional IOPE description, a profile also allows the specification of non-functional properties (NFP) of a service. These are properties that may influence the choice of the service when alternatives are available, but are not directly related to the IOPE functionality. There are two classes of NFP that can be defined in OWL-S:

1. The *category* of the service can be defined with respect to some existing standard ontology or taxonomy. For example, a service can be classified according to the United Nations Standard Products and Services Code (UNSPSC) taxonomy.
2. An unbounded list of *parameters* can be associated with a service. For example, quality of service, response time, and geographical location.

OWL-S does not place any restrictions on the types of parameters that can be represented.

We define an example service profile for our upload service in Figure 7.13. The presentedBy element provides a link from the profile back to the parent service description. Similarly, the has_process element links the profile to the model description. The serviceName, textDescription, and contactInformation elements form the human-readable part of the profile. These optional parts are intended to provide additional information about the service, e.g. for submitting bug reports, but are not intended to be used in automated discovery.

```
<service:presentedBy rdf:resource="&up_service;#UploadAgent"/>
<profile:has_process rdf:resource="&up_process;#UploadProcess"/>

<profile:serviceName>Photo Upload Service</profile:serviceName>
<profile:textDescription>
  This service provides a facility to upload a photograph file from
  a client to a photograph processing system.
</profile:textDescription>

<profile:contactInformation>
  <actor:Actor rdf:ID="MyCameraServices">
    <actor:name>MyCamera Company</actor:name>
    <actor:title>Upload Service</actor:title>
    <actor:email>services@myphoto.org</actor:email>
    <actor:webURL>http://www.mycamera.org/</actor:webURL>
  </actor:Actor>
</profile:contactInformation>

<profile:hasInput rdf:resource="&up_process;#FileLocation"/>
<profile:hasInput rdf:resource="&up_process;#FileName"/>
<profile:hasInput rdf:resource="&up_process;#FileType"/>
<profile:hasOutput rdf:resource="&up_process;#UploadResponse"/>
<profile:hasResult rdf:resource="&up_process;#UploadResult"/>

<profile:serviceParameter>
  <profile:serviceParameterName rdf:datatype="&xsd;#string">Region
  </profile:serviceParameterName>
  <profile:sParameter rdf:resource="&camera;#EuropeRegion"/>
</profile:ServiceParameter>

<profile:serviceCategory>
  <profile:categoryName rdf:datatype="&xsd;#string">DigitalProcessor
  </profile:categoryName>
  <profile:taxonomy rdf:datatype="&xsd;#anyURI">
    http://www.mycamera.org/processors.owl
  </profile:taxonomy>
  <profile:value>MyCamera Processor</profile:value>
  <profile:code>65536</profile:code>
</profile:serviceCategory>
```

Figure 7.13 *OWL-S profile description.*

The machine-readable part of the profile is provided by the `hasInput`, `hasOutput`, and `hasResult` elements. These elements specify the IOPE description of the service. We do not require any preconditions in our profile, but these would be defined using a `hasPrecondition` element. Our IOPE elements are simply links to the process model that we define later. In general, the IOPE descriptions in the profile will directly match those in the process model. However, it is possible to define different IOPEs in the profile, e.g. to customize the advertised description for specific applications.

Our example also defines two NFP. The first of these is a `serviceParameter` which states that the region for the service is Europe. This could be used by some external mechanism to restrict the service to clients in Europe. The second is a `serviceCategory` definition, which classifies the service as a Digital Processor within an imaginary `processors.owl` taxonomy. This classification may be used by some external mechanism to locate photo processors in different categories, e.g. digital, film, transparency.

7.5.3 OWL-S process model

The OWL-S process model is intended to describe how a service works, so that it can be used by external entities and composed with other services. Just as with the profile, OWL-S does not mandate how these tasks should be performed, but enables the service to be described in ways that are compatible with existing methods. This is accomplished by treating a service as a *process*, and specifying these processes in ways that are compatible with planning languages, workflow systems, and process modelling techniques.

A process in OWL-S should be viewed as a specification of the interactions between the service and a client, not as a program to be executed. OWL-S defines two kinds of processes: *atomic* processes and *composite* processes. An atomic process is a specification that takes an input and returns an output. Atomic processes are specified using IOPEs, as described in our discussion of service profiles. A composite process is a specification of a task that is enacted by a set of atomic processes. This will typically involve many interactions with the client, where each message from the client will advance the task. Composite processes are specified using a *task model* that we describe later.

We begin by discussing the specification of atomic processes, which correspond directly to services that can be invoked. This specification is essentially a definition of the IOPEs for the service. However, these definitions are not straightforward to define, as they cannot be completely represented in the standard OWL framework. In particular, IOPEs are defined using variables, but we recall from Chapter 5 that OWL is based on DLs that do not have variables. Thus, OWL-S defines a Parameter class that corresponds to variables in SWRL, and the Input and Output of a service are defined as subclasses of Parameter:

```
<owl:Class rdf:about="#Parameter">
  <rdfs:subClassOf rdf:resource="&swrl;#Variable"/>
</owl:Class>

<owl:Class rdf:ID="Input">
  <rdfs:subClassOf rdf:resource="#Parameter"
</owl:Class>
<owl:Class rdf:ID="Output">
  <rdfs:subClassOf rdf:resource="#Parameter"
</owl:Class>
```

An additional issue with the definition of parameters to represent variables is that OWL (and SWRL) have no notion of scope. Thus, by default all of the parameters that we define will have global scope. However, this can cause problems when we define composite processes as our definitions can be recursive. Thus, OWL-S defines an additional class of parameters called *local* parameters that are scoped to the process in which they are used, and are defined as follows:

```
<owl:Class rdf:ID="Local">
  <rdfs:subClassOf rdf:resource="#Parameter"/>
</owl:Class>
```

There is also an issue with the representation of preconditions and effects in OWL-S. These notions are taken from planning systems, and specified using logical formulae as discussed in Chapter 4. However, these logical formulae cannot be natively represented in OWL. Thus, OWL-S hides these formulae inside literals, and leaves their interpretation to the external tools that use the specification. For example, we can represent preconditions in OWL-S using PDDL notation as follows:

```
<hasPrecondition>
  <expr:PDDL-Expression>
    <expr:expressionBody rdf:parseType="Literal">
    (and (active ?client) (active ?upload)
         (knowabout ?client ?server))
    </expr:expressionBody>
  </expr:PDDL-Expression>
</hasPrecondition>
```

Preconditions and effects are defined by conditions expressed in a logical expressions language. This is indicated by the expr namespace in our example. Typically, these expressions will use the KIF, SWRL, or DRS

languages rather than PDDL. As shown in our example, it is often necessary to talk about the actual agents that are involved in the interaction.
OWL-S allows us to define these agents using `hasParticipant` definitions,
where the participant can be any OWL object. The OWL-S definitions for
conditions and participants are shown below:

```
<owl:Class rdf:ID="Condition">
  <owl:subClassOf rdf:resource="&expr;#Expression">
</owl:Class>

<owl:Class rdf:ID="hasParticipant">
  <rdfs:domain rdf:resource="#Process">
</owl:Class>
```

The OWL-S process model does not directly connect processes to their
effects. This is because, in practice, effects are often dependent on context.
For example, our photo upload service may either succeed or fail. In the
former case, the effect is that the file is transferred from the client to the
service, and in the latter case the service fails and there is no effect. Thus,
rather than specify the service for each possible output and effect, we
simply specify the service in terms of a result variable. This result variable
represents a coupled output and effect, and is specified by a `Result`, which
is another subclass of `Parameter`.

In summary, atomic processes in OWL-S are specified by their IOPEs,
which are represented by the types shown in Table 7.2. Inputs and
outputs are defined with `hasInput` and `hasOutput` respectively, and
are specified using `Input` and `Output` parameters. Preconditions are
defined with `hasPrecondition`, and specified by literal expressions. Effects are captured by results, and are defined by `hasResult`. Local variables are defined by `hasLocal`, and participants by `hasParticipant`
respectively.

We define an example process model for our upload service in Figure 7.14. This process model specifies an atomic process with three inputs, an output, and a result. These specifications match the profile that

Table 7.2 *OWL-S process specification.*

Property	Range	Type
hasInput	Input	Parameter
hasOutput	Output	Parameter
hasPrecondition	Condition	Expression
hasResult	Result	Parameter
hasLocal	Local	Parameter
hasParticipant	Participant	Thing

```
<process:AtomicProcess rdf:ID="UploadProcess">
  <process:hasInput>
    <process:Input rdf:ID="FileLocation">
      <process:parameterType rdf:datatype="&xsd;#anyURI">
      &camera;#PhotoLocation</process:parameterType>
    </process:Input>
  </process:hasInput>
  <process:hasInput>
    <process:Input rdf:ID="FileName">
      <process:parameterType rdf:datatype="&xsd;#string">
      &camera;#PhotoName</process:parameterType>
    </process:Input>
  </process:hasInput>
  <process:hasInput>
    <process:Input rdf:ID="FileType">
      <process:parameterType rdf:datatype="&xsd;#string">
      &camera;#PhotoType</process:parameterType>
    </process:Input>
  </process:hasInput>

  <process:hasOutput>
    <process:Output rdf:ID="UploadResponse">
      <process:parameterType rdf:datatype="&xsd;#boolean">
      &camera;#PhotoResponse</process:parameterType>
    </process:Output>
  </process:hasOutput>

  <process:hasResult>
    <process:Result rdf:ID="UploadResult">
      <process:withOutput>
        <process:OutputBinding>
          <process:toParam rdf:resource="#UploadResponse"/>
          <process:valueData rdf:datatype="&xsd;#boolean">true
          </process:valueData>
        </process:OutputBinding>
      </process:withOutput>
      <process:hasEffect>
        <expr:PDDL-Expression>
          <expr:expressionBody rdf:parseType="Literal">
            (uploaded ?client ?server ?file)
          </expr:expressionBody>
        </expr:PDDL-Expression>
      </process:hasEffect>
    </process:Result>
  </process:hasResult>
</process:AtomicProcess>
```

Figure 7.14   *OWL-S atomic process description.*

we previously defined in Figure 7.13. The inputs and outputs are very straightforward. For each, we specify the actual datatype, and a concept from an ontology that will classify the corresponding values. We assume that our camera ontology defines the concepts PhotoLocation,

`PhotoName`, `PhotoType`, and `PhotoResponse` for these inputs and outputs. The specification of the `UploadResult` is more complex. As previously noted, a result represents a coupled output and effect. Our definition should be read as stating that when the output of `UploadResponse` is true, then the PDDL effect (`uploaded ?client ?server ?file`) should be asserted.

7.5.4 OWL-S task model

The second kind of processes that OWL-S defines are composite processes. Unlike the atomic processes, composite processes are not directly invokable, instead they are *decomposable* into other (composite or noncomposite) processes. Composite processes are effectively workflows, which represent the composition of atomic processes into tasks. Once again, OWL-S only specifies these composite processes, it does not define precisely how the decomposition should be performed. The actual decomposition and invocation of the processes is left to external entities, e.g. planning agents.

It is useful to think of an OWL-S composite process as a recipe to accomplish service composition. The recipe describes how to unravel the composite process into invokable atomic processes. As the composite process is unravelled, the services that are referenced will be invoked, and service composition will be accomplished. There are many similarities between this approach and the simpler LCC approach to service composition that we discussed in Section 7.4.3. However, LCC protocols are designed to be directly executable, while OWL-S composite processes are just specifications. In effect, an LCC protocol defines the steps that *will* be executed during service composition, while an OWL-S composite process specifies the steps that *can* be performed.

To assist in the definition of composite processes, OWL-S introduces a third kind of process called a *simple process*. A simple process is similar to an atomic process in that it is treated as having a single-step execution. However, simple processes are not invokable. The purpose of a simple process is to provide a specialized view of an atomic process, or a simplified representation of a composite process. These abstractions are useful for hiding the complexity of the processes from external entities, and for simplifying the definitions of composite processes.

OWL-S defines a task model that specifies all of the different ways that processes can be composed to make up a composite process. Each composite process can be viewed as a tree, where the leaves are processes and the internal nodes are *control constructs* from the task model. The processes at the leaves of this tree can be either atomic processes, simple processes,

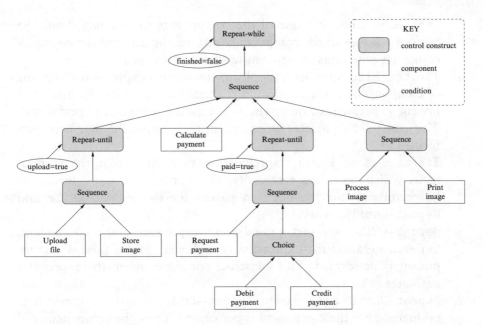

Figure 7.15 *Task model example.*

or further composite processes. Each control construct is associated with a
list of *components*, which are the children of the node within the tree. We
present an example in Figure 7.15 that illustrates a composite process as a
tree of control constructs, components, and conditions. This example is an
alternative view of our photo-processing application.

There are nine different kinds of control constructs in the OWL-S task
model, which we define below. The term *performed* is used to indicate
that the components are not necessarily atomic processes that can be
invoked, but may also be simple or composite processes that require further
expansion:

1. Sequence: specifies a list of components to be performed in order. This
    construct completes when all of the components have been performed.
2. Split: specifies a bag of components to be performed concurrently.
    The split construct completes as soon as all of the components have
    been scheduled.
3. Split-Join: specifies a bag of components to be performed concur-
    rently with barrier synchronization. This construct completes when all
    of the components have been performed.
4. Any-Order: specifies a bag of components to be performed sequentially
    in an unspecified order. This construct completes when all of the
    components have performed.

5. Choice: specifies that one of the components from a bag should be performed. Any of the components may be chosen, and the construct completes when this component has been performed.

6. If-Then-Else: specifies a (Boolean) conditional expression and a pair of components. If the expression evaluates to true, then the first component is performed, otherwise the second component is performed. This construct completes when one of the components has been performed.

7. Iterate: is an abstract specification that states that the components will be executed repeatedly. This construct is not intended to be performed directly, but is a parent for the Repeat-While and Repeat-Until constructs.

8. Repeat-While: specifies a conditional expression and a component. On each iteration the expression is evaluated, and if false, the component is performed. This construct completes when the expression evaluates to true.

9. Repeat-Until: is similar to Repeat-While, but the expression is evaluated after the component is performed. Thus, the component will always be performed at least once.

Each of the control constructs specifies the ordering and conditions under which their components are performed, i.e. the control flow. However, it is crucial that we also specify how data is transferred from the inputs and outputs of one component to the inputs and outputs of another. This is accomplished by a corresponding *data-flow* specification in the task model. OWL-S adopts a *consumer-pull* convention for the data flow. Each component specifies their input and output parameters, and how these parameters connect to the input and output parameters of the previous component that was performed. Thus, each component can be viewed as pulling their parameters from the previous component.

We illustrate the specification of control and data flow in Figure 7.16. In this example, we compose an image processing process ProcImage with an image printing process PrintImage using the Sequence control construct. This construct takes a list of processes as arguments, which is built recursively from first and rest elements. To construct a list with two elements we must use the following pattern: [first|rest[first|rest[nil]]]. Each process pulls its inputs from the previous process. The processing process takes its input from a previous image storage process, and the printing process takes its input from the processing process. The input sources are defined by the hasDataFrom element. Typically, we map a value generated by a previous process to an input on the current process. This is accomplished by creating an InputBinding, which specifies the output of

```
<process:composedOf>
  <process:Sequence>
    <process:components>
      <process:ControlConstructList>
        <list:first>
          <process:Perform rdf:ID="PerfProcImage">
            <process:process rdf:resource="#ProcImage"/>
            <process:hasDataFrom>
              <process:InputBinding>
                <process:toParam rdf:resource="#ProcImageIn"/>
                <process:valueSource>
                  <process:ValueOf>
                    <process:theVar rdf:resource="#StoreImageOut"/>
                    <process:fromProcess rdf:resource="#PerfStoreImage"/>
                  </process:ValueOf>
                </process:valueSource>
              </process:InputBinding>
            </process:hasDataFrom>
          </process:Perform>
        </list:first>
        <list:rest>
          <process:ControlConstructList>
            <list:first>
              <process:Perform rdf:ID="PerfPrintImage">
                <process:process rdf:resource="#PrintImage"/>
                <process:hasDataFrom>
                  <process:InputBinding>
                    <process:toParam rdf:resource="#PrintImageIn"/>
                    <process:valueSource>
                      <process:ValueOf>
                        <process:theVar rdf:resource="#ProcImageOut"/>
                        <process:fromProcess rdf:resource="#PerfProcImage"/>
                      </process:ValueOf>
                    </process:valueSource>
                  </process:InputBinding>
                </process:hasDataFrom>
              </process:Perform>
            </list:first>
            <list:rest rdf:resource="&rdf;#nil"/>
          </process:ControlConstructList>
        </list:rest>
      </process:ControlConstructList>
    </process:components>
  </process:Sequence>
</process:composedOf>
```

Figure 7.16   *OWL-S composite process description.*

the previous process using a `theVar` element, and the name of the previous process using a `fromProcess` element. In this way, we create a flow of data through our specification, which can be independent of the flow of control.

7.5.5 OWL-S grounding

The final part of an OWL-S specification is the grounding that specifies precisely how to access a service. A grounding is effectively a *mapping* from the abstract description of the service in the profile and process model, to a concrete specification. This concrete specification details the features which are required to invoke a service, such as the network protocols, messages formats, and addressing methods. In essence the OWL-S grounding details how the abstract inputs and outputs of atomic processes are realized concretely through message passing.

We recall from Section 7.3 that the messages and protocols for invoking web services are already represented in WSDL interface documents. Hence, the OWL-S grounding does not replace WSDL, but is defined as an extension to WSDL. We previously stated that WSDL does not mandate the format of the messages, but allows different message *bindings* to be defined, e.g. for SOAP and HTTP messages. Thus, the OWL-S grounding is defined as a new kind of WSDL binding, which permits messages containing semantic markup to be sent and received.

The construction of an OWL-S grounding involves the complementary use of both OWL-S definitions and WSDL definitions. There are three main points of contact between these definitions, which we outline below:

1. OWL-S atomic processes are mapped to WSDL *operations* as follows:
    *   An atomic process with inputs and outputs is mapped to a WSDL *request-response* operation.
    *   An atomic process with only inputs is mapped to a WSDL *one-way* operation.
    *   An atomic process with only outputs is mapped to a WSDL *notification* operation.
    *   A composite process that sends an output before receiving an input is mapped to a WSDL *solicit-response* operation.
2. The set of inputs, and the set outputs to an OWL-S atomic process are mapped to WSDL *messages,* i.e. a single input to an atomic process becomes part of a message to a WSDL operation.
3. The types of the inputs and outputs to atomic processes are mapped to WSDL *abstract types.*

The mappings above describe how WSDL definitions may be generated from OWL-S specifications. However, there is an additional mechanism that enables WSDL definitions to be referenced from within OWL-S. These definitions are only of limited use, e.g. when fine-control is required over the mapping between OWL-S and WSDL, and so we refer the reader to the OWL-S standard in the Suggested Reading section for details.

We have now outlined the three main components that are required to define an OWL-S specification: the profile, the process model, and the grounding. All three parts are required for a complete specification as these parts have a close correspondence. Nonetheless, generating a complete OWL-S specification for a service is clearly a complex process, particularly if an ontology must also be defined to represent the concepts in the service. Therefore, tools have been constructed to assist with this task, for example:

- WSDL2OWLS converts WSDL documents into OWL-S templates.
- The Java-based OWL-S API enables OWL-S specifications to be read, written, and executed.
- The OWLS2PDDL and OWLS-XPlan tools have been created to facilitate planning with OWL-S specifications.

OWL-S has been created specifically to support automated service composition, discovery, and invocation. However, as we have repeatedly emphasized, OWL-S does not state how these activities should be performed. Instead, the approach adopted by OWL-S is to provide a specification framework for web services, which is flexible and expressive enough to represent the knowledge required to perform such activities. The construction of techniques and tools to enable such activities is ongoing research at the time of writing.

7.5.6 Web services modelling ontology

The WSMO project is an alternative approach to the provision of semantic markup for Web Services. There are many conceptual similarities between WSMO and OWL-S. However, as the WSMO project began after the initial OWL-S proposal, it solves many of the open issues in the OWL-S approach. The WSMO project is still ongoing at the time of writing, and so we present only a high-level overview here as many parts of the project are in a state of flux. Nonetheless, WSMO is likely to play an important role in the future of the Semantic Web.

WSMO goes beyond simply providing an ontology for Web services. In addition, it attempts to provide a complete framework for the specification, construction, and execution of Semantic Web services, in which ontologies play a significant part. As previously discussed, WSMO is based on F-Logics and not directly on DLs. Thus, WSMO cannot readily be defined as a layer above RDF and OWL, as in the OWL-S approach. Instead, WSMO is recasting the fundamental standards of the Semantic Web using F-Logic. There are three related parts to the WSMO project, which are outlined below:

1. The WSML is effectively an F-Logic–based replacement for OWL, which nonetheless retains some compatibility with OWL ontologies. WSML essentially corresponds to an intersection between DL and Horn logic. This enables both ontologies and rules to be specified in the same formalism.

2. The WSMO is a formal ontology that is built using WSML. This ontology provides a formal vocabulary for semantically describing all relevant aspects of Web Services to facilitate the automatic invocation, discovery, and composition of these services on the Web.

3. The Web Service Modelling eXecution environment (WSMX) is a reference implementation of WSML and WSMO. This environment aims to validate these definitions by demonstrating how reasoning can be performed in WSML, and how WSMO specifications can be used in practice.

We only discuss the ontological part of WSMO here, as we can compare this directly with the feature set of OWL-S. A WSMO document provides a specification for a single web service, or a group of web services just as in OWL-S. The top-level elements that define a WSMO specification are illustrated in Figure 7.17. It should be clear from this diagram that WSMO includes additional concepts that are not present in OWL-S. At the top of this ontology is the *element* concept, which is defined simply as a part of the WSMO specification. The key concepts in WSMO are the four element subclasses that are outlined below:

1. The Ontology element is used to define the concepts and relationships that are relevant to the services being specified. In addition, this ontology can define instances, relations, rules, and functions. Therefore, the Ontology fulfils a similar role to the OWL ontology and RDF knowledge base associated with an OWL-S specification. However, the ability to define rules and functions directly makes the Ontology more expressive than OWL, even when augmented with SWRL rules.

2. The WebService element specifies the functional, non-functional, and behavioural aspects of services. Each service is specified in terms

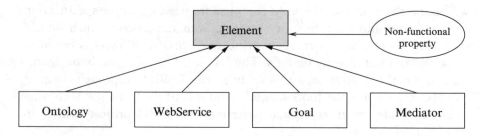

Figure 7.17 *WSMO top-level elements.*

of its *capability* and its *interface*. A capability specifies a service in terms of preconditions, assumptions, post-conditions, and effects (i.e. IOPEs). An interface specifies the *choreography* and the *orchestration* of a service. The choreography provides the necessary information to communicate with the service, and the orchestration defines how the service makes use of other services. Both the choreography and orchestration are specified using finite-state models. Thus, the capability and interface in WSMO have a similar function to the process model and grounding in OWL-S.

3. A Goal element is a representation of an *objective*. This objective may be something that a user would like to fulfil through the invocation of a service. A Goal can also be a description of a desired service in terms of its capability and interface. Therefore, a Goal in WSMO is similar to a profile in OWL-S.

4. The Mediator element is used to overcome interoperation problems between different WSMO elements. WSMO mediators have no direct counterpart in OWL-S. There are four different kinds of mediators that are identified in WSMO:

    *   ggMediators are used to link two Goals. They may define a refinement from the source Goal into the target Goal, and state the (partial) equivalence of Goals.
    *   ooMediators are used to link two ontologies. They may define mappings between concepts in these ontologies, and resolve mismatches between representations.
    *   wgMediators are used to link Web Services to Goals. That is, identifying Web Services which can (fully or partially) fulfil the Goals to which they are linked.
    *   wwMediators are used to link the inputs and outputs of two Web Services, and resolve any datatype issues between the services.

The final feature of WSMO that we discuss is the inclusion of NFP, which are defined for every WSMO element, and inherited by the top-level Element as shown in Figure 7.17. NFP are features of services that do not directly describe the functionality of the service, but may influence the choice of service. OWL-S enables two kinds of NFP to be defined: service categories, and service parameters. However, WSMO has many more categories of NFP, including: date, version, publisher, creator, coverage, performance, and quality of service. These additional NFP enable more flexible kinds of service matching and discovery to be performed.

In summary, there are essentially two main advantages that WSMO has over OWL-S. The first of these is the ability to specify the functional behaviour of services in a single common formalism. The IOPEs of services can all be specified in the ontology, without the need for external representations such as SWRL, KIF, or PDDL. The second advantage is the presence of mediators in the specification. These mediators provide the basis for a solution to the interoperation issues that arise when attempting to integrate services from different providers. This is one of the main issues that prevents automatic service composition, and on which OWL-S is entirely silent. Nonetheless, WSMO does not currently define how these mediators should be implemented. In particular, the mapping of concepts between different ontologies presents a number of significant challenges that we discuss in Chapter 8.

An additional advantage of WSMO will be realized when the WSMX reference implementation becomes available. One of the key challenges of using OWL-S is that it does not define precisely how its service specifications should be used in practice. Furthermore, the existing reasoning systems for OWL ontologies cannot perform effective inferences with the extended features of OWL-S. The WSMX implementation should illustrate how automated service invocation, discovery, and composition can actually be performed. Nonetheless, there are currently a number of challenges that must be solved before this goal can be fully realized, including the provision of efficient reasoning capabilities for the underlying F-Logic.

7.6 Summary

In this chapter we outlined how applications on the Semantic Web may be constructed from ontologies, reasoning systems, agents, and MASs. These techniques, and their associated technologies, can be effectively combined in an SOA. An SOA is a style of software architecture built dynamically from distributed components, called *services*, which facilitate three key activities:

1. The remote invocation of services.
2. The discovery of services that match certain criteria.
3. The composition of services to form applications.

The Web Services architecture is a kind of SOA that is particularly relevant to the Semantic Web. This is a specific set of technologies for constructing Web-based SOA. The key standard in this architecture is the WSDL, which defines an interface to a web service. A WSDL document specifies the operations within the service, the messages types required to access the service, the format of these messages, and the location of the service itself. WSDL is crucial to the invocation, discovery, and composition of web services.

We use the equivalent terms 'Knowledge Service' and 'Semantic Web Service' to refer to a web service which is designed specifically for the Semantic Web. These services can be divided into knowledge *providers*, and knowledge *transformers*. The key to constructing Semantic Web applications is to compose these services to accomplish specific tasks. We have illustrated how knowledge services can encapsulate agents, and how LCC protocols can be used to perform agent-based service composition. This approach enables us to build static Semantic Web applications.

In the second half of the chapter, we examined the challenges of automating the invocation, discovery, and composition activities to enable dynamic Semantic Web applications. The key approach is to specify the semantics of services using ontologies. The intuition is that we will be able to automate the three activities by performing reasoning over these ontologies. We examined two ongoing efforts to define these ontologies for Semantic Web services:

1. The OWL-S is an OWL-based ontology which can be used to provide a semantic specification for a web service, or group of web services. A service is specified in three parts: the profile, the model, and the grounding. The profile describes the capabilities of the service in order to advertise the service. The process model specifies the behaviour of the service, so that composition can be performed. The process model specifies atomic processes in terms of IOPEs. Composite processes, which are defined from groups of atomic processes, can also be specified using the OWL-S task model. Finally, the grounding specifies how to access the service so that invocation can be performed. The grounding provides a mapping between the abstract OWL-S specification and a concrete WSDL interface.

2. The WSMO project is currently building a complete framework for the construction of Semantic Web applications. WSMO uses an F-Logic semantics to specify services in terms of ontologies, relations, rules, and functions. The key differences between WSMO and OWL-S are the expressivity afforded by the use of F-Logic, and the use of mediators to address the compatibility issues between services, e.g. ontology mismatches.

7.7 Exercises

1. Construct a WSDL interface for a digital photo storage facility. You should assume that the facility will only be used by a single client. Your interface should contain operations for performing the following actions:

- Uploading an image with a descriptive name.
- Downloading a named image.
- Deleting a named image.
- Obtaining the number of uploaded images.
- Obtaining the names of all uploaded images.

2. Create a basic web service that matches your WSDL interface from Q1. You should use the JWSDP to construct this service, and Apache Tomcat to deploy the service. This software, and an informative tutorial that explains the Java-specific details of web service construction, are available at:

`http://java.sun.com/webservices/`

3. Extend the OWL-S composite process specification in Figure 7.16 to match the example shown in Figure 7.15.

4. Create an OWL-S specification for your photo storage application. You may find the WSDL2OWLS tool to be useful in creating the initial OWL-S template. The WSDL2OWLS tool is available at:

`http://www.daml.ri.cmu.edu/wsdl2owls/`

7.8 Suggested reading

1. D. Booth, H. Haas, F. McCabe, E. Newcomer, M. Champion, C. Ferris, and D. Orchard. *Web Services Architecture.* World-Wide-Web Consortium (W3C), Available at: `http://www.w3.org/TR/ws-arch/`, August 2003.
2. F. Brazier, D. Moback, B. Overeinder, S. van Splunter, M. van Steen, and N. Wijngaards. AgentScape: Middleware, Resource Management, and Services. In *Proceedings of the 3rd International SANE Conference (SANE'02)*, pp. 403–4, Maastricht, The Netherlands, May 2002.
3. G. Casella and V. Mascardi. From AUML to WS-BPEL. Dipartimento di Informatica e Scienze dell'Informazione, University of Genova, Italy, 2006. Technical Report DISI-TR-01-06.
4. The OWL Services Coalition. OWL-S: Semantic Markup for Web Services. Available at: `http://www.daml.org/services/`, November 2004.
5. D. Fensel and C. Bussler. The Web Service Modelling Framework (WSMF). *Electronic Commerce Research and Applications*, 1(2), 2002.
6. L. Fischer, editor. *The Workflow Handbook 2005.* Future Strategies Inc., 2005.
7. M. Gudgin, M. Hadley, N. Mendelsohn, J. J. Moreau, and H. F. Nielsen. *SOAP Version 1.2 Specification.* World-Wide-Web Consortium (W3C), June 2003. Available at: `http://www.w3.org/TR/soap12/`.
8. H. Lausen, A. Pollered, and D. Roman. Web Service Modelling Ontology (WSMO). Available at `http://www.w3.org/Submission/WSMO/`, June 2005.
9. D. Martin, M. Paolucci, S. McIlraith, M. Burstein, D. McDermott, D. McGuinness, B. Parsia, T. R. Payne, M. Sabou, M. Solanki, N. Srinivasan, and K. Sycara. Bringing Semantics to Web Services: The OWL-S Approach. In *Proceedings of*

the First International Workshop on Semantic Web Services and Web Process Composition (SWSWPC'04), San Diego, USA, July 2004.

10. M. Pistore, F. Barbon, P. Bertoli, D. Shaparau, and P. Traverso. Planning and Monitoring Web Service Composition. In *Proceedings of the 14th International Conference on Automated Planning and Scheduling (ICAPS'04)*, Whistler, Canada, June 2004.

11. D. Robertson. A Lightweight Method for Coordination of Agent Oriented Web Services. In *Proceedings of the AAAI Spring Symposium on Semantic Web Services (SSWS'04)*, Stanford, USA, April 2004. AAAI.

12. M. Singh and M. Huhns. *Service-Oriented Computing: Semantics, Processes, Agents*. Wiley, 2005.

13. K. Sycara, M. Paolucci, A. Ankolekar, and N. Srinivasan. Automated Discovery, Interaction and Composition of Semantic Web Services. *Journal of Web Semantics*, 1(1): 27–46, 2003.

14. K. Topley. *Java Web Services in a Nutshell*. O'Reilly, June 2003.

15. C. Walton. Uniting Agents and Web Services. In *AgentLink News*, Number 18, pp. 26–8. AgentLink, August 2005.

8 Conclusions

At the start of this book we outlined the challenges of automatic computer-based processing of information on the Web. These numerous challenges are generally referred to as the 'vision' of the Semantic Web. From the outset, we have attempted to take a realistic and pragmatic view of this vision. Our opinion is that the vision may never be fully realized, but that it is a useful goal on which to focus. Each step towards the vision has provided new insights on classical problems in knowledge representation, MASs, and Web-based techniques. Thus, we are presently in a significantly better position as a result of these efforts.

It is sometimes difficult to see the purpose of the Semantic Web vision behind all of the different technologies and acronyms. However, the fundamental purpose of the Semantic Web is essentially large scale and automated *data integration*. The Semantic Web is not just about providing a more intelligent kind of Web search, but also about taking the results of these searches and combining them in interesting and useful ways. As stated in Chapter 1, the possible applications for the Semantic Web include: automated data mining, e-science experiments, e-learning systems, personalized newspapers and journals, and intelligent devices.

8.1 The Semantic Web vision

The current state of progress towards the Semantic Web vision is summarized in Figure 8.1. This figure shows a pyramid with the human-centric Web at the bottom, sometimes termed the Syntactic Web, and the envisioned Semantic Web at the top. Throughout this book, we have been moving upwards on this pyramid, and it should be clear that a great deal of progress that has been made towards the goal. This progress is indicated by the various stages of the pyramid, which can be summarized as follows:

- The lowest stage on the pyramid is the basic Web that should be familiar to everyone. This Web of information is human-centric and

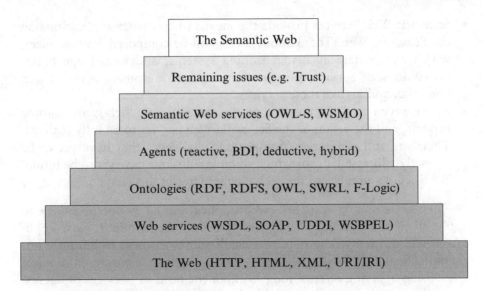

Figure 8.1 *Semantic Web progress pyramid.*

contains very little automation. Nonetheless, the Web provides the basic protocols and technologies on which the Semantic Web is founded. Furthermore, the information which is represented on the Web will ultimately be the source of knowledge for the Semantic Web.

- Web Services provide us with the first stage towards the notion of a computer-processable Web. Web Service technologies do not themselves provide the Web with any additional intelligence in the way that information is processed. However, they do provide a standard way for computer programs to access Web-based information, a standard wrapper for these programs, and a means for these programs to interoperate via message passing.

- Ontologies are the key to defining computer programs which can comprehend and reason about Web-based information. These ontologies provide us with a means to semantically annotate and classify Web-based information in useful ways. An ontology enables us to structure information as a knowledge base, and the logical foundations of the ontology enable us to perform inferences over this knowledge base.

- The Agency paradigm is key to the definition of intelligent programs on the Semantic Web. Agents are programs which act on behalf of entities, such as humans and other agents. Therefore, these agents will be responsible for automatically gathering and exchanging knowledge on the Semantic Web. Individual agents are equipped with autonomous and rational behaviours and can interact through communication with other agents to form powerful MASs.

- Semantic Web Services provide the means to construct applications on the Semantic Web. These applications will be composed from services, which encapsulate agents, reasoning systems, and knowledge bases. Semantic Web Services give us the means to automatically discover, compose, and invoke these services.
- As we have noted, the construction of the Semantic Web is an ongoing process, and the vision of the Semantic Web has yet to be fully realized. There are still a number of important challenges that have yet to be properly addressed, or for which suitable solutions have yet to be found. We discuss a number of these challenges later in this chapter.

When constructing Semantic Web applications, it is not necessary to apply all of the techniques that we have described. Indeed, each application will normally only require a small subset of these techniques. For example, Semantic Web applications can be built at a purely ontological level, using querying or reasoning, without the need for services or agents. Similarly, it is possible to build MASs without directly constructing any ontologies. Thus, a key issue in the construction of applications is the selection of appropriate technologies, through a careful consideration of the alternatives.

In this book we have attempted to give a broad overview of all of the current techniques and technologies which are presently being applied to the challenges of the Semantic Web vision. In doing so, we have steered the reader through all of the main issues in the field, from low-level knowledge representations to high-level service specifications. Throughout the book we have been guided by the following dual goals:

1. To educate the reader on the various technologies so that they can construct Semantic Web applications.
2. To give the reader a suitable theoretical grounding, and to highlight the key issues, so that they can perform further research in the area.

On the assumption that we have met these goals, the reader should now have gained a reasonable level of understanding of the field, and be suitably prepared to begin constructing basic Semantic Web applications. We note that it was not the intention of this book to serve as a detailed manual for all of the different techniques and tools. Instead, we have presented a summary of the main features of each approach to give the reader a feeling for the key advantages and limitations. The reader is referred to the Suggested Reading section at the end of each chapter for specific implementation details.

It should be evident from our presentation that the Semantic Web is still a work in progress. New techniques and technologies are being developed at a surprisingly rapid pace, and there are still many issues and unsolved problems that must be addressed before the Semantic Web vision can be realized. In the remainder of this chapter we outline two important challenges, which are currently the focus of much research effort in the field. These challenges are concerned with *ontology mapping*, and *trust* in the Semantic Web respectively.

8.1.1   Ontology mapping

Throughout this book we have emphasized the crucial role that ontologies play in the management of knowledge on the Semantic Web. Ontologies are used to represent knowledge, and provide a formal basis for reasoning about this knowledge. Without ontologies, we simply have unstructured collections of information that we cannot readily make inferences about, or understand in a wider context, as illustrated by the present-day Web. Thus, the majority of the techniques that we have defined in this book have revolved around ontologies in one form or another.

As we have shown, ontologies are certainly useful in addressing many of the challenges in the construction of the Semantic Web. However, they are no magic bullet for solving all of the knowledge management problems that we might face. For example, in Chapter 5 we showed that ontologies can lack the expressivity required in some applications. Nonetheless, even when the expressivity of our ontologies is sufficient, their use can still present us with additional challenges. We discuss one of these here, which is the challenge of ontology mapping.

A key assumption of the Semantic Web is that there will be many ontologies available. These ontologies will be constructed for different collections of information, and different kinds of applications. At the present time, in the infancy of the Semantic Web, the Swoogle search engine has indexed over 10,000 ontologies. There are many reasons for this rapid proliferation of ontologies. For example, it is often easier to construct a new ontology, than find an existing one which is appropriate for a given task. Similarly, there is often a desire for direct control over the ontology for a particular domain, rather than having the structure dictated by external forces.

A direct consequence of having large numbers of ontologies available is that we will want to integrate knowledge which is represented in different ways. Thus, in addition to the problem of integrating knowledge from different sources, we are now faced with the challenge of coping with different ontological representations of this knowledge. This issue goes beyond simply coping with ontologies which are represented in different formats, e.g. OWL-DL verses KIF ontologies. We also require some way to integrate the concepts of one ontology with another, where these concepts

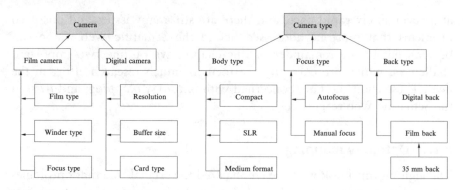

Figure 8.2   *Ontology mapping example.*

may overlap. This challenge is termed the *ontology mapping problem* as the key issue is the mapping of concepts (and relationships) from one ontology to another.

To illustrate why ontology mapping is a problem in the Semantic Web, we consider the two ontology fragments shown in Figure 8.2. Both of these ontology fragments are intended to be used to classify different types of camera, and both are structurally sound. The ontology on the right is taken from our earlier examples, while the ontology on the left classifies cameras according to specific features. By examining these two ontologies, it should be immediately clear that we have (at least) the following five problems:

1. Concepts may have different names, e.g. the 'Camera' concept is equivalent to the 'Camera type' concept.
2. Concepts may only be present in one or other of the ontologies, e.g. 'Card type' and 'Medium format'.
3. Concepts may be similar but not identical, e.g. 'Film camera' and 'Film back'.
4. Certain concepts are related but not equivalent, e.g. 'Film type', and '35 mm back'.
5. There may be unstated assumptions in the ontology, e.g. all 'Digital cameras' are 'Autofocus'.

An ontology mapping can be formally defined by a collection of functions (or bridging rules) which map the symbols of one ontology to another. These functions may perform computations on the instances of the ontology. For example, if one ontology defines a 'Date' concept and another defines 'Year', 'Month', and 'Day', then string decomposition will be required. Furthermore, ontology mapping only constitutes a fragment of the following more ambitious tasks which may be required in certain applications:

- Ontology *translation* is the process of completely transforming the instances of one ontology to another.
- Ontology *alignment* is the process of establishing binary relations between a pair of ontologies, i.e. a bidirectional mapping between all of the concepts and relationships in both ontologies.
- Ontology *articulation* is the process of expressing the concepts and relationships of two ontologies in a third common ontology.
- Ontology *merging* is the process of integrating together all of the concepts, relationships, and instances of two ontologies.

A further challenge on the Semantic Web is that we would like these processes to happen in an automated (or semi-automated) manner. This is because knowledge will often be processed by agents without direct human intervention. These agents should be able to automatically integrate and compare knowledge from different sources regardless of the representation used. A key part of this process is *semantic matching*, which is the identification of equivalent or similar concepts. For any pair of concepts, there are five possible outcomes, which are illustrated in Table 8.1. The equal case is when the concepts are identical, and the more general/specific cases are when there is an overlap between concepts. The disjoint case is when no overlap can be inferred, and the unknown case is where a connection cannot be either established or dismissed.

It should now be clear that the ontology mapping problem is certainly non-trivial. This is particularly true if we attempt to automate the mapping process. However, the situation is far from hopeless, as there are a wide variety of techniques that can be used, and we can often make simplifying assumptions. For example, we may only require partial mappings between ontologies, i.e. only the parts of the ontology which are directly relevant to the task being solved, or our agents may be able to communicate with other agents to interpret certain concepts, or to establish common ground. In the remainder of this section we outline a number of approaches that are currently being applied to the ontology matching problem, though this list is by no means exhaustive:

Table 8.1 *Semantic matching.*

Operator	Meaning
$=$	Equal
$\sqsubseteq$	More specific
$\sqsupseteq$	More general
$\perp$	Disjoint
$\mathcal{U}$	Unknown

1. The ontology matching problem can be lessened or avoided altogether by the adoption of *common ontologies*. We previously discussed the need for common ontologies to enable agent communication in Chapter 6. To this end, a number of efforts have been proposed with the intention of creating top-level ontologies, or definitive ontologies for a particular domain. An example of a top-level ontology is the IEEE Suggested Upper Merged Ontology (SUMO). Examples of domain-specific ontologies include: the Gene ontology, the Enterprise ontology, the OWL-Time ontology, and the Standard Ontology for Ubiquitous and Pervasive Applications (SOUPA). There are also a number of repositories for common ontologies, such as Ontolingua, and OntoWeb.

2. A key feature of the OWL standard is that ontologies can be linked together through the use of URI. This means that ontologies can be constructed with links, in much the same way as web pages. Thus, an ontology designer can define explicit links to equivalent concepts in other ontologies, or directly use parts of these ontologies in the definition. Therefore, this information may subsequently be used to infer connections between ontologies. For example, if two ontologies are derived from a common source, then their concepts are likely to be similar. We term this approach *link inference*, though it is largely dependent on the designers of the ontologies to make the appropriate links.

3. The difficulty of the ontology mapping problem is related to the expressiveness of the language in which the ontology is defined. In other words, the mapping problem is more difficult in a language which permits a large vocabulary to be expressed. Thus, it is possible to address the mapping problem by restricting the ontologies under consideration to certain less expressive forms. For example, there are many existing techniques for *schema matching* which have been developed for combining databases. Similarly, mappings between taxonomies can readily be accomplished by *linguistic matching* techniques, e.g. mapping between synonyms obtained from WordNet, and *structural mapping* techniques which examine similarities between the graphs.

4. A number of tools have been developed which are based on the notion that humans are best equipped to perform ontology mappings. Thus, these tools are designed to present the task in such a way as to make it straightforward to define mappings, e.g. by drawing links between concepts in a GUI. These tools may also be combined with automated methods, which generate candidate matches for the user. Examples of such tools include: ConcepTool, PROMPT, and MAFRA.

5. The final approach that we outline is based on the definition of theoretical frameworks for ontology mapping. This is generally accomplished

by considering the underlying DL on which the ontologies are founded. Examples include formal concept analysis (FCA-Merge), information flows (IF-MAP), and translations frameworks (TOVE).

8.1.2 Trust

The final challenge that we discuss is that of *trust* in the Semantic Web. This is an umbrella term which covers a wide range of interrelated issues. The provision of trust in the Semantic Web will be crucial to its long-term success, as trust is inextricably linked to the usefulness of the results that we hope to obtain. To give a flavour of the various issues, we now outline four important areas where trust has a direct impact on the Semantic Web:

1. A key task in the Semantic Web is the integration of knowledge from different sources. Up to now, we have assumed that all of these sources will be treated equally. However, in reality, certain sources of knowledge will be definitive or authoritative, while other sources may be considerably less reliable. For example, a scientific journal is likely to contain more accurate information than a blog. Thus, we often want to take into account the source of the knowledge to assess its trustworthiness. The origin of the knowledge is termed the *provenance* of the knowledge.

2. When we perform inferences over collections of knowledge, we are often attempting to answer specific questions. In some situations, we may require very accurate answers, while at other times a 'good enough' answer may be appropriate. For example, if we are making a purchase then we usually require precise answers, while if we are researching a topic, then we may tolerate a good enough answer. A key issue which affects the trust that we have in our inferences is *context*. This is meta-knowledge which describes properties, such as how the knowledge was originally obtained, and in what situations it can be applied.

3. In an MAS, each agent is responsible for their own private knowledge. For example, beliefs are a kind of private knowledge that is used by an agent to guide their decisions. When an agent communicates with another agent, parts of this private knowledge may be exposed to the other agent, and this private knowledge may be augmented or altered. Thus, there is an issue as to whether an agent is willing to trust another agent with its beliefs, e.g. when these beliefs may be bank details, and how much the agent is willing to trust the beliefs of another agent, e.g. when the other agent believes that they are owed money. An important issue here is that of *reputation* of agents, i.e. if an agent has acted in a

trustworthy manner in the past, then it is likely to continue with this behaviour.

4. The Semantic Web is designed as an open environment, with no central control or authority over the agents and services which participate. Therefore, there is a strong possibility that malicious agents or services could be introduced into this environment. These entities may attempt to provide misleading information, or to disrupt the workings of the environment. The behaviours of services and agents can be partially controlled through the definition of *norms* and *deontic* notions, such as policies, permissions, obligations, security, and commitments. By adhering to these notions, entities can demonstrate their trustworthiness within the environment.

As we have shown, the issues of trust can have an effect at all levels of the Semantic Web. However, many of the current standards for the Semantic Web have been designed without any real consideration of trust or security. For example, there is no definitive security model in the Web Services architecture. Nonetheless, as the techniques for the Semantic Web have risen in popularity, trust issues have become more apparent, and these shortcomings are being addressed. We conclude with a brief overview of several proposals for increasing trust in the Semantic Web:

• Trust on the present-day Web is established through the use of digital signatures, and secure transfer of information. Therefore, the first approach that we discuss is the extension of these techniques to the Semantic Web. This may be accomplished directly, i.e. RDF data can be digitally signed, and knowledge can be transferred between entities in a secure manner. Such a system would enable the provenance of knowledge to be established, and the authenticity of services and agents to be determined. A variant of this approach is proposed in the WS-Security and WS-Trust proposals for the Web Services architecture. The use of digital encryption techniques may be extended further to establish a *web of trust* for the Semantic Web, similar to that used by Public Key Infrastructure (PKI). A web of trust is essentially an interconnected set of entities who are deemed trustworthy. To join a web of trust, it is necessary to be certified as trustworthy by an entity who is already part of the web. There is generally a central authority who is responsible for starting and maintaining the web, and certification is performed by the exchange of digital signatures. Many such webs can exist at the same time, and bridges can be created between these webs through membership. Using such techniques it would be possible to construct a trusted subset of the Semantic Web.

- A variety of different techniques have been proposed for establishing the reputation of agents or services on the Semantic Web. Much of this work is derived from past research on reputation in MASs. Reputation-based techniques attempt to use past performance as an indication of the trust-worthiness of an entity. The simplest system is a form of ranking, such as used on a popular Web-based auction system to rate the reliability of buyers and sellers. Alternative metrics are also possible, e.g. response time, analysis of results, and adherence to policy. The effectiveness of such systems can be increased by integrating reputation information from a variety of different sources. In particular, the following four kinds of trust may be obtained about an entity:

    1. Interaction-based trust from past experience of direct interactions.
    2. Role-based trust by observing the behaviour of the entity in different roles.
    3. Witness reputation obtained from a third party about past behaviour.
    4. Certified reputation of past behaviour from an authoritative source.

    The key advantage of the reputation-based approach is that trust can be established in a P2P manner, without the need for a central authority.

- The final approach that we outline of the use of *contracts* to enforce trust on the Semantic Web. A contract is a precise statement of agreement between two or more entities. The contract commits the entities to a particular course of action. The terms of the contract can be established through a process of negotiation between the entities, which will typically include the following:

    1. The entities involved in the contract.
    2. The actions that the entities agree to undertake.
    3. Temporal aspects of the contract, e.g. the start and end of the contract, and any intermediate milestones.
    4. Norms to which the entities should adhere, e.g. obligations, rules, and permissions.
    5. Penalties for breaking the contract, e.g. rule x was broken, so rule y now applies.

The advantage of the contractual approach to trust is that trust can be established through proof, i.e. it is possible to prove that a contract was satisfied or broken. The WS-Policy, and WS-Agreement proposals are an attempt to define a contractual framework for the Web Services architecture. However, the unsolved issue for the Semantic Web is how to compel the entities to adhere to such contracts. Ideally, these contracts would be enforced by legal machinery.

8.2 Suggested reading

1. D. de Roure, N. R. Jennings, and N. Shadbolt. The Semantic Grid: A Future e-Science Infrastructure. In F. Berman, G. Fox, and A. J. G. Hey, editors, *Grid Computing—Making the Global Infrastructure a Reality*, pp. 437–70. John Wiley & Sons, 2002.
2. J. Hobbs and F. Pan. An Ontology of Time for the Semantic Web. *ACM Transactions on Asian Language Processing (TALIP): Special Issue on Temporal Information Processing*, 3(1): 66–85, March 2004.
3. T. D. Huynh, N. R. Jennings, and N. Shadbolt. FIRE: An Integrated Trust and Reputation Model for Open Multi-Agent Systems. In *Proceedings of 16th European Conference on Artificial Intelligence (ECAI'04)*, pp. 18–22, Valencia, Spain, August 2004.
4. Y. Kalfoglou, H. Alani, M. Schorlemmer, and C. Walton. On the Emergent Semantic Web and Overlooked Issues. In *Proceedings of the 3rd International Semantic Web Conference (ISWC'04)*, Hiroshima, Japan, November 2004.
5. Y. Kalfoglou and M. Schorlemmer. Ontology mapping: The State of the Art. *The Knowledge Engineering Review*, 18(1): 1–31, January 2003.
6. D. McGuinness. Why Should You Trust Answers from the Web? In *Proceedings of the Joint Conference on Information Sciences, Web Intelligence and Security Track (JCIS'05)*, Utah, USA, July 2005.
7. K. O'Hara, H. Alani, Y. Kalfoglou, and N. Shadbolt. Trust Strategies for the Semantic Web. In *Proceedings of the 3rd International Semantic Web Conference (ISWC'04)*, Hiroshima, Japan, November 2004.
8. M. Singh, A. Chopra, N. Desai, and A. Mallya. Protocols for Processes: Programming in the Large for Open Systems. *ACM SIGPLAN Notices*, 39(12): 73–83, December 2004.

Index